Locating Your Roots

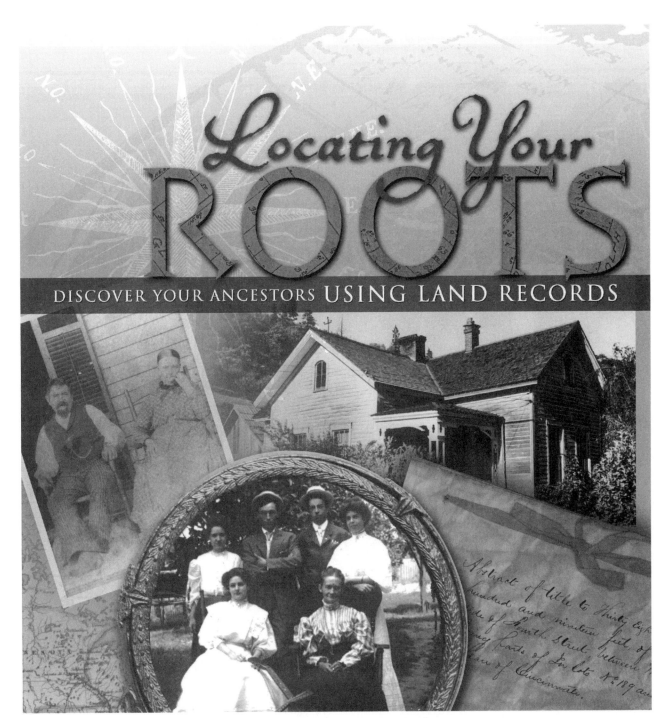

Locating Your ROOTS

DISCOVER YOUR ANCESTORS USING LAND RECORDS

Patricia Law Hatcher

BETTERWAY BOOKS
CINCINNATI, OHIO

www.familytreemagazine.com

Other fine Betterway books are available from your local bookstore or on our Web site at www.familytreemagazine.com.

07 06 05 04 03   5 4 3 2 1

Library of Congress Cataloging-in-Publication Data

Hatcher, Patricia Law
  Locating your roots: discover your ancestors using land records / Patricia Law Hatcher.
    p. cm.
  Includes bibliographical references (p.) and index.
  ISBN 1-55870-614-3 (pbk.: alk. paper)
    1. United States—Genealogy—Handbooks, manuals, etc. 2. Land titles—United States—Handbooks, manuals, etc. 3. Deeds—United States—Handbooks, manuals, etc. I. Title.
CS49 .H38 2003
929′.1′072073—dc21   2002153185
                                                                          CIP

Editor: Sharon DeBartolo Carmack, CG
Production editor: Eric Schwartzberg
Production coordinator: Michelle Ruberg
Interior designer: Sandy Conopeotis Kent
Cover designer: Stephanie Strang
Icon designer: Cindy Beckmeyer

DEDICATION
To my ancestors, who lived on the land.

Acknowledgments

I wish to thank especially my technical reviewer, Anita Anderson Lustenberger, CG, whose love of land records is equal to my own.

Myrtle Stevens Hyde, FASG, and William Bart Saxbe Jr., CG, FASG provided examples.

About the Author

PATRICIA LAW HATCHER, CG, FASG is a professional genealogist specializing in problem solving. She is a Certified Genealogist, certified by the Board for Certification of Genealogists; a former trustee of the Association of Professional Genealogists; and in 2000 was elected a Fellow of the American Society of Genealogists.

Her oft-migrating ancestors lived in all of the original colonies prior to 1800 and in seventeen other states, presenting her with highly varied research problems and forcing her to acquire techniques and tools that help solve tough problems. Land records have been key to solving many of those problems.

A popular lecturer and instructor, Pat has spoken at many conferences, institutes, and workshops. With Mary McCampbell Bell, Birdie Monk Holsclaw, and Anita Anderson Lustenberger, she has developed and presented a variety of land-platting workshops.

She is the author of *Producing a Quality Family History*, editor of *The Pennsylvania Genealogical Magazine*, consulting editor to Newbury Street Press, consulting editor to *The New England Historical and Genealogical Register*, contributing editor to *The Maine Genealogist*, author of *A Rhoads Family History—The Family and Ancestry of Jay Roscoe Rhoads*, and author and publisher of the four-volume *Abstract of Graves of Revolutionary Patriots and Barren County, Kentucky, Deeds 1798–1813*. Her articles have appeared in more than a dozen publications, including the *National Genealogical Society Quarterly*, *The American Genealogist*, *The Maine Genealogist*, the *New Hampshire Genealogical Record*, *The New York Genealogical and Biographical Record*, *The Pennsylvania Genealogical Magazine*, the *Genealogical Journal*, *The Virginia Genealogist*, the *Arkansas Historical and Genealogical Magazine*, *Ancestry* magazine, *Ancestry Daily News*, AGLL's *Genealogy Bulletin*, and the Federation of Genealogical Societies' *Forum*.

Icons Used in This Book

 CD Source
Databases and other information available on CD-ROM

 Printed Source
Directories, books, pamphlets, and other paper archives

 Definitions
\di'fin\ *vb* Terminology and jargon explained

 Reminder
"Don't-Forget" items to keep in mind

 For More Info
Where to turn for more in-depth coverage

 Research Tip
Ways to make research more efficient

 Idea Generator
Techniques and prods for further thinking

 Sources
Where to go for information, supplies, etc.

 Important
Information and tips you can't overlook

 Step By Step
Walkthroughs of important procedures

  Internet Source
Where on the Web to find what you need

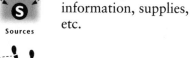 **Timesaver**
Shaving minutes and hours off the clock

 Library/Archive Source
Repositories that might have the information you need

 Tip
Ways to make research more efficient

 Microfilm Source
Information available on microfilm

 Warning
Stop before you make a mistake

 Notes
Thoughts, ideas, and related insights

Table of Contents At a Glance

Table of Contents

ONE

Why Use Land Records?

T hey are statements too often overheard in libraries and archives. "One of these days, I'll check the deeds." "I know I should learn more about land records, but . . ." "I need to find the headstone (or birth certificate or will) for William first; *then* I'll think about land records." "I just want to find out who the father of my John is; I don't want to read microfilmed deeds."

The saddest thing about these statements is that the speakers may have been denying themselves access to the very information about their ancestors that they were seeking.

One of the strongest motivators for American immigration was land. Our ancestors came because we had available land. In Europe, land was in private hands. To own property outside of inheritance, you had to buy it from someone, which meant that you had to find someone who wanted to sell it—not an easy task. Furthermore, land in Europe was expensive; it was definitely a seller's market.

In America, the opposite was true. The colony, state, proprietor, or federal government was often actively trying to dispose of land, either to encourage settlement or to raise money. From the beginning with New England town proprietors and the Virginia headright system continuing through to the homestead acts that helped settle the American heartland and plains, the potential emigrant from Europe knew that land would be easier to obtain in America. Because the potential purchaser had options and wasn't forced to buy from a specific individual, prices were affordable to many. Furthermore, competition between sellers helped keep prices reasonable—a buyer's market.

Land was important in other ways. In many places in early America, only landowners could vote and hold public office.

The availability of land continued to be a motivating factor for generations. Not only was land a significant factor in immigration; it was the primary factor in migration within America. A farm that supported one family quite nicely simply couldn't sustain the families of all four sons. Inevitably, the push of overcrowding and the pull of newly available land drove settlement westward. Land had a lot to do with dreams, with *the future*. Anyone who read the stories

Important

1

There weren't many family records in the drawers of the old library table at the farm where my grandparents lived. A few photographs, a family record written on free notepad from the local grain company (my grandfather never forgot the birthdays of us grandkids), and two items that silently speak volumes about what mattered to my family.

There was an old *Atlas and Plat Book of Merrick County, Nebraska*. This is a booklet, produced regularly by the county for tax purposes, showing the current ownership of each parcel of land, including the land that would become my grandfather's farm in section 23 Township 15 North, Range 6 West and the parcels owned by my extended Gregg family. It was from this plat book that I first learned that "the crick" that flowed behind the barn had a name—Prairie Creek—and the fact that it meandered its way across most of the county. Nebraska is a public-land state. (Chapter twelve, Public-Land Survey System, discusses township/range land descriptions.) See figure 1-1.

There also was an old piece of paper—a *very* old piece of paper—taped with adhesive tape to a shirt cardboard (the gray cardboard that new shirts come wrapped around). It was a *metes-and-bounds* drawing of a piece of land. (See figure 1-2.) Below the drawing it says:

> A draught of a survey made December 9th 1825 containing 100 Acres strict measure it being the land sold by Hugh Willson to Jas Kerr situate in Cumberland Township in Greene County.
>
> —John Fordyce

Greene County is in Pennsylvania, which is a state-land state. (Chapter eleven, Metes-and-Bounds Land Platting, discusses metes-and-bounds descriptions and platting.)

On the back of the shirt cardboard, in the handwriting of my grandfather James Stanley Gregg, is written:

> Boundry lines on Grand Father's Gregg Farm. I believe it was north & maby a little west. Went through covered bridge going out to farm. Grand Father James K Gregg had two jersey cows that he took out to farm every day to pasture, get them at night, put yoke on them. Just over a mile out to farm. Rented Buildings, Farm Land, lived in Carmicales on acerage. Big Barn on Farm, House too. 3 story barn built into Big Hill. Barn 3 stories Bottom for cows, horses, stored grain threshed on second floor. 3 top story for odds & ends grain hay drove into each floor from hill which barn was built against.

My grandfather was referring to a trip he made from Nebraska to Pennsylvania as a child, probably around 1903, to visit his grandfather James Kerr Gregg, who was farming the land purchased by *his* grandfather James Kerr. Notice that what my grandfather talked about was *farming*. It's what he knew; it was his life. If your ancestors included farmers, land was probably very important to them, also.

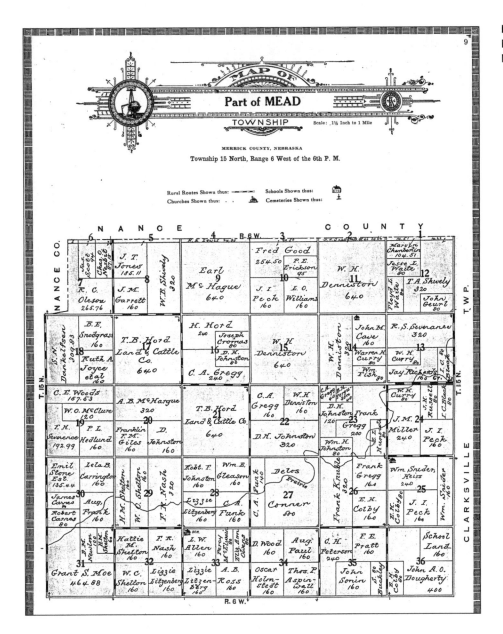

Figure 1-1 Atlas and Plat Book of Merrick County, Nebraska, 1921.

of Laura Ingalls Wilder will remember that the family relocated several times, each move prompted by Pa's desire to settle new land.

Land records are the most common records available for pioneer ancestors. For many, they may be the only records. In frontier areas, land records were the first records to be carefully recorded and hence predate other records.

Land was often the most important thing to our ancestors, so it should be equally important to us in our research. **To get closer to our ancestors, we should get closer to their land.**

Important

WHY DO RESEARCHERS AVOID LAND RECORDS?

Land records can tell us much more about our ancestors than that they bought and sold land. They can prove ancestry and family relationships. They can point to new research paths. They can tell us about the lives of our

Figure 1-2 Surveyor's plat of the land made in 1825, showing land sold by Hugh Wilson to James Kerr in Greene County, Pennsylvania.

ancestors. They can do so much for us—but there are no guarantees, and the research may require effort.

Land Records Can Be Confusing

This statement is both true and false. Deeds—the basic transaction that encompasses the greatest volume of land records—are easy to access and easy to use, once you become familiar with the legal jargon. However, deeds are but one type of land record. The ownership of land involves many types of transactions and record keeping.

Tip

- The most basic land records are records of *transfer*. **In theory, any ownership of property should have generated two records of transfer:** the first when your ancestor acquired the land, the second when it left his possession. The most common records of transfer are a grant or a deed for acquisition and a deed for disposition, but there are many other possibilities. You've probably already encountered land being transferred by a bequest in a will.

- The transfer itself may have created records of *process*. These include such items as warrants, surveys, partitions, and even nasty court battles. Many of the more common types of transfer, the processes involved, and the records created are discussed in chapter two, Where Are the Records?, and chapter five, First Transfer—Getting Land Into the Hands of Individuals.
- Additionally, there are records of *ownership*. Tax lists of persons owning real property (land is called *real property*, as opposed to *personal property*, which is moveable property) can be a valuable resource. You may not have paid much attention to it, but the columns on the 1850, 1860, and 1870 censuses indicating "value of real estate" are records of landownership; the 1890, 1900, and 1910 censuses had check boxes related to ownership of real property.

Land Records Can Be Difficult to Locate

The location of records is determined by the jurisdiction involved, the types of records the jurisdiction kept, and any subsequent transfers of custody. Sometimes, to obtain the information from a document, our research must first determine the location of the document. (See chapter two, Where Are the Records?, for suggestions.)

It's always good to remind ourselves that the actual document of transfer—the grant or deed—was a private document, a contract between two individuals. You probably have the deed to your own house locked away in a safe-deposit box, right? As researchers, when we refer to "deeds," we're usually referring to the copy of the deed recorded in the deed book. Recording deeds hasn't always been a requirement. Recording required a fee, funds that our ancestors didn't always have readily at hand.

Researchers Don't Know What Wonderful Stuff Is in Them

I was team-teaching a class on problem solving, and we had recommended that one of the students search the deeds for a particular county. She hadn't used land records before. It was a new area for her, so she inquired, "What will deeds tell me?" In perfect unison, my team teacher and I shrugged our shoulders and said, "I don't know." **The reality is that land records can contain valuable information beyond the basics of the transaction, but it is totally unpredictable.**

We know what to expect from, say, a marriage certificate: names of bride and groom, date and place of marriage, who performed the ceremony. We know what to *hope* for: additional information such as names of parents, residence of bride and groom, and age of each. With land records, the types of additional information you find are much less predictable. Let's look at some of the possibilities.

WHAT CAN LAND RECORDS TELL US?
Anchor Your Ancestor in Time and Place

Unless your ancestor was a speculator, his deed or grant securely anchors him to a specific location—not a state, county, or township, but a very small, very real acreage.

For More Info

LEARN ABOUT THE CENSUS
See Kathleen W. Hinckley, *Your Guide to the Federal Census.*

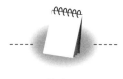

Notes

You can use this information to identify nearby churches, cemeteries, and schools that might lead to additional records. By examining the geographical features and transportation routes, you can determine the most convenient courthouse and the town or hamlet in which he bought household supplies.

Killian Kreek bought 288 acres on Tamhauck [Tomahawk] Creek in Pittsylvania County, Virginia, in 1779. I had platted his land (see chapter eleven, Metes-and-Bounds Land Platting), located it on the map, and carefully studied the area. Therefore, an entry in the card catalog for the Manuscript and Document Section of the University of Virginia Library caught my eye. The card was for store records of Samuel Calland. Callands is the name of the crossroads near Tomahawk Creek and the site of the courthouse from 1772 through 1777 (when Chatham became the county seat). This building was acquired by Samuel Callands to use for his store. It was a place I was confident that Killian Kreek had known. These particular records, however, were for a store at Piney Mount near John Smith's *Pocket* plantation on the Staunton River, far away from Tomahawk Creek.

I decided that this was a good opportunity to learn more about store records, so I requested the archive box. Inside the cover of the last volume, I found an item not listed in the box inventory. It was a small copy book, "A List of Debts due Saml Calland for Dealing at his store on Tomahawk taken 15th Nov 1784," that ran for nine months. On 27 November "Killion Kreek per self" (on his own account) bought a number of items for £7.8.3, including men's shoes and buckles, saddle straps, a cuttoe knife (a large knife, somewhat like a machete), a variety of fabric and items made of fabric—and a quart of rum.

Killian made purchases several other times and appears to have received credit for hauling tobacco. A careful examination of the purchases told me much about Killian's life. He wore shoes—his wife and children didn't (or they wore well-worn shoes). He owned a horse. The family purchased little foodstuff, but had to purchase all their cloth.

I would not have found this record if I had not researched Killian Kreek's land and identified the nearest store.

Determining the precise location of your ancestor's land can help you in a variety of ways. For example, you may realize that, because of county-boundary changes or new county formations, your ancestor's land was in another county during part of his ownership, leading you to additional records.

Learn About the Land

In chapter seven, What's in a Deed?, you'll learn that one of the tricks about using land records is to *read every word*. **Pay close attention to the detailed location description of the land.** It will often provide bits of physical information about your ancestor's property.

Tip

The general land description may mention a road or waterway, "a lot near the crossroad," "on both sides of Pigg River Road," "adjoining the mill pond," or "on Branches of Christophers Run and Tomerhawk Creek." Corners in metes-and-bounds land descriptions are often described as "a chestnut oak," "a clump of pines," "a persimon in edge of old field," "a black gum sassafras & Ash," or even "a pile of rocks formerly a hickory." Lines might be described as along "the meanders of the Creek" or "the great road leading toward Fredricks Tavern." Each of those descriptions gives a mental picture of one portion of the land.

Even in public-land states, physical characteristics may be used to describe the land. For example, we learn a lot about both the *topography* and the use of the land when Jacob Halsey and his wife Laura sold one acre of Township 4 Range 12 section 33 in Meigs County, Ohio, "on the middle branch of Shade River at the mouth of Jacob Halsey's lane on the north side of the creek at the fording that now crosses to Jervis Halsey's. The land is sold for the purpose of erecting a mill and mill dam." (See chapter ten, Maps, Atlases, and Gazetteers, to learn more about topography and topographic maps.)

Visit the Ancestral Home Place

Some of us, particularly those whose background isn't that far removed from the farm, may want to visit, to see, to walk on the dirt our ancestors owned. Others find that seeing the land gives them a stronger sense of connection to their ancestors.

In a public-land state, the land description in a grant or deed is usually sufficient for you to locate the land and drive straight to it (see chapter twelve, Public-Land Survey System). In a state-land state, the problem may be more difficult but not impossible (see chapter eleven, Metes-and-Bounds Land Platting).

LAND RECORDS SOLVE PROBLEMS!

As with any genealogical record, **land records are most powerful when used in conjunction with other records.** Genealogical problem solving is based on *synergism*; the total effect is greater than the sum of the individual parts. Land records can be one of the most important elements of this synergism.

You can often use land records in breaching a brick-wall problem or in building a case when there isn't a single record with an explicit statement of relationship.

Tip

Establish Dates of Residence

Land records can help you determine when your ancestor lived where. This seemingly trivial fact often is ignored. Such information frequently highlights the reasonableness—or unreasonableness—of a genealogical claim.

For example, if your ancestor owned land in Ohio from 1810 through 1845, he probably is *not* the man of that name who married a gal in North Carolina in 1823, even if he was born there. It isn't conclusive proof, but be practical. If your ancestor had been farming the land in Ohio for thirteen years, why would he suddenly decide to return to North Carolina to seek a bride? That's taking the phrase "childhood sweethearts" a bit too seriously. There were plenty of eligible women in his own neighborhood. The marriage record is most likely for a cousin of the same name.

On the other hand, if you can show that he returned to North Carolina to settle matters of his father's estate—and land records are one of your best possibilities—you can build a case that he *is* the groom.

Establish Age Estimates

From a practical point of view, most men were at least twenty-five, often thirty, before they had enough money to purchase real estate. Some men labored most of their productive years before saving enough for their first purchase. Thus, if your ancestor John Jones bought land in 1830, you suspect that he was born before 1805 or even earlier.

Use this information in conjunction with other records. If your John Jones was the only John Jones in the county, then the census probably provided a rough age estimate for him already. But what if there are two men of that name and several additional Jones households? Maybe by using the records together, you can identify your ancestor on the census.

Both boys and girls were considered old enough to witness documents at fourteen, although in practice this rarely happened.

Learn Your Ancestor's Occupation

There were many more men of the same name, even in the small communities of our ancestors, than we at first realize. Clerks and scribes were well aware of the potential for confusion and used various identifiers to help with the problem. The majority of deeds written before preprinted forms gave the place of residence (always the county, often the township in areas with named townships) and often the occupation.

Of course, given that the area of interest here is land records, it isn't surprising that the most common occupation given was that of *farmer*. The terminology varied, though. In early Delaware, for example, he might have been styled a *yeoman* or *planter*. Do not read more into these terms than should be there. For instance, do not interpret *yeoman* in an American deed as having the old English meaning of a retainer in a noble household, nor assume that a *planter* was wealthy.

What is interesting, though, is how many men who were clearly buying and selling land on which they were residing had occupations other than farmer, usually a skilled trade. We often see a carpenter or a blacksmith or a cordwainer (a leather worker) identified in deeds, suggesting that they earned ready cash (or bartered for needed items) to supplement the highly seasonal earnings and expenses of farming.

Establish Earlier or Later Residences

When someone moves, they generally sell their real property (real estate) shortly before they move. When they arrive in a new locale, they generally buy property soon thereafter (if they have the money to make a purchase). These typical patterns allow us to suggest the possible dates for moves and migrations.

Sometimes things don't follow this pattern precisely. Perhaps your ancestor didn't get his property sold before he moved—or maybe he just wanted to be sure that Texas was a place worth settling down in. Conversely, he may have been a careful planner who purchased his land before pulling up stakes.

The latter was the case with George Law. On 24 July 1856 he purchased 120 acres in Monroe County, Illinois. In the deed he is called "George Law of Philadelphia and State of Pennsylvania." This description was again used when he bought an additional forty acres on 26 August 1857. This immediately suggested searching Philadelphia records. The city directories listed him from 1848 through 1858 as a stonecutter, residing in the area north and west of Rittenhouse Square. When I visited Philadelphia, I was able to walk to each of his residences. Written inquiries to the City Archives produced copies of his naturalization intention and naturalization, including signatures.

His 1858 will, in which George left everything to his wife, Tamar, reiterates that he was "late of the City of Philadelphia, and State of Pennsylvania, now residing in Munroe County, in the State of Illinois."

In 1887 "Tamar Law of the County of Monroe and State of Illinois" sold forty acres of George's land. In 1895 "Tamar Law, a single woman of Milwaukee State of Wisconsin" sold another forty acres. It hadn't been necessary to read the deeds to learn of George's earlier residence since he repeated it in his will, but there was no other way to learn of Tamar's *later* residence.

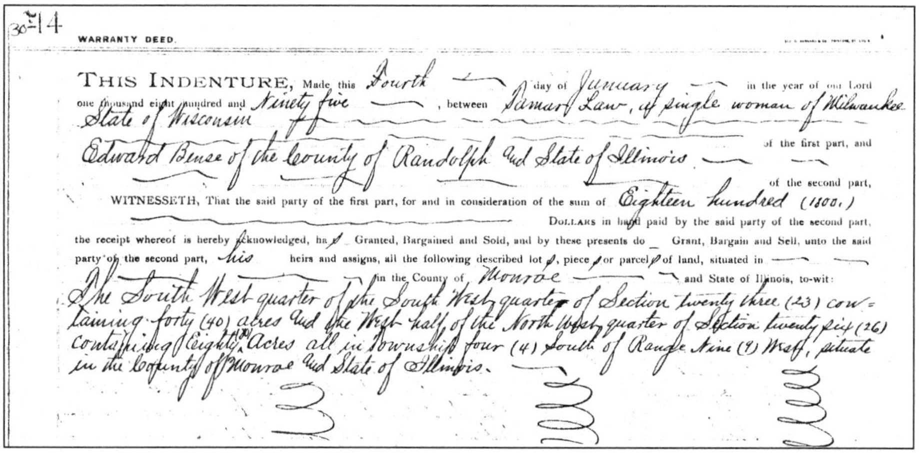
30-14

WARRANTY DEED.

THIS INDENTURE, Made this Fourth day of January in the year of our Lord one thousand eight hundred and Ninety five, between Tamar Law, a single woman of Milwaukee State of Wisconsin of the first part, and Edward Bense of the County of Randolph and State of Illinois of the second part,

WITNESSETH, That the said party of the first part, for and in consideration of the sum of Eighteen hundred (1800.) DOLLARS in hand paid by the said party of the second part, the receipt whereof is hereby acknowledged, has Granted, Bargained and Sold, and by these presents do Grant, Bargain and Sell, unto the said party of the second part, his heirs and assigns, all the following described lots, pieces or parcels of land, situated in the County of Monroe and State of Illinois, to-wit:

The South West quarter of the South West quarter of Section twenty three (23) containing forty (40) acres and the West half of the North West quarter of Section twenty six (26) containing Eighty (80) Acres all in Township four (4) South of Range Nine (9) West, situate in the County of Monroe and State of Illinois.

Figure 1-3 Tamar Law deed

Once again, land records had pointed to a new locality and new records. The index to Milwaukee death certificates reported that Tamar died 1 February 1899. They also noted a death for James W. Law on 30 June 1895, whom I suspected might be their son, probably born in Philadelphia. The certificates showed that he died of pneumonia, was indeed the son of George and Tamar, was born 11 July 1854 in Philadelphia, and had followed his father's occupation as a stonecutter.

Tamar's Milwaukee death certificate reports that she died of pneumonia, her maiden name was Weston, and she was born 2 July 1819 in England, the daughter of William Weston and Mary W.

Yes, death certificates can provide wonderful information—but you may need to use deeds to find them. This is a typical example of using land records in conjunction with other genealogical records.

Figure 1-4 The death certificate for Tamar Law, giving the names of her parents and exact age at death, was found only through the deed from Randolph County, Illinois, showing she had moved to Milwaukee, Wisconsin.

451

THE N. O. HAZALL MFG. CO., STATIONERS, MILWAUKEE, WIS.

REGISTRATION OF DEATH.

(To be returned within 30 days to the Register of Deeds of the County in which the Death occurs.)

No. 1248

1.	Full name of deceased	*Tamar Law*
2.	Maiden name (if wife or widow)	*Weston*
3.	Color	*White*
4.	Sex	*Female*
5.	Race (a)	
6.	Occupation of deceased	*Housewife*
7.	Age (years, months and days)	*79 yrs 6 mos 29 days*
8.	Name of father	*St— Weston*
9.	Birthplace of father	*England*
10.	Name of mother	*Mary H.*
11.	Birthplace of mother	*England*
12.	Birthplace of deceased	*do*
13.	Name of wife of deceased	
14.	Name of husband of deceased	*George Law*
15.	Date of bearth of deceased	*July 2 - 1819*
16.	Condition (single, married or widowed)	*Widow*
17.	Date of death	*Feb 1 - 1899*
18.	Residence at time of death	*Milwaukee*
19.	Cause of death { Primary / Secondary	*Pneumonia*
20.	Place of death	*1916 - Prairie St.*
21.	Duration of disease	
22.	Was the deceased ever a Soldier or Sailor in the service of the United States	
23.	Place of burial	*Red Bud, Ills*
24.	Name of undertaker or other person conducting burial	*Brett & Son*
25.	Date of Certificate	*Feb 2 - 1899*

Research Tip

Identify the Wife—or Wives—of Your Ancestor

Even if the wife is not named in the body of the deed, there may be a dower release from her recorded after the deed and acknowledgment. If a woman could not come into town to give her release, due to age, pregnancy, or illness, for example, a justice of the peace took her statement at home.

Not all states and colonies required dower release in all time periods. Additionally, the clerk's personal interpretation may have affected how rigorously the requirement was followed. One clerk may have been meticulous about requiring the dower before recording the deed, while another may have obtained the release and recorded it only at the landowner's insistence. You should examine many deeds in the deed book to see which kind of clerk you're working with.

Remember, the dower release is only for the wife of the seller. The wife of the buyer was not a party to the deed unless she was there for a specific reason, which is not usual.

Carefully read all deeds of sale for your ancestor. Note the name of the wife in the dower release—or the lack thereof. Let's say you have a marriage between John Jones and Mary Smith in 1815 and a will in 1843 in which John names his wife Mary. Your ancestor, their daughter, was born in 1828. Your ancestor is the daughter of Mary Smith, right? Maybe not. Suppose you have the following deeds of sale for John Jones:

1817	dower release by Mary
1821	no dower release
1825	dower release by Alice
1826	dower release by Alice
1832	dower release by Alice
1841	dower release by Mary

The picture is quite different, isn't it? John married three times, and you are descended from the middle wife, Alice. Never skip reading deeds because you think they have nothing to tell you.

DOWER, DOWER THIRDS, AND DOWRY

Dower was the lifetime interest that the law allowed a widow to retain in the real property of her deceased husband in order to maintain herself and her children. Under English common law as interpreted in America, women had a one-third lifetime *dower interest* in the real property of their husbands. Because *dower rights* represented real property rather than personal property, in much of early America a husband couldn't sell land—thereby selling his wife's protection—without his wife's consent to give up her *dower thirds*.

Therefore, we find the *dower release* of the wife recorded in deed books. She usually was questioned out of the presence of her husband (or at least that's what the records *say* was done).

Don't confuse dower with *dowry*, the property that a woman brings to her husband in marriage. In America, dowry rarely included land.

Establish Death Dates

If a deed shows land being sold on by the *estate of* John Jones or by William Jones, *executor of* (or *administrator of*) John Jones, then clearly John died before the date of the deed. There should have been a will or administration, but it isn't uncommon to find such a land record without the associated probate. On your family group sheet for the death date, you can enter "before 2 January 1848."

An even more interesting example is that of the death of the widow. Because of the widow's dower interest, her husband's three hundred acres couldn't be "sold out from under" her after he died. A couple of options existed. The land could be partitioned (more on this process in chapter two, Where Are the Records?), or the widow could retain her dower right to her portion of the three hundred acres. When the widow died, her dower rights went to the named beneficiaries in the will or to the heirs of the deceased husband (not to the widow's heirs, because she only owned an interest during her life).

Either way, you may find a deed from the heirs written shortly after the death of the widow. Once again, you can say that the widow died probably shortly before the date of the deed. The trick is spotting the deed. It probably won't be indexed under the name of the deceased husband or the widow. The dower interest usually ended up with the couple's children and is indexed under their names. Not all indexes list all parties (more on this in chapter four, Finding a Deed in a Courthouse). You should always scan the surname in the index for additional interesting possibilities. Deeds marked *et al* (and others) or identified as *quitclaims* are quite possibly prompted by a widow's death. The trickiest ones to find are those for which the first child named—and the only one indexed—happens to be a married daughter.

These deeds rarely state that the land is being sold because the widow has died. Your evidence is a bit of reverse logic—the land couldn't have been sold without her being a party to the deed *unless* she had died.

Find Statements of Relationships

The big payoff in deeds, and the reason it is so sad that more researchers don't use them, is that they so often contain the only statement of relationships we will find. For the colonial period, few areas outside of New England have vital and church records to establish family relationships. We must rely on land records in order to reconstruct families.

Important

Two types of records—*deeds of gift* and *maintenance agreements*—usually derive specifically from family relationships.

"For natural love and affection" is the standard phrase found in *deeds of gift*. Occasionally the relationship is stated explicitly, sometimes it isn't. Be careful when making notes and reporting findings that you do not insert wording such as "their son" that in any way could be construed as having been part of the original record. Sometimes the consideration (payment) included a token monetary value, such as one dollar or five shillings. This doesn't mean anything special; they were just trying to ensure that the document couldn't be challenged. Often several deeds of gift were made at about the same time. Records about women can be difficult to find, but deeds of gift to a daughter when the husband is named prove both father and marriage for her. The following deeds of gift are all for land in Barren County, Kentucky. The slight variations in wording are typical.

29 May 1807 John Garnett and Betsy his wife to Richard Garnett of Barren Co. *for natural affection and $1.*

11 May 1811 Elizabeth Wright to *her son* Thomas Wright *for natural love and affection.*

19 June 1811 Thomas Hardy to George Hardy *for $10 and the love & esteem he bears unto his son* George Hardy.

19 June 1811 from Thomas Hardy to Nancy Burks (wife of John Burks) *for $10 and love and esteem for his daughter.*

[no month or day] 1811 Thomas Hardy to Jeduthan Hardy *for $10 and love and esteem for his son.*

Maintenance agreements usually are seen between elderly parents and one of their children. Sometimes the child is the eldest son, while at other times it may be the youngest daughter.

On 23 June 1795 Adam Wahle and his wife Maria Ablonia of Warrington Township, York County, Pennsylvania, sold to their son Michael Wahle of Warrington 131 acres, plus timberland in Warrington. In exchange, Michael agreed to pay £425 and support his parents in their old age.

Things don't always work out, and maintenance agreements often were

I knew that the given name of the wife of Jeremiah Claypoole was Sarah. Early genealogies even said her last name was Shepard, but without a hint as to the source of this information. It was quite by accident that I found the deed with the answer while I was reading microfilm for another problem. (Recently, abstracts of that deed book have been published, which could have saved me many hours struggling with the problem of Sarah's identity. With modern personal computers, more and more abstracts are being published. This is a promising time to investigate land records.)

I had figured out that Sarah was born in the early 1690s. The deed with her lineage was from a series of three deeds executed in 1743.

. . . between Jacob Kollock of the town of Lewes in the County of Sussex upon Delaware Esqr and Comfort Kollock widow and relict of Simon Kollock late of the same place Esqr of the one part and Thomas Gordon of the County of Sussex afsd yeoman of the other part Whereas Jacob Kollock by virtue of a former marriage with Alice Shepherd and also by purchase made from Jeremiah Claypool and Sarah his wife . . . the afsd Comfort Kollock sister of the afsd Sarah and Alies which three sisters where [*sic*] the daughters and coheirs at law to a certain Hercules Shepard late of the County afsd who intermarried with Mary Avery one of the daughters and coheirs at law of John Avery late of the County of Sussex afsd decd . . . which said land did descend and came to the afsd Comfort Kollock, Sarah Claypoole & Alies Kollock from the afsd John Avery in whom the rights was invested and also the father of the afsd Mary Shepherd mother to the afsd three sisters . . .

Sarah, Comfort, and Alice Kollock were the daughters of Hercules Shepard and Mary Avery; Mary Avery was the daughter of John Avery. Connections between three generations proved in one deed. Pretty nifty, huh?

changed. In this instance, it was probably because Michael was relocating to Monaghan Township, where he bought land in 1801, a move his parents didn't want to make. No subsequent agreement was found in the land records, although a guardian was appointed for Adam in 1801.

> On 22 August 1799 Michael Wiley of Warrington canceled the 1795 letter of agreement with Adam and Mary Wiley of Warrington.

Notice that these two documents accomplished something else. They turned what was thought to be a Scotch-Irish family into a family of German immigrants by proving that Adam, Mary, and Michael *Wiley* were the same as Adam, Maria Ablonia, and Michael *Wahle*. These two deeds are the *only* records that tell of this, or for that matter, tell us that Michael is the son of Adam and Maria Ablonia.

Deeds sometimes contain statements of relationship in the chain of title, explaining how the land was inherited. Occasionally the statements can be quite extensive, covering multiple generations and identifying an assortment of spouses and siblings. This is most common in early records in the original colonies.

Reconstruct the Community

Deeds contain names—lots and lots of names. To solve genealogical problems, such as the father of an ancestor or the maiden name of a wife, you should use land records to gather names of friends, relatives, neighbors, and associates.

The other party to a deed may be a stranger to your ancestor, or he may be a close connection. It is always a good idea to do a quick record scan to determine who the person was and if he might be connected to your ancestor.

The adjoining property owners were your ancestor's neighbors. Your ancestor might have known some of them before he purchased the property. He surely knew them while he lived there. He might have been related to some of them before he owned the land. He might have become related by marriage to some of them *after* he lived there awhile.

Research Tip

If you don't know where your ancestor came from, investigating the origins of his neighbors isn't a bad place to start. Often a man purchased a particular piece of property because someone he knew told him about it. That person was quite possibly someone from back home who either wrote the news to your ancestor or mentioned it to him when your ancestor stopped by to visit and said he was looking to buy some land.

When looking for a potential spouse, you should begin by looking for someone within "kissin' distance." Young couples needed time to court, time that was available only after the day's chores were done or on Sunday. They couldn't go far, so their options were limited. Look for nearby families with similarly aged young people. In your own research, you've probably encountered situations where several siblings in one family married several siblings in another family. An investigation into land records would probably show that they were close neighbors.

Prepare to Research

To make the most of your research efforts, invest a little time before heading for the library or courthouse. It may save you lots of time in the future.

STEP 1. Get focused. Research into land records can be quite involved. Select a single problem, and write a problem statement.

STEP 2. Review. Don't go rushing off seeking new documents when you may not have gleaned everything there is in what you've already found. During this review, focus particularly on potential land-related events and items. For example, was there a value in the real-estate column in the 1850 census?

STEP 3. Create a chronology. Again, focus on land. Include events for your ancestor's siblings and extended family. You may find important information to help you in their land records.

STEP 4. Study the time and place. Create a political chronology. New counties were formed—and existing counties changed boundaries—frequently during settlement. Compare your political chronology and maps to your family chronology so that you will be sure you are searching in the right place. Collect maps (see chapter ten, Maps, Atlases, and Gazetteers) to help you in this effort.

Step By Step

Date	Place	Event
by 1824	Rocky Run, Greene Co.	acquired 100 acres ***find this***
1824–33	Rocky Run, Greene Co.	owned 100 acres [tax lists]
after 1833	Rocky Run, Greene Co.	disposed of 100 acres ***find this***
1830	Greene Co.	census, 010001–110001
by 1839	Cripple Creek, Greene Co.	Acquired 150 acres ***find this***
11 Dec 1839	Cripple Creek, Greene Co.	150 acres sold to John Jones. [Deeds B:333]
1840	Greene Co.	census, 0001001–0010001
1841	*Brown Co. from Greene Co.*	*new county formation*
1850	Brown Co.	census, John 55, Mary 51

STEP 5. Review family group sheets. Make sure you have the names of your ancestors' siblings, children, and in-laws—and their spouses—readily at hand. You may need to use them in searching for quitclaims, and you want to recognize them when they appear in a document.

STEP 6. Learn. This book will give an overview. Review the portions that relate to your selected problem. Many additional resources are listed in this book. Examine those that apply.

STEP 7. Create a land chart. List the pieces of property that your ancestor

Figure 1-5 Make a chart to ensure that for every piece of land owned by your ancestor that you have found the record by which he acquired it and the record by which it passed out of his ownership.

Description	Acquire	Dispose
Greene County 100 acres on Rocky Run, listed on taxes 1824–33	??	??
Greene County 150 acres on Cripple Creek	??	sold to John Jones, 11 Dec 1839. Greene Co. Deeds B:333
Check for other Smith deeds in Greene Co. 1820–1840		
Check for Smith deeds in Brown Co. 1840–1860		

owned, the document that shows how he got it, and the document that shows how he got rid of it.

STEP 8. Design a research plan. Based on your chart, list where to search and what to search for.

STEP 9. Have fun researching land records!

TWO

Where Are the Records?

Reminder

T he answer to "Where are the records?" is determined by a different question, "How was the land transferred?" There are many ways to transfer land. Each type of transfer generated as few as none and as many as half a dozen records. This chapter provides an overview of the most common types of land transfers. You may have to do a bit of research to find where the records are housed and to access them most conveniently. **For any piece of land, you will look for two transfers:**

- When the land came into your ancestor's possession—*acquisition*.
- When the land left your ancestor's possession—*disposition*.

You will need to investigate a variety of transaction types.

ACQUISITION	DISPOSITION
Patent or grant	Deed
Deed	Quitclaim
Quitclaim	Will
Inheritance by will	Intestacy
Inheritance by intestacy	Silent inheritance
Silent inheritance	Court suit
Court suit	Division/partition
Division/partition	Assignment
Assignment	Escheatment

In addition to these events of acquisition and disposition, there also may be records of ownership or of possession, such as mortgages, leases, or agreements. Records concerning rights or interest in land, which occur when land is inherited jointly, are of special importance to genealogists.

Researching the Records
As with anything in genealogy, you can't just research people—you also must research the records.

For More Info

LEARN ABOUT THE FAMILY HISTORY LIBRARY

See Paula Stuart Warren and James W. Warren, *Your Guide to the Family History Library,* and their video, "The Video Guide to the Salt Lake City Family History Library." Hurricane, Utah: The Studio, 2002, <www.123geneal ogy.com>.

Printed Source

Appendix A: Locality Reference points you to resources that will help you learn about the records and researching in your state of interest.

Appendix B: General Resources lists a number of resources that you will want to use to survey what is available. I always begin with the Family History Library Catalog (FHLC), which is part of the FamilySearch system of The Church of Jesus Christ of Latter-day Saints (LDS).

More than half a century ago, the Genealogical Society of Utah (GSU), the family-history entity of the church, began microfilming records to help its members research their ancestral families. The GSU agreed to make the microfilm readily available to the public through the Family History Library (FHL), so many state, county, and local jurisdictions agreed to the microfilming.

The record holders received a copy of the microfilm, thereby helping to preserve their own records at no cost to themselves. If you visit a courthouse or archives, you may be surprised to discover that you will be seated at a microfilm reader and handed a roll of FHL microfilm (which you could have read without leaving your hometown).

When GSU took their microfilm cameras into a courthouse, they didn't film every record in the building. They had a list of the records considered "genealogically significant." Fortunately, the early planners of the microfilming program understood the importance of land records in piecing together families, so deeds were on the "to-be-filmed" list. Not all land records were filmed, however. Sometimes volumes with labels such as "Mortgages," "Agreements," or "Leases" were skipped. In counties that had suffered severe record losses, the "to-be-filmed" list included everything.

The microfilming parameters didn't extend into filming more recent records. Early microfilming (mostly in the eastern states) often terminated after the deed books containing the year 1850. Later on, particularly for midwestern states, filming extended later. Most deed indexes, however, are consolidated and cover extensive time periods, often into the twentieth century. If the index points to deeds you want, you can write a letter to the Recorder of Deeds to order copies.

There are many published abstracts of or indexes to deeds at the county level, particularly for eastern states. Your best survey source for these is the FHLC, although you should always check other library catalogs, *Periodical Source Index* (PERSI—see page 47), and online sources. (See chapter three, Finding a Deed Without Using Vacation Time.)

Specific records of land transfer belong to the jurisdiction that had authority over that transfer of that land at that time. The governmental level might be federal, state, county, parish, or town. It is also possible that the authority was private. Within each government level, there may be several offices that might have jurisdiction.

Deed Books

Most land transfers were by deed between two individuals and are recorded in deed books.

Land records other than deeds, such as quitclaims, mortgages, leases, assignments, and divisions, are also routinely found in deed books.

Additionally, some actions may have been recorded originally in the records

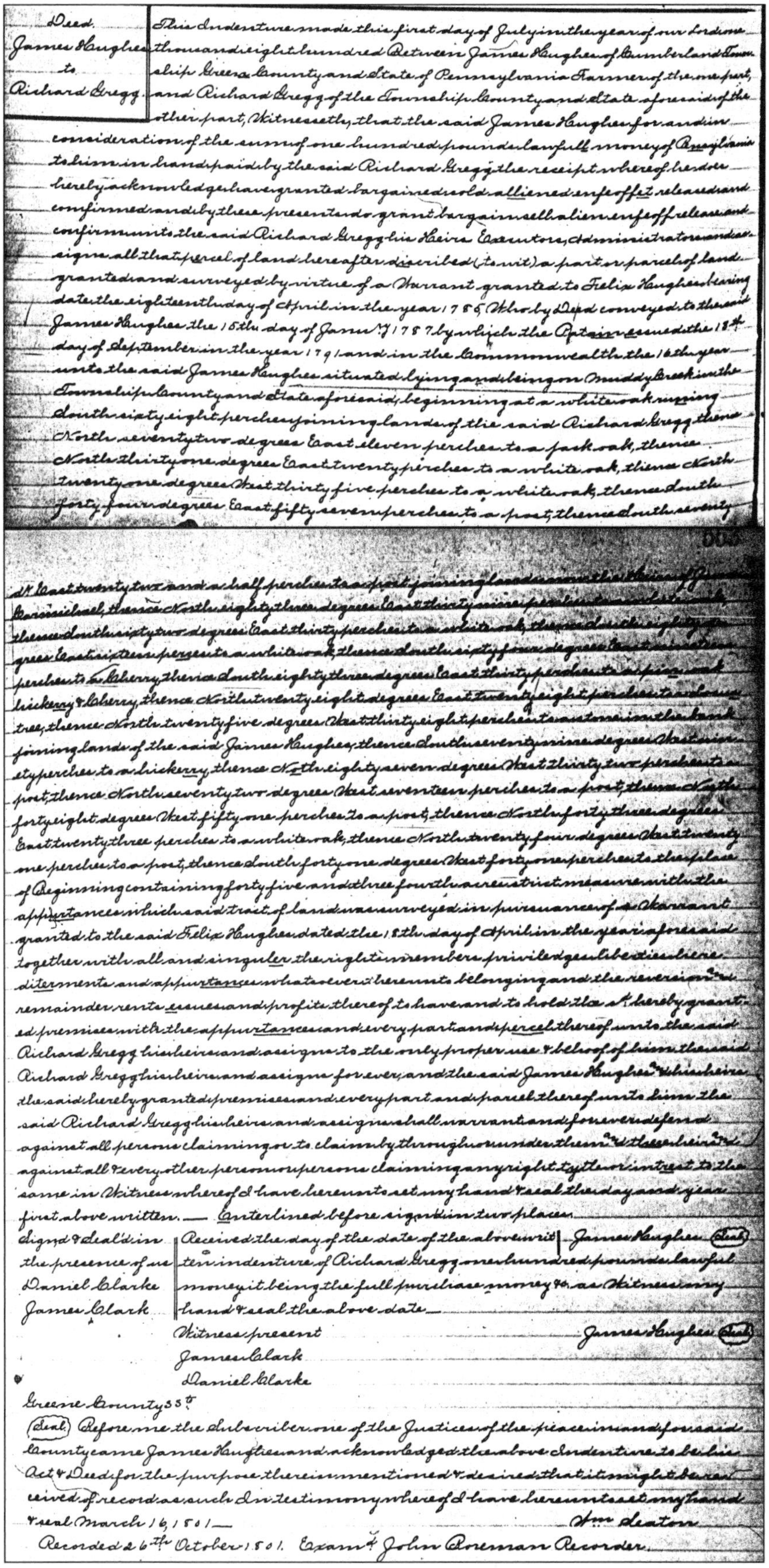

Figure 2-1 Deeds such as this one from 1801 are the most voluminous type of land records. Unfortunately, few are as legible as this one.

Figure 2-2 Amos Janney's surveys in Virginia's Northern Neck included an ornate compass rose—with north at the left on this example. This survey is for a woman, and the name of her husband is given.

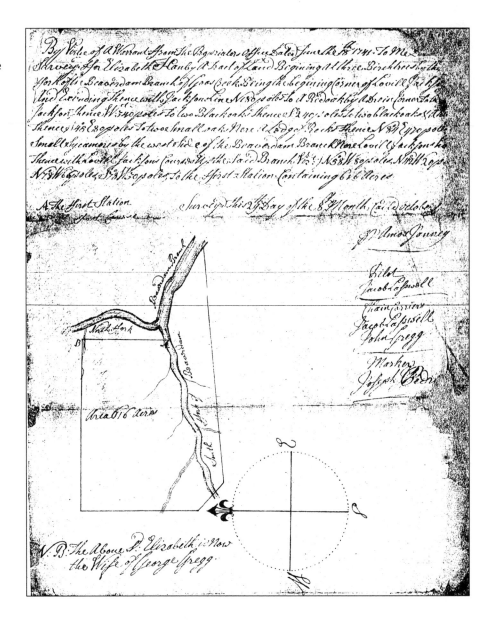

of the probate or civil courts (see "Courts—Probate and Civil" on page 21), then re-recorded in the deed books.

Other Land Books

As the record volume grew, some jurisdictions began recording some types of documents in a designated volume of their own.

It is, for example, routine to find early mortgages amidst the deeds but later mortgages in dedicated volumes.

Surveys were usually kept in separate volumes. Sometimes (but not always) these became the property of the county. Sometimes, as in the case of the surveys for Virginia's Northern Neck, they are loose papers. The metes-and-bounds descriptions in deeds derive from these surveys. An initial survey was made when the land was granted. Subsequent resurveys were often required because of the inaccuracies of earlier surveys or because the land was subdivided. A word of warning if you can find a survey book showing your ancestor's land—

the surveyor oriented the drawing in whatever position was most convenient, so north was not necessarily at the top.

Courts—Probate and Civil

Land was usually a family's most valuable asset. **Upon a landowner's death, the land might transfer in a variety of ways,** leaving an even greater variety of records (or lack thereof).

- Some landowners clearly identified in their wills who was to inherit which parcel. This record of transfer is recorded in a will book, which is a record of the probate court.
- Some landowners never got around to making a will, dying *intestate*. In this case, the law determined who inherited the land. The law varied by time and place. Records of intestacy also are found in the probate court. They may refer to land transfers or have detailed descriptions of land partitions, or they may not mention the land explicitly at all.
- Some landowners left land jointly to two or more of their children, or they neglected to mention all parcels of land. Records in this case might be found in a probate court, in deed books, or in a civil court.
- Not all families got along amicably. In any of the previously mentioned circumstances, you may find squabbles about land in the records of a civil court, known as the court of equity or chancery. In some times and places, this court also was used to record friendly divisions of land.

HOW WAS THE LAND TRANSFERRED?

Land transferred between individuals in a variety of ways, far too many for this book to consider in-depth. We will discuss the most common transfers—and the most interesting.

My Ancestor Was an Original Owner—Grants and Patents

The first transfer of a piece of property was from some government entity into the hands of an individual. There is such variety in these records that they are the topic of two other chapters:

- Chapter five, First Transfer—Getting Land Into the Hands of Individuals, discusses the original thirteen colonies, plus Alaska, Hawaii, Kentucky, Maine, Tennessee, Texas, and Vermont, and bounty land.
- Chapter six, Public Lands, discusses the thirty public-domain states.

My Ancestor Was Typical—Deeds

It is quite possible that your ancestor's only purchase of land was a straightforward purchase from another individual. The recording of the purchase might not have been as straightforward, however.

For example, suppose Abraham Abbott sold land to Benjamin Butler in exchange for money. The record that states that Abraham Abbott transferred title of the property to Benjamin Butler is called a deed. A deed is a piece of paper, signed by Abraham Abbott, which is then given to Benjamin Butler.

That piece of paper was Benjamin Butler's private property, but he probably wanted protection against the possibility of loss of this precious document, so his deal with Abraham Abbott included that Abraham would have the deed recorded in the county in which the land lay. The deed couldn't be recorded until Abraham acknowledged in front of an official that he had signed the document (hence Benjamin couldn't have the deed recorded without Abraham's cooperation). See chapter seven, What's in a Deed?, to learn more about acknowledgments and recording.

Reminder

Early in America's history, there was no requirement that deeds be recorded, although a recorded deed might be considered more binding or to have precedence over an unrecorded deed. Eventually laws were passed requiring deeds to be recorded, in part to help the county in tax collection. Needless to say, there was no great rush to comply. You will find that in some localities almost all deeds were promptly recorded, but that in other localities (or other time periods), the opposite may be true.

In some instances, such as when land was sold within the family, our ancestors didn't feel overly motivated to rush to the courthouse and pay the filing fee. We often find these deeds recorded years, even decades, later, when the land was finally sold out of the family.

Suppose, for example, that Benjamin Butler sold the land to his son-in-law Charles Cooper. They never bothered to record it, since Benjamin continued to live with his daughter's family and helped out on the farm until his death. Twenty years later, Charles Cooper (whose only son wanted to be a sailor), decided it was time to sell the farm and move into town. Donald Dooley, who bought the land, wanted to be sure that his title was clear, so he required that the deed from Benjamin Butler to Charles Cooper be recorded at the same time as his own deed of purchase.

When reading deeds, it is always wise to look forward and backward through the deed books to see if related deeds were filed at the same time. There may be an unrelated deed or two recorded in between. Some clerks seem to have put loose deeds into a stack to be copied into the book later, not always in the expected order.

My Ancestor Left a Will—Testate Estates

Most fathers wanted the land they had worked so hard to acquire and improve to stay in the family. Do not make assumptions.

- Some fathers, echoing the concept of primogeniture (a common law principle that the eldest son inherited all real property), thought the home place should go to the eldest son.
- Many fathers lived to be quite old, perhaps even outliving their eldest son. This practical consideration means that it was often the youngest son or sons to whom a father left the home place.
- Some fathers (those who were the most successful financially) often tried to provide for each son as he came of age. Some gave each son money to buy land. Others had been systematically buying parcels of land (often widely dispersed), which they deeded to their sons. Often they had disposed of all land before they wrote their will.
- Some fathers left their land to all—or several—of their children jointly.

They may have included instructions that the land not be sold until the youngest child came of age or the mother died or remarried. When this was the case, you may find much additional information about the family in deed books, probate records, or civil court records.

- A few fathers ordered that their land be sold. I have been surprised to see how often this was true. Perhaps it was a practical matter for large families where the land represented a major portion of the value of the estate. The only way all of the children could receive a reasonable share was to sell the land.

My Ancestor Didn't Plan Ahead—Intestacy

Personally, when a father owned land, I'm usually happier to see an intestacy than a will, especially in the pre-1850 era. In a will, a man could simply leave his land to "my son John" with the rest of the estate divided among "all my children," whom he all too often didn't bother to name. In theory (but, alas, not always in practice), if he died intestate, the land would have to go through a probate court.

The name of the court, the jurisdiction, and the terminology might vary. Over time, probate cases have been heard at many court levels, initially in the catch-all county court. As examples, in Pennsylvania and Delaware, the probate court is at the county level and is called the Orphans' Court; Connecticut has probate districts, and one class of probate records in the parishes of Louisiana is called succession records.

Intestate records should include the names of all the heirs of the land, which (except under primogeniture) included all of the children—although in many places, the eldest son got a double portion of the land. Furthermore, if any of the children were minors, they had to have guardians. Our twentieth-century concepts of orphans and guardians can get in the way here. An *orphan* could still have a living parent. A *guardian* wasn't to guard the child, but the *property* of the child. Guardianship records often help us sort out the relative ages of the children in a family. Sometimes specific ages, or even birth dates, are given. Children under fourteen had guardians appointed for them. Those between fourteen and twenty-one could choose their own guardian.

My Ancestor Had Siblings—Joint Ownership

Like many fathers, Johannes Buke wanted his land to go to his sons. His will, written 27 April 1779 and probated 10 June 1786, stated:

> First I leave my whole Estate in my beloved wife Margaret Books possession untill my youngest son Micheal is sixteen years of age, and then . . . I give and bequeath to my oldest son Jacob and youngest son Micheal Book the plantation I now live on the land to be Equally divided. Jacob to have the home part at the time my youngest son is sixteen years of Age . . .

Jacob and Michael could have requested a partition (see "My Ancestor Had Siblings—Partitions" on page 28), or they could have held the 296 acres jointly and sold it together. They chose the latter. As with any deed, it is wise to read every word, because things aren't always written as they ought to be.

> This Indenture made the Seventh Day of June in the year of our Lord one thousand seven hundred and Ninety six Between Jacob __ & Michall Book in the County of Washington and State of Pennsylvania and Mary, Jacob Books wife of the one part and William Forgison of the County and State aforesaid of the other part.

We learn that Jacob has a wife Mary. You should immediately add to your family group sheets or computer database the information that Jacob married *by* 7 June 1796 Mary –?–.

When we get to the end of the deed, there is a surprise. Although it clearly says that Michael, Jacob, and Mary are signing, there also is a mark for an Elisabeth Book. Could it be that their sister Elizabeth signed? No, she clearly had no interest in this land. Following the deed are several other sections that researchers all too often ignore (see chapter seven, What's in a Deed?, to learn more about receipts, acknowledgments, and dower releases). From the first section, we learn there was a slight delay in finalizing the sale.

> Present 28 Day of march 1798 whin [*sic*] the said Michal Book was come to full age and acknowledged his signature.

Johannes may have felt that Michael was old enough to inherit the land at sixteen, but Pennsylvania required that Michael be twenty-one to sell it. The last section explains who Elizabeth was. (Don't forget to record that Michael married Elizabeth –?– *by* 28 March 1798.)

> Personally came before me the subscriber one of the commonwealths Justices of the Peace in and for said County the within named Michael Book and Elisebeth his wife She being previously examined apart from her Husband the said Michael now being of full age the[y] acknowledged the within Indenture to be their Act and Deed and desires it may be executed as such. Given under my hand and Seal this 28th Day of March 1798.

The inventory for the estate of John Book does not list his land. This is common, but many researchers don't realize this. Inventories are of "goods and chattels, rights and credits." The inventory of the goods of John Book, for example, didn't list the items sold at an earlier sale either, which were listed in a separate document; they included several books and seventy-six gallons of whiskey. This is the locality of the Whiskey Rebellion, after all!

Notes

Many deeds include a chain of title, which may recite a number of transactions. The transactions may be between family members and include both deeds and inheritances. Careful reading shows that the chain of title in this deed has several useful bits of information.

> Whereas John Bouch in the year of our Lord one thousand seven hundred and eighty eight by virtue of sundry good conveyances and assurances in law had and executed obtained a pattant for a certain tract of land called "Devisees" situate on the waters of Pegen Creek in the County of Washington ajoining lands of Jacob Forward, George Meyers, John Lyda, Nicholas Platter, and John Hill containing two hundred and nenety six acres and a

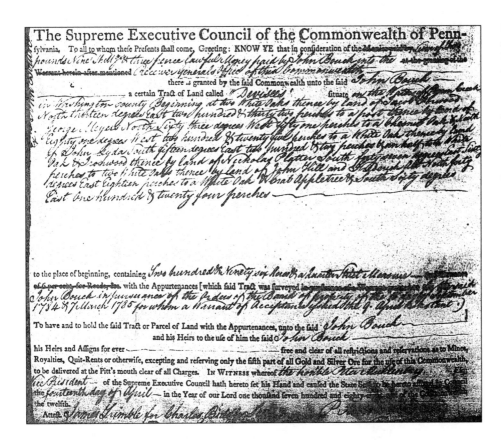

Figure 2-3 This 1788 Pennsylvania patent for *Devisees* in Washington County provides the names of adjoining landowners of John Bouch/Bouck, which are clues for further research. In some areas patents were given names, which may provide further clues for research, but not in this case.

quarter strict measure as by the pattant now inrolled in the Rolls Office in Philledelphia in Pattant Book No 14 page 132.

We learn that John was the original patentee of the land. This tells me that there is another record to check. Furthermore, there is a citation to the patent, which saved much time and effort.

The detailed metes-and-bounds description of the land that Jacob and Michael were selling identifies the adjoining property owners as Jacob Forwood, George Myers, John Lyda, Nicholas Platter, John Hill, and Fredick [*sic*] Ault. Notice that with the exception of Ault, these were the same as the neighbors identified in the patent as cited in the chain of title. I'm always interested in who the neighbors were when my ancestor moved into a new area. It is not at all unlikely that one or more of those neighbors also were kin or that they came from the same prior location of residence. A little investigation into probates shows that Nicholas Platter's daughter married one of John Bouch's sons, and John Huffman was married to John's daughter (not Elizabeth). Huffman was an executor of Johannes' will, and George Meyers was a witness.

The patent itself contains much of the same information as the deed (patents are covered more fully in chapter five, First Transfer—Getting Land Into the Hands of Individuals). It's recorded in a book of preprinted forms, two per page. The Supreme Executive Council, which was the administrative body of the Commonwealth of Pennsylvania at this time, granted the land. We also learn that although the patent was issued in 1788 (after Johannes's death!), the land was surveyed "for the said John Bouch" in 1784 and 1785. (See figure 2-3.)

The patent book provided additional information of value to the research. As with deed books, it is wise to examine the documents preceding and following the one for your ancestor. I didn't look for names, though—I looked for patents for Washington County, particularly those on Pigeon Creek. The patent immediately above that of John Bouch/Bouck was to John Huffman for land on Pigeon Creek adjoining land of Rudolph Huffman. I also found patents to Nicholas Platter and Thomas Fawcett. These names may provide leads into tracing Johannes's origins.

Do not confine your research into land records merely to those records of your ancestor. I am potentially descended from Elizabeth, sister of Jacob and Michael, who may have been the wife of James Kerr. If I had not checked the deeds of her siblings, I would know considerably less about her family.

Important

My Ancestor Had Siblings—Quitclaims

When a single individual owns a piece of land, he can sell it easily without involving other parties (other than his wife's release of dower). Suppose, however, that many individuals own the land. Such is the case when a man wills his farm "to all my children," for example. All owners (in this case, all the children) must be named as parties to the sale, and they all must sign the deed. From a practical point of view, this is inconvenient, especially if not all parties lived in the same town. The buyer just wants to get his land. Obviously the process would be easier if he could deal with just one person.

The *quitclaim* transaction solves this problem. It allows a person to sell his or her undivided interest in a piece of property. *Undivided interest* means that the individual owns, say, one-fourth of a one-hundred-acre plot, as opposed to a specific twenty-five acres of the plot. Quitclaims also are used when one of the owners wants possession of all of the property and the other owners are agreeable.

Definitions

Quitclaims transfer the rights an individual has in the property, or the *future* rights he or she has in the property, or any rights that he or she *may* have in the property. They are very flexible. We often see future rights in a quitclaim when the widow is still living and still has her dower interest. If the title to property is cloudy or under litigation, a quitclaim can be used to consolidate interest into the hands of a single person for efficiency.

I have even seen quitclaims used when the grantor did not have any legal title, but it seemed best to make it clear that he or she was not going to try to make a claim later. When a landowner with no descendants died leaving living parents, siblings, and half siblings, many people didn't understand all the nuances of the laws of inheritance—which varied by time and place—so a quitclaim could be given, even by those who legally had no right to transfer.

We most often see quitclaims resulting from inheritance (both testate and intestate). When experienced land researchers see the designation "QC" or "quitclaim" in an index, we often must exercise great discipline to continue recording the index entries, instead of immediately rushing to read the quitclaim. We *know* there's probably going to be "good stuff" therein.

On 1 July 1864, Alford Gregg of Cumberland Township, County of Greene and State of Pennsylvania, wrote his will. In it he mentioned:

3. I will to my sons Ellis B. Gregg, John W. Gregg, Edwin C. Gregg each $100 dollars or a horse worth $100 dollars this to be paid as the Boys come of age. [John and Edwin were under age at this time.]

. . .

6. My Son Ellis sent home $30 which if unpaid at my death mus [*sic*] then be paid.

Since Ellis "sent home" money, he clearly wasn't living at home. Where was he? The possible answer lies in a quitclaim recorded in Greene County thirty-five years later, on 11 August 1899.

> Know all men by these presents that I, Ellis B. Gregg, and my wife of the County of Elk and State of Kansas for and in consideration of the sum of One hundred Dollars to us in hand paid by James K. Gregg of Cumberland township Greene County Pennsylvania, . . . doth remise, release and quit-claim unto the said James K. Gregg . . . all the right, title, interest, claim and demand whatsoever which the said party of the first part may have by virtue of being an heir of Olfred [*sic*] Gregg Dec'd of, in and to the following described piece or parcel of land Situate and lying in Cumberland township Greene Co, Penns bounded and described as follows to Wit—on the East by lands of N. H. Biddle on the north by Thomas Crago, on the west by lands of James S. Kerr—and on the south by lands of John W. Hathaway Containing one hundred (100) Acres more or less this being the same tract of land owned and occupied by Olfred Gregg Dec'd in his lifetime. . . .

> Ellis B. Gregg
> Mary E. Gregg

This is the same piece of land, by the way, for which my grandfather had James Kerr's original survey plat as shown in chapter one, Why Use Land Records?

Earlier I mentioned that you should glance at deeds recorded on the pages before and after your ancestor's deed to look for related deeds. This is especially true of quitclaims. Filed together, sequentially, were eight quitclaims—or deeds that were for the purpose of quitclaiming. In addition to learning the names of their spouses, we learn from these quitclaim deeds that these siblings lived far apart.

> Ellis B. and Mary E. Gregg of Elk County, Kansas; A. E. and Elizabeth Gregg of Carmichaels; William and Sarah M. Flenniken of Carmichaels; Joseph and Susan McMillin of Monongahela, Washington County; Alexander and Ruth B. Rodgers of Wymore, Gage County, Nebraska; John W. Gregg of Randolph, Coos County, Oregon; Ann E. Gregg of Elmwood, Illinois; William C. and Ellen Gregg of Uniontown, Fayette County; and Aaron and Lucy A. Gregg of Scranton, all to James K. Gregg of Cumberland Township, Greene County, Pennsylvania.

The documents showed some of the variety you will find in deed books and indexes. Two were called quitclaims; the rest were called deeds. Most of them were listed as *et ux* (and wife), but Susan's was styled *et con.* (and consort). Ann E. signed her deed as Ann E., but signed her receipt as Anneliza, which is how it was indexed. The siblings received varying amounts, ranging from one hundred dollars to two hundred dollars, even though they were each giving up an equal portion of the land.

Why do these quitclaims exist? Another element of the will tells us:

> 5. If when my youngest son comes of age my Widow and the Executor think best to sell the farm they may do so to the best possible advantage, and in such case my Executors shall procede [*sic*] to sell all the property belonging to my estate except so much of the household goods as she may wish to keep; and pay unto my Widow Mary Gregg the interest (annually) of one third of the procedes [*sic*] of such sale while she lives, and the two thirds of the procedes [*sic*] of such sale to be divided between my children Ann Eliza Armstrong, Sarah Margaret Flennikin, Susannah McMillin, Aaron Gregg, James Gregg, Ellis B. Gregg, Wm Gregg, Ruth B. Rogers, John Gregg and Edwin Gregg, share and share alike, and at the death of my Widow the remaining one third to be divided among the above named children share & share alike.

Alford's children were to inherit his land equally and also to inherit the widow's third equally. The quitclaim is dated about one month before Mary's death. Apparently she wanted to see the estate settled before she died, consolidating it into the possession of her son James Kerr Gregg.

My Ancestor Had Siblings—Partitions

When land was inherited jointly, some method had to be found for getting each child his or her share. Often, when there was an intestacy, one of the heirs petitioned the probate court for a division of the land. The court would appoint several men (usually three) to view the land and decide how to partition it. Much of the time they returned an opinion that the land could not be divided without harm to its overall value. It may have been readily apparent to anyone that the land couldn't be divided, but the court still went through the steps of appointing the viewers and recording their opinion.

When the land could not be divided, the court often ordered a valuation of land, usually by the same men. Then, one of the heirs could buy out the other heirs at the court-recorded value. If none of the heirs wanted—or was able—to buy out the others, one of the heirs would usually petition for a public sale of the land. This generated more records when the sale was publicized. The deed of sale may be found recorded in both the probate book and the deed book—or in only one. In the deed book, the grantor may be named as the deceased, as the executor (in the case of land jointly owned through a will), as the administrator (in the case of an intestacy), or even as the public official who oversaw the sale.

If the land could be divided, a survey was made. The original survey may be found in the probate packet. A copy might be made in the probate book or in the deed book. Sometimes the children's names were written in their assigned section of the land (which was often determined by a random drawing), sometimes they were lettered with the associated child named in the text, and sometimes we don't learn who got which part until we investigate later deeds.

The acknowledgment by each child (and usually his or her spouse) of his or her share of the land or money was recorded, which can provide valuable genealogical information.

Notice in the land partition shown (see figure 2-4) that neither the surveyor nor the clerk was very picky about "right way up." The acknowledgment of one of the heirs is recorded sideways in one partition, and in another, the majority of the writing on the survey is upside down. The plot does not have an arrow indicating north—and north is not at the top!

Sometimes the land could be divided, but into fewer parcels than there were children. In this instance, you might find a combination of the options described previously.

Other options for joint inheritance are discussed in more detail below.

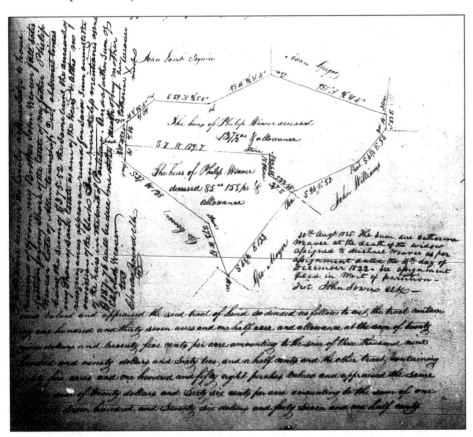

Figure 2-4 Philip Weaver's Pennsylvania farm could not be divided into separate parts for each heir, but it could be partitioned into two parts. The payment from one of the siblings for another's portion is recorded next to the plat in the deed book.

My Ancestor Spoke Latin?—et al., et ux.

As we look at indexes, we should keep alert for magic notations in the index that point toward genealogically valuable deeds.

- **The first common Latin phrase is *et ux.*, which is shorthand for *et uxor*, or "and wife."** An *et ux.* deed should, at the very least, tell you the wife's given name, which in the pre-1850 period might not be recorded elsewhere. If you have several men named John Jones in the area, using the wife's given name in conjunction with the land location can help you untangle their records.

\di'fin\ *vb*

Definitions

- The second Latin phrase you should look for is *et al.*, which is shorthand for *et alius* or *et alii*, and means "and another" or "and others." Obviously, a deed in which the clerk couldn't fit all the names onto one line in the index might contain genealogically significant information about those people. The exception would be routine deeds from trustees or commissioners for a town. Some clerks also used *et al.* for deeds that should have been indexed as *et ux*.

- Several phrases are used to identify land transactions when the owner is deceased. Look for *est.* for "estate of," *admr.* or *excr.* for "by administrators" or "by executors," or simply *heirs* for "by heirs of."

- *Quitclaims* are not always identified in the indexes as such. If they are, they may be coded *QC*.

- Any index is likely to have its own set of abbreviations. A clerk who didn't like Latin might use *& w.* (and wife), *& H.* (and husband) and *& ors.* (and o[the]rs). You'll routinely find *WD* (warranty deed), *PoA* (power of attorney), but it may take a bit of thinking to figure the meaning of *BS* (bill of sale) or *RoD* (release of dower).

- An *agreement* could cover just about anything. Since it probably is not a straightforward deed, it is also a prime candidate to contain "good stuff." Land sales contingent on maintenance and support for elderly parents may be indexed as agreements.

In discussing the quitclaim on page 26, I mentioned that this was the same land we saw in the earlier plat. But why did Alford Gregg have James Kerr's land? James Kerr left no will; I don't even know when he died, although he was apparently deceased by the 1840 census. An entry in the Greene County Deed index highlighted the answer. First, let's look at the index entry from the "K" Grantor index:

Grantor: Kerr, James Est
Grantee: Alford Gregg
Year of Inst.: 1842
Date of Record: Aug 11 1899
Recorded: 64:547
Location and area: Muddy Crk 100 A

Of course, any deed with "Est" is of interest. However, this deed was recorded more than fifty years after it was written, and Alford Gregg had been dead for more than three decades. This seems odd, doesn't it? Late-recorded deeds often indicate land that has stayed in the family.

Reminder

Because it wasn't required that deeds be recorded in a timely manner, and because it cost money, our ancestors often waited until they had a good reason, a need, to pay for the recording. This deed, which was dated 29 October 1842, was filed on the same day as the Ellis B. Gregg quitclaim and was recorded in the deed book immediately before the quitclaims.

By reading the deed, we learn the identity of Alford's widow, Mary. It tells us the name of her father and the names of her siblings, with their spouses and residences.

> This Indenture . . . By and between Margaret Kerr, and Rachel intermarried with William Wilson, William Kerr and Elizabeth his wife, Isabell Intermarried with Benjamin Grooms, Sarah intermarried with John Wiley, Archabell Kerr and Hannah his wife, Emely Intermarried with Samuel Moredock and Ann Kerr, Children and heirs at law of James Kerr Dec'd all of Greene County P.A. except William wilson and wife who is of Washington County Pennsylvania of the first part, and Alford Gregg of cumberland township Greene County P.A. of the other part. And Whereas the said James Kerr with (Mary wife of the said Alford Gregg her having an undivided Moyety in common with the other children) was in his lifetime Seised & possessed of a certain tract of land lying on the waters of Muddy Creek in Greene County aforesaid purchased from Hugh wilson of the Burrough of washington in washington county P.A. and conveyed by him the said Hugh wilson and wife unto the Said James Kerr Dec'd Bearing date the 14 day of apil [sic] 1826 and recorded in Greene County in book . . .

Whew! There are a lot of family relationships packed into this deed, aren't there? What was it we overheard a researcher saying? "I just want to find out who the father of my John is; I don't want to read microfilmed deeds." So sad.

Some of the statements in this document are ambiguous if not used in conjunction with other records. I found this deed early in my research and hadn't realized that it might not say what I thought it did until I was working on this chapter.

There is a weird parenthetical clause in the middle. At first it appears that Mary is the sister of the deceased James, especially since "moiety" usually means "half share." Fortunately most of these family members survived into the 1850s and are buried in two cemeteries, so we are able to determine relative ages and I know that Mary is James's daughter. The scribe apparently had realized at this point that he had forgotten to mention Mary's right to the land and decided to stick it in.

It was also unclear to me whether Margaret was the widow of James (deeding her dower interest) or a daughter (as other researchers had told me). I immediately dug into my other Kerr records. They conflicted. Margaret was age forty to fifty in 1840, but only forty-seven, living with Anna, in 1850. Furthermore, there was a gap between Anna and her next oldest sibling. Perhaps Anna was Margaret's daughter by James's second marriage and half-sister to the others. William said in his biography that he was the fourth of eight children, which would fit. Fortunately, the matter was resolved smoothly by Anna's obituary from Oregon, which states, "she was the youngest of the nine children of James and Elizabeth Kerr," hence Margaret was the ninth child.

My Ancestor Isn't in the Records—Silent Transfers

It is possible that land passed silently through inheritance. The silent transfer may have been through primogeniture, it may have been through inheritance where no one saw a need to involve the court system, or it may be an unrecorded deed. Primogeniture applied to some extent in the colonial period in Georgia, New Jersey, New York, Rhode Island, North Carolina, South Carolina, and Virginia.

This is probably what Donald Lines Jacobus—a New Englander who is considered to be the founder of the modern scientific model of genealogy—was thinking when he said, "in Virginia in the early decades, . . . often the first two to four generations of Virginia families have to be built on land evidences." However, the usefulness of land records in building families goes far beyond the early decades of Virginia.

It may be necessary to establish the ownership of the land to establish descent. If you're lucky, there may be sufficient records to identify the land. Often, however, you may need to work with records that concern your ancestors and records for the neighbors. It can be done. By tracking a piece of land over time, platting it (see chapter eleven, Metes-and-Bounds Land Platting, to learn how), identifying the neighbors, and platting the neighbors' land, I identified the maiden name of a woman in North Carolina and her parents—the significant bits of evidence being the corners marked by a dead beech and a post oak in several land descriptions for transactions involving neighbors' property.

Primogeniture is unfamiliar to many genealogists, yet so important for certain colonies. Under English common law, land was considered to pass automatically in whole to the eldest son (unlike personal property, which had different rules). This applied whether or not the father made a will. In colonies with primogeniture, if John Jones died without a will (intestate), his eldest son, William, received all of his land. Period. If John Jones wrote a will, then any land he didn't bother to mention in the will automatically passed to William. Period. In other words, the land transferred title because it *wasn't* mentioned in a document.

This concept that the land by right belonged to the eldest son was so strong that early Virginia statutes allowed the eldest son to challenge provisions in his father's will that gave land to someone else.

To follow a silent transfer of land, track the neighboring parcels, watching for changes in the names of landowners. When land that formerly belonged to John Jones is described as belonging to William Jones, but you have found no deed, it is likely a case of silent inheritance.

Be forewarned, though. One trap that can catch you is a practical matter of how business was done. When a man sold land, he probably contacted the scribe, handed him his current deed, and gave him the details of the new sale. He may not have mentioned that "Oh, by the way, my neighbor John Jones died ten years ago and his son William now has the land," so the scribe copied "along John Jones' line north 27 degrees east 100 poles."

My Ancestor Needed Money—Mortgages

Our ancestors took out mortgages for pretty much the same reasons that we do. Some of them had to borrow money to buy land, and they put up the land as security. Others got into financial trouble later and borrowed money against their land.

In the South, where the economy was dependent largely on a single, large cash crop of cotton or tobacco, mortgages were more common and frequent. You will often find a landowner obtaining a mortgage every year. Depending on how well he managed his affairs, he may have mortgaged just the crop, or he also may have had to mortgage slaves and land.

Mortgages were recorded in deed books. **As they became more common, they were recorded in a separate book labeled "Mortgages."** Many recorders left a blank space in the deed book, often a box at the side in which the release of the mortgage could be recorded. Other clerks just wrote the release in the margin. A few recorded them chronologically as separate instruments. However, not all releases were recorded.

In theory, a mortgage would contain wording concerning the repayment and other special language identifying it as a mortgage. In practice, however, I find that mortgages often look just like deeds, with the differences, if any, being subtle. I will find two nearly identical documents filed on the same day (or close together), with the names of the grantor and grantee exchanged. I have even found instruments where it looked like my ancestor sold the same land more than once. Other records usually make it clear which document is the deed and which is the mortgage.

Research Tip

My Ancestor Feuded—Land Transfers in Court

Disputes over land, whether between relatives or between individuals, are not criminal matters; they are civil matters. As such, they are considered in equity court or chancery court. Some ended up in appellate courts.

Sometimes these weren't really disputes. When a family needed to partition land legally, or to obtain an order so it could be sold efficiently, often one or more family members would petition the court.

It can be difficult to tell whether any specific case was a friendly suit or a family feud (unless it was appealed—that's a pretty good clue that it wasn't just a matter of convenience), so don't make assumptions. Even the standard language can sound a bit harsh. Sometimes enough details are given that you can get a good picture.

The chancery courts in Virginia heard so many land suits that some clerks decided to record those cases in separate books. Chancery suits related to land are called land causes. Separate land-cause books are found scattered in a few other localities, as well.

One of the best things about chancery suits is that they often give you information, especially about individuals other than adult males, that you can find in no other place. Consider these two entries from Accomack County, Virginia, Land Causes:

> 1800 March 3. Partition suit. Charles Leatherbury, father of Charles Leatherbury, Thomas Leatherbury, Nancy Leatherbury, John Leatherbury, Susanna Leatherbury, and Perry Leatherbury, died intestate [date blank, 17__], seized of 636 acres on Onancock.
>
> 1803 July 28. Partition suit. Nancy Leatherbury died intestate in 1802, seized of 66 acres on Onnancock Creek. She was underage without children, father, or mother, but left siblings Charles Leatherbury, Thomas Leather-

bury, John Leatherbury, Susanna Leatherbury, and Perry Leatherbury, all children of Charles Leatherbury from whom the land descended.

If there had been a will, it might not have named daughters. If it did name daughters, you would not have known that Nancy died without heirs.

Another type of land suit often heard in court was that of boundary disputes. Early surveying methods and tools were not very accurate, in part because they weren't well adapted to the reality of the American countryside. Additionally, many surveyors didn't have the best of mathematical skills.

Boundary disputes didn't usually result in a transfer of land (except in the earliest times with overlapping or "shingled" surveys), but you should still look for them because of the important details and depositions that may have been given. Boundary disputes in metes-and-bounds colonies and states, especially in the South, were so numerous that the court systems were overloaded. Processioning—walking the bounds—was one solution. In Virginia, for example, the law provided for regular processionings in which appointed officials, along with the landowners or tenants (and usually one or more long-time resident of the area), walked the perimeter of a parcel of land, refreshing corner markers such as blazes on trees (slashes made in the bark with an ax or tomahawk) or piles of stones.

My Ancestor and the Speculator

There has almost never been a time when the American land system didn't include speculators. They came from all stations of life. Many speculators were, to put it bluntly, in it for the money, but many were average individuals.

Don't consider speculation a pejorative term. Land jobbers, agents, and brokers functioned as an important part of the land-transfer process. The federal government originally intended to sell the land in the Northwest Territory to speculators and let them get it into the hands of the common man; the government thought this would be the most efficient mechanism.

The interpretation of the term *speculator* was definitely in the eye of the beholder. To many small farmers, it meant a city-residing, back-East landowner who made money from the land sale, while the farmers could barely afford enough land to support their families. To the government, it often meant an individual or a group willing to buy a large amount of land, promote it, and sell it to individuals, relieving them of some of the small-sale details.

Speculators often served a purpose that helped the ordinary man (while usually turning a profit). Many farmers considered the railroad and canal companies, who received broad swaths of alternating sections of land to promote western advancement of transportation, to be speculators. Yet those farmers or their children may have used these same railroads to move west.

Important

Recipients of military bounty-land warrants rarely settled on their land. Speculators bought up almost all of the warrants and scrip. But since bounty-land was generally not readily available for settlement until long after the military service was rendered, it is likely that the serviceman getting cash in hand felt like he had gotten the better deal.

Although we tend to think of land in agrarian terms, America had many cities and towns and villages. In many cases, these were begun by speculators. For example, in the early nineteenth century, local farmer and carpenter William Anderson laid out the town of Andersontown on the rise of a hill on the York County side of Yellow Beeches Creek. The plans show more ambition than the reality, but eventually the village had a post office, a stage stop, a church, and a cemetery. Today it has just a few houses. However, without Anderson's speculation, there would have been only fields on the top of that hill.

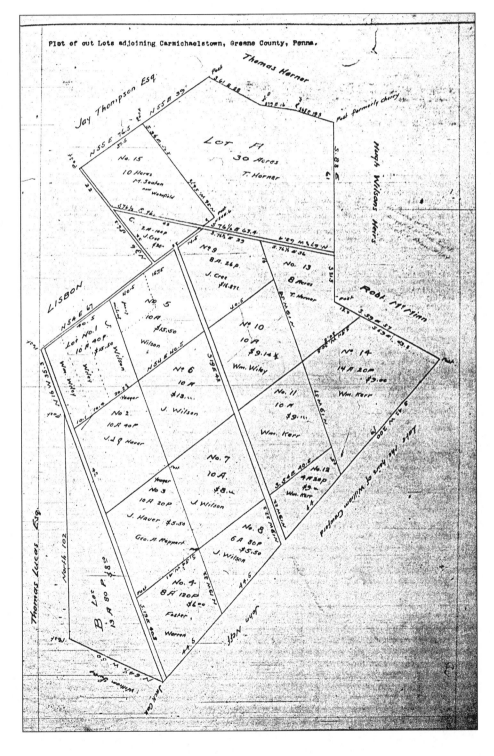

Figure 2-5 As towns grew, subdivisions were sometimes formed from adjoining land, as in this case, land adjoining Carmichaels, Pennsylvania. The plat is found in the deed book.

Many a lowly farmer engaged in speculation. Whether he squatted on land hoping for a successful preemption claim, bought a bit more land than he needed in the hopes of selling the extra at a profit to a new arrival, or bought up entries and surveys for the same reason, he was speculating.

Few genealogists seem to want to claim a speculator in their ancestral family, yet it would be a rare pioneer family who didn't deal with a "speculator" in one form or another.

My Ancestor Lost His Land—Taxes and Escheatment

We're all familiar with paying taxes on real property. When a landowner becomes in default, the governing unit wants to recover the money owed to it. Therefore it can force a public sale of the land. It doesn't just take back the land, because the value of the land may exceed the taxes owed.

A process was followed: Appropriate notification was given to the landowner, who was given an opportunity to make amends; the county court announced the foreclosure, which was recorded in the court minutes; appropriate public notice of the forthcoming sale was given, usually by a posting at the courthouse or an ad in a newspaper; and finally the land was auctioned—usually by the sheriff and often on the courthouse steps—with excess funds, if any, returned to the original owner.

The proverbial sale on the courthouse steps isn't just proverbial. A colleague of mine recently made a research trip to a courthouse and found the main entrance blocked by the crowd of people attending just such a sale.

The deed of sale may be entered under the sheriff's name or his title, rather than that of your ancestor, which can make it difficult to find. However, it was often noted in the county court minutes, so sometimes you can find the deed based on the name of the grantee or on the date of the sale.

If your ancestor lost his land in a court suit, a similar process was followed, but the court of record would be the equity court, rather than the county court.

Many colonial land grants contained stipulations. Requirements for annual quitrents and lease payments or for settlement, clearing, cultivation, and construction were common. Technically, if the conditions were not met, the land would *escheat* (return to the colony, state, or proprietor). Usually these requirements weren't strictly enforced unless someone coveted the land or speculation was involved.

Land escheated for another reason—one that family researchers are apt to forget because of their focus. If a man possessed land, but no heirs could be found upon his death, the land eventually escheated to the government (more quickly if it was good land that a neighbor wanted).

Keep this in mind. If you're researching the adjoining property owners mentioned in an ancestor's grant but can't find any further information on that adjoining property, it may have escheated. You will need to research, instead, the person to whom it was later granted. If you thought you were descended from John Jones who was granted land that later escheated, study the reason for escheatment. You may need to find a new ancestor.

My Ancestor Kept His Land—Mineral and Other Rights

Landownership included a number of facets. Usually ownership is considered to include everything above, below, and on the land. The owner could sell or lease some of those rights while still retaining the land. Mineral rights were a common right to sell. The clump of Gregg-Kerr deeds recorded in 1899 that we looked at on pages 26–31 culminated in the following deed.

> This Indenture made this eighteenth day of August AD 1899 between Hiram H Cree and Alexander Kerr, executors of the last will and testament of James Kerr, late of Cumberland township, Greene County, Pennsylvania, deceased, and David Kerr and Susan his wife, and Elizabeth Cree and Hiram H Cree her husband and Alexander Kerr, unmarried man, and Huston Kerr and Amanda his wife and Archibald Kerr and Fanny his wife, the said David, Elizabeth, Alexander, Huston and Archibald being five children and devisees of said James Kerr deceased, all of said Green County, parties of the first part, And Josiah V. Thompson, S. Leslie Mestrezat, Isaac W. Semans, James M. Hustead, Henry C. Huston, Alltia L. Moses and William A. Longanecker all of Fayette County, Pennsylvania, parties of the second part.

The deceased James Kerr in this case is the son of the earlier man of that name.

> . . . it being the desire as well of said executors as of said children and devisees that the hereinafter mentioned coal property etc be sold . . . All the Coal of the Pittsburg or River Vein in and under all those certain tracts of land, situate in Cumberland township, Greene County, Pennsylvania, bounded and described as [a lengthy land description follows, referring to six earlier deeds of purchase] . . . Together With the free and uninterrupted right of way into, upon and under said land at such points and such maner [*sic*] as may be proper and necessary for the purpose of digging, mining, draining, ventilating and carrying away said coal hereby waiving all surface damages or damages of any sort arising therefrom or from the removal of all of the said coal, together with the privilege of mining and removing through said described premises other coal belonging to said second parties their heirs and assigns or which may hereafter be acquired; reserving, however, the oil and gas in said land with the privilege of boring for the same without cost, but so as not to interfere with the safe mining of said coal, all holes to be securely cased.

Notice what is and what is not transferred in this deed. The coal can be removed (and a substantial mess made), and the grantees also could transport coal from other property through the Kerr property, but oil and gas must be left alone. Furthermore, the Kerr heirs could own the land, live on it, raise livestock, and farm it (if the coal company didn't make that impractical).

Other types of rights that your ancestor might sell are right-of-way (such as a road, a path, or in modern times, power and phone lines) and water rights. These documents are deeds and are recorded in deed books, although if there were many of one kind, the county may have decided to segregate them into a separate book for convenience.

My Ancestor Leased His Land

The concept of individual ownership of land (*fee simple*) wasn't used in early proprietaries. Instead, an individual leased the land, but not year by year as we do today. Many leases were for a very long time. A most interesting kind was a lease for three lives, used in the Northern Neck of Virginia and the manors of New York. In this example, the three lives are those of Samuel and Elizabeth Gregg and their first son, Thomas. This lease tells me that the couple had married probably by mid-1743.

> 1744 May 1. Fairfax County Deeds. William Fairfax Esqr and Samuel Gregg for rents, farm let, survey by Amos Janney, 150 acres on north side about two poles from the Bever Dam branch of Kittockton, for the natural lives of Samuel Gregg and his wife Elizabeth Gregg, and his son Thomas Gregg and the longest liver of them; paying to Fairfax for the first three years, the quitrents and one good turkey or fat capon to be delivered yearlly at the mansion house of William Fairfax Esqr and in that time build a dwelling house at least 20 feet long and 16 feet wide and other outhouses as his way of husbandry, thence paying every year before the first day of May the som of 49 shillings six pence sterling to be discharged in cash or tobacco at ten shillings sterling or wheat at 2 shillings and six pence the bushel, delivered at some public landing on the navigable part of the Potomac river.

Notice the lord-and-tenant requirements for annual tribute and also the specific requirements for house construction.

The three parties named in a lease for three lives didn't all have to be related to the lessee—some leases named prominent people. Those people had nothing to do with the land; the lessee just hoped that they were healthy and would live for a long time.

The document above is really a land grant, but its language is that of a lease. With a lease, technically the land still was the property of the proprietor (who was trying to retain his rights to quitrents or taxes). Thus, when the grantee/lessee wanted to transfer the land, of which he technically had only possession but not ownership, there was a problem. The instruments of lease and release were used to solve this. This involved two transactions, executed one day after the other, between the same two parties, one of which was for a nominal sum, such as one dollar. Sometimes only one of the two instruments was recorded. Usually only one instrument recorded the full land description (too often the unrecorded document).

RECORDS IN DEED BOOKS THAT AREN'T DEEDS

This is one of my favorite categories. In early times, clerks were thrifty. (I'm descended primarily from pioneers who settled in an area before the record keeping got overly standardized.) They didn't have one book for deeds, another for mortgages, another for cattle brands, and so on. Therefore, deed books contain wonderful nuggets beyond the sales of land.

The documents recorded in deed books weren't even always about land. We find sales of personal property, usually valuable property such as slaves, recorded in deed books.

In Barren County, Kentucky, jumbled right in with ordinary deeds, I found agreements, apprenticeships, bills of sale of nonreal property, bonds, contracts, deeds of gift, partitions, leases, a manumission, mortgages or securities, plats, powers of attorney, prenuptial agreements, and quitclaims. The following distinctly nonland records (notice the details restricting market area) were quite interesting:

> Power of attorney [blank] March 1809 from Edward Richardson to John Richardson of Warren Co. for divers good cause: to sell patent rights for *improvements on stills* in Kentucky, except in Logan, Warren, Barren, Cumberland, Adair, Garrard, Green, Washington, Nelso[n], Wa[y]ne, Lincoln, Mercer, Pulaskey, Jessamine, Woodford, Scott, Bourbon, Harrison, Franklin, Jefferson, Fayatt [Fayette] Counties and 1 right in Christian Co. (already sold).
>
> Patent right 23 June 1808 from Joseph Dodge to Daniel Peaton/Payton and James Harrod of Barren Co. for $120: full and exclusive right and liberty of making, constructing, using and vending to inhabitants of Barren Co., Wayne Co. and Adair Co. a *washing machine* (patented by Simon Willard for 14 years), except Gabriel Ament may make 1 machine for himself.

Powers of attorney and other documents recorded in the deed books linked families back to their origins in Georgia, Illinois, Indiana, Kentucky, North Carolina, Ohio, Pennsylvania, South Carolina, Tennessee, Virginia, and even Ireland.

Apprenticeships were frequently recorded in deed books. They usually gave the name of a parent and sometimes stated the age of the child.

> Apprenticeship 17 December 1810 binding George Gladwell (age 15 months), orphan of Hannah Gladwell, until he is 21, to William Trigg of Barren Co. to learn farming, reading & writing with common Arithmetic including the rule of three.

Prenuptial agreements are sometimes found in deed books, especially when the bride-to-be came from a well-to-do background or it was a second marriage for one or both parties. This unusual agreement was drawn in Livingston County, New York, but filed in Champaign County, Ohio, because the mature couple, both of whom resided in Ohio, met while visiting relatives in New York.

> Marriage Contract. An agreement made and entered into in the 9th day of May in the year of our Lord 1866 between Warren Freeman of Champaign County State of Ohio of the first part and Lucy Saxbe of the same place of the second part wittnesseth that the above named parties agree to marry each other the same being first cousins on the following condition: that the party of the second part shall receive from the party of the first part $1,000 provided that the party of the first part shall be in possession at the time of

his decease three times that amount free and clear of all demands of whatsoever name or nature—if not in possession of that amount a less sum in the ration of 1 to 3 shall be paid to the party of the second part by the executor administrator or assigns of the party of the first part and further that the party of the second part is to hold in her own possession the property she now occupies . . .

Deed books contain many types of agreements between individuals. Occasionally they were used when there was no other pertinent place to record the document. For example, in Brent Holcomb's abstracts of Union County, South Carolina, deed books, I noticed the following statement:

Joseph McJunkin, Esqr. and Major Thomas Young . . . saith they were present at the house of John Hughley . . . on the day before his death when he named he had an anxiety to make a will but there being no Ink, he named in the presents of these deponants that he first wishes his body to be decently buried, next that his just debts should be paid, next wishes that his son Alexander should have his real estate. . . .

The next document is an agreement:

We, the persons named are hereunto subscribed heirs & legatees of the estate both real and personal of John Hughley lately deceased do hereby agree that his last request as communicated and published by him in the presence of Joseph McJunkin and Thomas Young and Mordicai Chandler shall bind and be obligatory upon us, 13 March 1819. [The widow, children, and daughters' spouses signed.]

A third document, a quitclaim from the widow and children, sold their rights in the real estate to the son Alexander, as father John had designated. In this way, the family tied up any potential loose ends of a nuncupative (oral) will—in a deed book.

THREE

Finding a Deed Without Using Vacation Time

B egin your at-home research by clearly identifying your goal. At the end of the first chapter, Why Use Land Records?, is a section called "Prepare to Research." The first three steps are get focused on a single problem, review what you've found, and create a chronology of the family events. In this chapter, we'll pick up with step four: Study the time and place. In our efforts, we will use local facilities, the Internet, the U.S. mail, and a combination of printed, microfilmed, and online sources. Each problem is different. The resources you'll use depend on the time and place of your problem, plus the holdings of the library collection closest to you.

FOCUS ON PLACE AND TIME

We'll begin with something pretty basic—make sure you are looking in the right place. You may have been told that your great-great-grandfather was the first person to break ground on the family farm in Washington County, when in fact he bought it from an uncle who decided to move "back home." It may seem pretty obvious that the next step is to look at Washington County land records. However, land that is now in Washington County was in Jefferson County during your great-great-grandfather's lifetime if Washington County wasn't formed until five years after his death.

Learning About the Locality

How do you learn about county formations? (I will use *county* generically in this section, but in some areas, deeds are found at the town or city level, and in Louisiana the county-equivalent jurisdiction is a *parish*.) **Some popular printed sources are The Handy Book, the Red Book, the Genealogist's Handbook for New England Research, and the Map Guide to the U.S. Federal Censuses, 1790–1920** (see "Resources" on pages 53–54 for full reference information).

A typical entry in *The Handy Book* or the *Red Book* would tell you (among other information) the year Washington County was formed, the county—or

Printed Source

counties—from which it was formed (i.e., the *parent* county), the county seat, the zip code of the county courthouse, and the first year for which the county has land records. These books also have maps showing *present-day* county boundaries. For New England states, consult the *Genealogist's Handbook for New England Research* to understand the peculiarities of land jurisdictions in that region.

Some counties were created from two or more other counties. If you know where the family land is, you may be able to locate it on a modern map and then determine which county it came from. If you don't even know if your ancestor had land, you will want to check all parent counties.

The *Map Guide to the U.S. Federal Censuses, 1790–1920* shows the county-formation process visually in ten-year snapshots. Personally, I find it the most informative place to start, since I can quickly get a mental image of the process of county formations (many states had finalized their county structure by 1860, for example). Then I check the other sources as needed.

If you have the name of the township where your ancestor lived, you will find the *Township Atlas of the United States* especially helpful, since it will let you focus on an area much smaller than a county.

The Family History Library Catalog

The Family History Library Catalog (FHLC) is another place where you can learn about county basics. It is available online at <www.familysearch.org>. Additional information about the Family History Library and its valuable holdings is given later in this chapter.

Select Place Search from the FHLC home page. Enter the name of the county (you don't need the word "county") in the Place field and the name of the state in the Part of field. The Place Search Results screen appears with a list of matches. Click on the match that has just the county and state. The Place Details screen that appears has Place, Notes, and Topics. People often ignore the Notes. They shouldn't. That's where you'll find an overview of county formation and other helpful information. Some examples:

[Nebraska, Garden] Created in 1909 from Deuel County.
[Nebraska, Deuel] Created in 1888 from Cheyenne County.
[Nebraska, Cheyenne] Created in 1867 from unorganized lands in western Nebraska (some sources say it was organized in 1871 from Lincoln County).
[Kentucky, Monroe] 1820, created from Barren and Cumberland counties. Disasters in 1863 and 1887 destroyed most records.

Check More Than One Source

These are typical of the notes you may find in many sources. Entries such as these are quite brief, so you may need to investigate further. There may be a wealth of additional background that you need to know.

For example, the FHLC notes for Sussex County, Delaware, indicate:

[Delaware, Sussex] Created in 1682 from Deale County and Durham County, Maryland. In 1742 Worcester Co., Maryland, was created from

Sussex Co., Delaware. Prior to 1769 information on lands south of Nanti-coke and Indian Rivers should be sought in Maryland records.

But when we follow up on each place mentioned in the notes, the FHLC entries modify our first impressions of the entry on Sussex County, Delaware:

[Delaware, Deale] Created in 1680; renamed Sussex County in 1682.
[Maryland, Durham] No matching places found.

It's sad, but true—information is not always totally correct, no matter where you find it. Worcester is an original Maryland county; I've never heard of Durham County. With further research, you'll learn that Maryland and Delaware were engaged in a serious argument over the location of a medallion nailed to a tree, which is what determined the southern boundary of William Penn's property. Until you are past the 1769 date mentioned in the FHLC note, it would be wise to look in both localities, plus Somerset County, Maryland, which wraps around the southwestern portion of Sussex, and also includes disputed land.

Appendix A: Locality Reference will point you to several general guides with detailed information on each state and also to state-specific books that you will want to examine. Do not neglect these sources. The more you read, the more likely you are to locate *all* of the records that you need and to do so most efficiently. Not all states have state-level guides.

Maps are a big help. See chapter ten, Maps, Atlases, and Gazetteers, for more information.

Do you see now why it is wise to investigate the place and time before proceeding with your research? It can save hours of misdirected effort and weeks of waiting for a reply from the wrong county courthouse.

FIRES AND OTHER DISASTERS

Don't give up when you're told that "a fire burned the records." First of all, fires didn't necessarily burn all records. Citizens didn't stand by and let the courthouse burn without attempting to save it. Land records were important to the county (they were, after all, the source of their tax base). Therefore, if time permitted, the deed books may have been literally thrown out on the lawn to save them. Furthermore, due to considerations of space or convenience, the records you seek might not have been stored in the location of the disaster.

A final note should be made on disasters and land records. Deeds are private property. The document belongs to the owner of the land. The owner had the deed recorded in the county deed books to protect his title, especially in the event that *his* home suffered a disaster. Therefore, when a disaster occurred, you may find that owners brought their deeds in to be rerecorded. Sometimes they also brought the earlier deeds to the property, which had been successively signed over from one owner to the next.

WHERE ARE THE DEED BOOKS?

Our instinct is to reply to the question "Where are the deed books?" by saying "At the county courthouse, of course." That answer may be incorrect—or it may not be the *only* correct answer. This chapter focuses on finding deeds. If your ancestor acquired land directly from the government, the records would be at that level (see chapter five, First Transfer—Getting Land Into the Hands of Individuals). However, the general process of identifying and obtaining records of original landowners parallels that described here.

Land records are accessible in a variety of formats—the original record books, microfilm, online images, and printed abstracts.

S

Sources

Original Record Books

Deed books originally belonged to the jurisdiction that created them, most commonly the county. However, things change over time. As counties became more mature and more populous, the number of record books grew and grew. Fortunately, land records (at least, deeds) were rarely discarded. Landownership is an important asset and one on which many facets of county business are based, from tax collection to the location of roads and easements.

To deal with the ever-growing volume of records, some counties built bigger courthouses. Some counties consigned older records to basements or attics. Some counties began storing them off-site (sometimes with ready access, sometimes not). Some counties, in effect, moved the records "up" a jurisdiction. In a few states (Illinois being a prime example), regional archives were established where counties could send their old records for safekeeping. A number of states established programs in which the state archives accepted older records. This is generally an ongoing process. Not all counties have transferred records. Not all records have been transferred. Some counties are working on it; others intend to keep their records. In other words, you need to be open to a wide range of possibilities as you seek the land records of your ancestors.

This transfer process may be influenced by whether or not the originals have been recorded on microfilm, microfiche, or other storage media. If a county knows it can still refer to its records quickly and easily, it may be more likely to transfer the originals to another locality, either off-site storage or a regional or state archives. Some counties that still possess their original record books won't let you look at them. You will have to look at the microform version.

Microform

Commercial vendors of microform systems have long seen the problem of record storage and retention for county offices as a business opportunity. Many counties purchased some kind of microform system in which the vendor made copies and provided equipment to access the copies. To say that there's a wide variety of systems would be an understatement. Many of them are heavily proprietary. In other words, the vendor's equipment is required to read the records. Some systems do not lend themselves to efficient duplication of microform, so the county has the only usable copy.

A number of state archives also undertook microfilming programs for the records in their possession. Some of these programs are ongoing, but many were a one-time effort, hence records deposited later may not be microfilmed.

For microfilming done at the state level, a copy may have been given to the county, and vice versa.

LDS Microfilm

The largest coordinated microfilming effort is that of The Church of Jesus Christ of Latter-day Saints (LDS). You can learn more about using the Family History Library and its resources from *Your Guide to the Family History Library* by Paula Stuart Warren and James W. Warren, so only an overview is provided here.

The members of the LDS church believe that they have an obligation to search for their ancestral families and to perform "temple work" called *sealings* to link individuals into families within the church for eternity. To aid in this, more than six decades ago the Genealogical Society of Utah (GSU), which was the family-history entity of the church, began microfilming records that would help its members research their ancestral families.

Because GSU agreed to make the microfilm readily available to the public, many state, county, and local jurisdictions agreed to the microfilming. The jurisdiction received a copy of the microfilm (without having to pay a commercial vendor), the master copy went into the LDS vault (you've probably heard about "the mountain where all the records are stored"), and a copy of the microfilm became part of the Family History Library (FHL).

The microfilming program worldwide, plus an active purchase program, has to date grown to more than two and a half million rolls of microfilm, with new rolls being added constantly. **For the United States, land records are an important—and voluminous—portion of the collection.** In general, the microfilming process started in the oldest areas of the country, so most counties in the original thirteen colonies and the first tier of trans-Appalachian states have been microfilmed. The microfilming units have not yet been to as many counties in the Midwest and West.

Library/Archive Source

The best news is that you can access the microfilm without going to Salt Lake City, where the FHL is located. The LDS church has more than 3,400 Family History Centers (FHC) located at local churches, plus they have granted FHC microfilm-loan privileges to some public and private libraries. For a nominal fee (usually less than four dollars), you can borrow a roll of microfilm to read on a microfilm reader at the local FHC or FHC-designated library.

As an added bonus, because the filming program began so long ago, you may find that the LDS microfilm includes a volume that has "gone missing" in the years following the filming or that they filmed pages that have since fallen out or crumbled away from use.

Published Abstracts

You may be lucky. A dedicated genealogist may have read entire deed books for the county and time period in which you are interested, abstracted all of the deeds, and published them in one or more books. Volunteers may have abstracted deeds for publication in the county genealogical society's periodical. Published abstracts are valuable in two ways.

- First, it's easier and faster to check the index of a book than it is to crank microfilm or drag heavy volumes from the shelves in courthouses.

- Second, information about your ancestor may be buried in a deed in which neither the seller's name nor the purchaser's name is familiar to you. The every-name index in a book of abstracts may lead you to a deed you would have overlooked otherwise.

Researchers in state-land states south of the Mason-Dixon line have been most appreciative of the value of land records and therefore have been proactive in publishing abstracts. Land records in public-land states are usually less useful for researchers because they tend to contain less information on the family and neighbors. New Englanders had vital records and thought they didn't need to use land records. (They were incorrect, of course, but as a result they've never gotten as enthusiastic about publishing abstracts.) Southerners, on the other hand, often must rely on land records to learn anything about their ancestors, so the need for published abstracts has long been recognized. In fact, you may find that more than one set of abstracts exists for your area of interest.

Warning

Land Records Online

There are few land records available online, especially at the county level. One reason is the sheer volume of records. As an example, just the indexes to Philadelphia County, Pennsylvania, deeds through the beginning of the twentieth century occupy about 150 rolls of microfilm. Needless to say, the deeds occupy many times that number of rolls. The record books of rural counties are, of course, much fewer in number, but they are never minimal. The older the county, the greater the volume.

In a few cases, volunteers may have abstracted deed indexes to be placed on Web sites, subscription services may have abstracts, and counties or archives may have placed their indexes online, but don't expect it. See "Online Searching" on page 50 for suggestions.

Step By Step

STEP BY STEP

Where should you start? Begin by determining if there are published abstracts for your area of interest. Second, look for microfilm. Third, see what's online. Fourth, do it the old-fashioned way—contact the county.

What's in Print?

I like to start my searches with the FHLC because it lists more published deed abstracts than does any other single source, and it is straightforward to use. On page 42 we saw that the **Place Results** screen had frames for **Place, Notes,** and **Topics.** Scroll down, if necessary, until you see the entry under **Topics** for **Land and Property.** There also may be an entry for **Land and Property—** Indexes. If the categories aren't there, the library has no land-record holdings for that county.

Click on **Land and Property** (repeat for the indexes later). There may be only one or two items listed—or there may be dozens. Remember that at the moment we are looking for published abstracts. Each item lists the equivalent of a title and an author. For now ignore the items that say something like "Deeds 1788–1861. Washington County, Clerk of the County Court." Look instead for items that are more like "Washington County Deed Books A and B, 1788–1797. Abstractor, Abbie."

Most titles have a range of years. Because you have carefully defined your years of interest in your problem statement, you should be able to tell if items cover your time period or if they are too early or too late. You may find later that you need to expand your focus, so make a mental note that the abstracts exist.

Once you find an item that seems likely or needs further exploration, click on the title. The screen that appears contains a detailed catalog entry. The catalog Notes usually tells exactly what is covered by the book, even if the title did not. Write down the title, author, and all publication information (it's at the bottom of the screen, so you may need to scroll down to get it all).

Do not quit with the FHLC. They don't own every book. Many genealogical publications are done in very limited productions. Check the online catalogs for the library nearest you with a genealogical collection, for libraries with good genealogical collections around the country, for the state library in the area of interest, and for smaller libraries in the area of interest (don't neglect to search for historical and genealogical society libraries). Don't forget the Library of Congress online catalog, <www.lcweb.loc.gov>. The online catalogs of libraries vary widely in their search techniques, so this step may take time.

You also might try the Web sites for genealogical book distributors. There may be newly published abstracts available that haven't had time to show up in library catalogs yet.

FINDING CONTACT INFORMATION FOR COURTHOUSES, LIBRARIES, AND SOCIETIES

Several printed sources, such as the *County Courthouse Book* and *Ancestry Family Historian's Address Book,* often are used to obtain addresses, phone numbers, and e-mail addresses or Web sites. Many genealogical collections have these books. The addresses for genealogical and historical societies seem to change relatively often, as the officers change.

• To get more current information, most genealogists rely on Cyndi's List, <www.cyndislist.com>. The site lists a category for Libraries, Archives, and Museums and another for Societies & Groups. I usually go to the United States Index category, select my state, and then browse to find everything that might be applicable.

Periodicals

Finding abstracts in periodicals is now relatively simple using the *Periodical Source Index* (PERSI). The Allen County (Fort Wayne, Indiana) Public Library has the largest collection of genealogical and historical periodicals in the country. To

CD Source

facilitate access to this wonderful collection, they developed PERSI. Originally, it was published in book form with annual updates. There were more than two dozen large volumes in 1999 when they worked with Ancestry to produce electronic versions of the constantly growing database. Many libraries have either a CD-ROM version or a subscription to Ancestry.com that you can use to search PERSI.

PERSI has three major sections: surname, locality, and general subjects. Finding land records is easy. Search the U.S. Locality section for the record type "land," and enter the name of the state and the county. There are about twenty thousand such entries in PERSI. The article may be an index or an abstract—or it may be a single deed. There may be many references when the series is continued from one issue to the next. You may be surprised to note that some of the references occur in states other than that in which the county is located.

When you find a periodical article that looks interesting, you can click on the name of the periodical to display a list of some major libraries that hold the periodical.

Accessing a Printed Book or Periodical

First, find out if the genealogical collection nearest you has a copy. If not, you may need to try several options.

- Consult with your local librarian about interlibrary loan. Although most genealogical collections do not circulate their books, a few do. State libraries may loan their books to residents within their state. To request a book through interlibrary loan, you should supply as much of the publication information as possible, as precisely as possible—author, title, publisher, place and date of publication, and volume number or edition, if applicable. You usually must have a library card, and you may have to pay a processing fee.
- If you found the item on the FHLC, go back and look in the upper right corner of the Title Details screen. Most books say, "There are no film notes available for this title." A few will have a button labeled View Film Notes, which means that the book is on microfilm. This is good news. You can borrow the microfilm at your local FHC, as described on page 45.
- If the book is still in print, consider purchasing a copy. After you've completed your research for that locality, you can donate it to the genealogy collection nearest you.
- You may wish to hire a researcher to check the book for you (see "Hiring a Professional Researcher" on page 50).
- Contact the library and genealogical society in the area of interest to ask if they would check the index for you. Inquire about fees and getting copies. You should consider joining the society, especially if you will have much research there. Sometimes research services are available to members but not nonmembers. If the society is helpful to you, please consider making a donation.

Reading Microfilm

In the FHLC, we skipped entries like "Deeds 1788–1861. Washington County, Clerk of the County Court." If your search for published abstracts was unsuccessful, go back and check those entries. The Title Details page provides information similar to that for books. Click the View Film Notes tab. A list of many rolls of microfilm appears. There are, in general, two series.

- At the top of the list are the indexes (usually with grantors first, followed by grantees). These are consolidated indexes, covering a broad span of years, often more than a century.
- Below the indexes are the microfilm rolls for the deed books. If there are only one or two films covering the years you need, you may be tempted to order the deed books and skip ordering the index first. Don't. Because they had filmed the consolidated indexes, the filming crews often did not film the indexes to the individual volumes. Believe me when I tell you that you don't want to read an entire deed book.

Write down all the information about the index rolls that you want (order both the grantor and the grantee volume), and go to your local FHC to order the films. They will call you when they arrive.

Read the index to identify all the deeds of your ancestral family. See the next chapter, Finding a Deed in a Courthouse, to learn about the idiosyncrasies of deed indexes. Write down every entry—in full—for every family member. Once you've identified the deeds you want to look at, return to the FHLC to get the microfilm numbers and order them.

If you have access to a microfilm reader at the local library, you also can consider borrowing or buying microfilm from the state archives if it is available. Your interlibrary loan librarian can advise you about borrowing microfilm. If your library permits it, you may choose to buy the needed microfilm from the state archives to read at the library—and I'd suggest you donate it to the library for other researchers to use. If you buy the microfilm, it will be there for you to use at a later time.

Idea Generator

TIPS FOR SUCCESSFUL SEARCHING

- Search both grantor and grantee indexes.

- Don't wear blinders. Don't focus on only your ancestor.

- Remember that your ancestor's siblings had the same parents as your ancestor did. Consult your family group sheets for the names in the extended family.

- Make a list of the names of brothers-in-law and sons-in-law. It's easy to forget them in a surname-focused search.

- Copy all index entries for the surname. You may later discover that they are relatives, and it will save you a step.

Online Searching

As mentioned previously, there aren't many online indexes to land records. However, you should always check. Look for indexes done by volunteers—and for indexes done by the county.

The three major Web sites to check are:

- Cyndi's List. <www.cyndislist.com> Select the United States Index category.
- RootsWeb. <www.rootsweb.com> Select the Web Site tab.
- The USGenWeb Project. <www.usgenweb.org> Select The Project's State Pages.
- Also do a general Web search for the name of the county and the state.

Internet Source

The Old-Fashioned Way

We used to find deeds for our ancestors in one of two ways: We visited the courthouse (see chapter four, Finding a Deed in a Courthouse), or we wrote to the courthouse. These options are still available to you.

When you write to a courthouse, remember that answering mail from out-of-state family researchers is not the primary job of courthouse employees. Their primary job is to serve the citizens and taxpayers of their county and to perform the needed county tasks. Keep this in mind, and be patient and polite when contacting them. Also be brief and to the point.

Remember to be both concise and complete in your request. Don't impart extraneous information—and make sure you've provided all the needed information. Be neat and check your spelling. This is also true if you contact the courthouse by e-mail. Show that you respect the county employee—do not ask the "Wahsington country clerk" to search for the "deads of my ancestrs."

I wrote many courthouses in my early days of genealogical research. I must say that I almost always got courteous replies, many going far beyond what I would ever have expected them to do for me. Sometimes they replied that they could not do research, but they provided a list of local researchers available for hire. There are many more people interested in genealogy today and county populations have grown, so I expect that fewer clerks will be able to check the indexes and make the copies for you.

Reminder

SASEs

It is common genealogical courtesy to provide an SASE (self-addressed, stamped envelope) in any correspondence. Look for no. 9 envelopes at an office supply store. They're slightly smaller than no. 10 envelopes. One no. 9 envelope can be dropped neatly inside a no. 10 envelope without having to fold it in thirds.

Hiring a Professional Researcher

You may find that the best (or only) option available to you is to hire someone to examine books and records or to obtain copies. For example:

- The county has not been microfilmed. The county does not do research, so it can provide you with only minimal information by mail.
- The county has been microfilmed by the LDS church. You found a number of deeds of interest in the indexes, which you borrowed at your local FHC. However, the deeds are on many rolls of microfilm, you want copies, and your FHC doesn't have a reader-printer.
- You may not be able to read old handwriting and want a professional to abstract the records for you so that you don't overlook anything.

IMAGES ONLINE

In a few cases, institutions have put images of land records online. Three notable instances—all representing the earliest transfers to individuals—are

- Early Essex County, Massachusetts, deeds, <www.salemdeeds.com>. There is no index; you must have the book and page number from another source. (Since the pages have been numbered more than once, it may require patience to find the deed you seek.) You must be able to read seventeenth-century handwriting. Modern deeds are indexed and linked separately elsewhere on the Web site.

- The Library of Virginia <www.lva.lib.va.us> has computerized and linked its name index (including the names of adjoining landowners) to images of the Virginia patent and grant books and the Northern Neck grant books. You will need to be able to read seventeenth- and eighteenth-century handwriting to take advantage of the images if your family resided in Virginia in the 1600s or 1700s. The Web site, which has been operating for several years, has been a great boon to those working on ancestry in early Virginia.

- The Bureau of Land Management—Eastern District <http://glorecords.blm .gov> has been indexing and imaging public land grants. See chapter six, Public Lands, for more information.

In every case, don't just look for your ancestor's records. Spend some time with the Web site. The sites all offer much explanatory material that will help you use each site more effectively and help you learn more about the records.

If the records have been microfilmed by the LDS church, you could choose to hire a researcher either in Salt Lake City or in the county or state.

Communicating With a Professional Researcher

Hiring a researcher usually requires two steps. First, contact the researcher by e-mail, mail, or phone. Not all professionals do simple record searching (I do not, for example), so begin by asking if he or she will find and copy deeds. Ask about the person's availability and schedule (a backlog may prevent an immediate response). In a rural area, a researcher may visit some courthouses infrequently. Inquire about financial details, such as hourly rate, billing units, minimum charges, retainers, travel costs, and charges for copies.

Tip

When you forward information to the researcher, follow these guidelines:
- Provide concise, accurate, and complete information on the family. This means no rambling letters, phone calls, or e-mails about the family history and its interesting legends.
- List for the researcher exactly what you've already found.
- Be specific about what you want done.

FINDING A PROFESSIONAL RESEARCHER

There are three organizations of professional researchers that you should check. The members of all three organizations have signed codes of ethics. Two of the three have testing procedures. Each organization has a Web site that explains about the organization and lists its researchers.

- Board for Certification of Genealogists <www.bcgcertification.org>

- International Commission for the Accreditation of Professional Genealogists <www.icapgen.org>

- Association of Professional Genealogists <www.apgen.org>

For example, let's say that you've searched the indexes for the Abercrombie family and found entries for eight deeds in the right time period. List all the information as you abstracted it from the index, not just the book and page number—if there is a problem (deed indexes on microfilm can sometimes be difficult to read), it will take less time for the researcher to rectify the error. Tell the researcher that you want photocopies of these deeds, including the acknowledgment and recording information.

Let's say that you now realize that you also need deeds from the collateral Brightwell family, for which you have not examined the index. Tell the researcher that you want a list of all Brightwell deeds in the index and that you want copies of the Brightwell deeds between 1840 and 1860—unless there are more than ten deeds, in which case you would like to see the index entries first.

LEAVING HOME

This chapter is about finding deeds without leaving home, and the next chapter is about finding deeds in local courthouses. There is a third option, favored by those of us who have traced our ancestry back to areas for which the LDS church has done lots of microfilming. We take our vacations in Utah instead!

Early in my genealogical research, I began adding several days onto ski trips in order to remain in Salt Lake City and peer into a microfilm reader. During the summer, families can visit national parks and hike in the mountains. The researcher in the family can stay for a few extra days to search for ancestors. *Your Guide to the Family History Library* offers extensive, helpful advice on planning a trip, including information on hotels, restaurants, and activities for the nongenealogist.

On my visits to the FHL, land records have always been a focus of my research because of the large number of rolls of microfilm I need to check. It isn't exactly instant gratification, but it is much more efficient to read an index and walk forty steps to retrieve the film for the deed book than it is to wait several weeks for each microfilm. I justify it to myself financially by thinking of how many film-rental fees I'm saving!

RESOURCES

Andriot, Jay. *Township Atlas of the United States*. McLean, Va.: Documents Index, 1991. Earlier editions by John L. Andriot. McLean, Va.: Andriot Associates, 1979, 1987.

AniMap Plus software from The Gold Bug, P.O. Box 588, Alamo, CA 94507. <www.goldbug.com> Shows changing county boundaries over time.

Bentley, Elizabeth Petty. *County Courthouse Book*. 2d ed. Baltimore: Genealogical Publishing Co., 1995.

The Church of Jesus Christ of Latter-day Saints. The Family History Library Catalog in FamilySearch. <www.familysearch.org> A fast and easy-to-use CD-ROM version is available for purchase from the Web site at the extremely reasonable price of five dollars (as of this writing). Also published on microfiche and available at the Family History Library and Family History Centers (the microfiche is no longer available for purchase); microfiche is the fastest version to scan, especially for localities with many entries or with lengthy entries.

Cyndi's List. <www.cyndislist.com>, created by Cyndi Howells, is the starting point for exploring what land information is available online and for accessing local Web sites of courthouses, archives, and libraries.

Eichholz, Alice, ed. *Ancestry's Red Book: American State, County and Town Sources*. Rev. ed. Salt Lake City: Ancestry Incorporated, 1992. Organized by state, with each state covered by a local expert.

Elliott, Wendy B., and Karen Clifford. "Printed Land Records." In *Printed Sources: A Guide to Published Genealogical Records,* edited by Kory L. Meyerink. Salt Lake City: Ancestry Incorporated, 1996.

Everton Publishers. *The Handy Book for Genealogists*. 10th ed. Logan, Utah: Everton Publishers, 2002.

The Library of Virginia Web site. <www.lva.lib.va.us> The library has automated the consolidated card file index to all Virginia colonial patents, Virginia grants, and Northern Neck grants with links to scanned images of the original patent books.

Melnyk, Marcia D., ed. *Genealogist's Handbook for New England Research*, 4th ed. Boston: New England Historic Genealogical Society, 1999.

Luebking, Sandra Hargreaves. Chapter eight, "Research in Land and Tax Records." In *The Source*, rev. ed., edited by Loretto Dennis Szucs and Sandra Hargreaves Luebking. Salt Lake City: Ancestry Incorporated, 1996. The latter part of the chapter has state-by-state discussions of land sales and records.

Periodical Source Index (PERSI). An enormous project of the Allen County (Fort Wayne, Indiana) Public Library, which has a substantial periodical collection. PERSI identifies the primary topic of each article in each publication. More than 1.5 million entries (PERSI 2000), available on CD-ROM and online subscription at <www.ancestry.com>.

RootsWeb. <www.rootsweb.com>, an organized, linked system of Web sites created by volunteers, some of which include land-related information or information on research in the locality; now owned and hosted by Ancestry with free access.

Smith, Juliana Szucs. *Ancestry Family Historian's Address Book*. Salt Lake City: Ancestry Inc., 1997.

Thorndale, William, and William Dollarhide. *Map Guide to the U.S. Federal Censuses, 1790–1920*. Baltimore: Genealogical Publishing Co., Inc., 1987. Available in hardcover and softcover; has been revised. Absolutely necessary to ensure that you're looking in the right locality, and to identify other likely localities.

The USGenWeb Project. <www.usgenweb.org>, an organized, linked system of Web sites created by volunteers, some of which include land-related information or information on research in the locality.

Warren, Paula Stuart, and James W. Warren. *Your Guide to the Family History Library*. Cincinnati: Betterway Books, 2001. And their video, "The Video Guide to the Salt Lake City Family History Library." Hurricane, Utah: The Studio, 2002.

FOUR

Finding a Deed in a Courthouse

our trip to the ancestral county will probably be jam-packed. You won't want to waste a minute of time—and you probably have places to visit beyond the courthouse, such as cemeteries.

SCOPING OUT THE TERRITORY

Use printed sources, online sources, and the telephone to plan your visit to the courthouse effectively. Note that this chapter uses the terms "county" and "courthouse" generically, to include "parish," "town," and so forth.

Research the Records and the Courthouse

Chapter three, Finding a Deed Without Using Vacation Time, is a prerequisite for this chapter. It discusses some recommendations for preliminary research. Some of your questions will include:

- Do land records for your time period of interest still exist?
- What jurisdiction were they created in? (There may be a parent county.)
- Are the records still in county custody? (They may be at the state archives.)
- What is the county seat? (It isn't always the biggest town in the county.)
- What is the name of the "deed office"? (See Appendix A: Locality Reference for help.)
- Are the old records in the main courthouse—or in some other building?
- Where (exactly!) is the courthouse? You can waste a lot of time driving around looking for a courthouse in a county seat without an obvious town square.
- Where do you park? (Even small towns abound in one-way streets with parking that can be entered from only one direction.)
- Is parking free?
- What are the hours of operation? (They usually are not 8 A.M. to 5 P.M. Many county offices open after 9 A.M. and close around 4 or 4:30 P.M. Some even close for lunch.)

- **What days is it open?** (Rarely are courthouses open on Saturday. Additionally, there may be state holidays—always unknown to visitors—on which the courthouse is closed. Renovations such as asbestos removal may cause closure or restricted access.)
- If you have any physical difficulties, inquire about handicap access. The ramp may be at the side or rear of the building, especially in old courthouses with impressive flights of front steps. If you have a handicap-only parking permit, check about the location of handicap parking. Be forewarned that researching deeds will require lifting heavy volumes and possibly even climbing on ladders. Research space may be awkward.
- Where are related offices, such as the tax or revenue office? You may be able to obtain inexpensive, detailed maps of modern property holdings at the tax office.

Research the Region

Contact the local chamber of commerce (or office of tourism in larger towns). Find out everything you can from them.

- Ask for the special events calendar. You don't want to plan a quick trip to the courthouse on the day of the Pioneer Parade.
- Ask for lists of hotels and motels. Chances are you're going to do more than visit this one courthouse. You may have visits planned to several nearby courthouses and cemeteries. I like to choose one centralized location. I may do more driving, but I don't waste time packing and unpacking or cut short a research session to check in or out. This also leaves me more flexible for adjusting my plans based on what I discover.
- Ask for lists of restaurants. Make a preliminary plan for where you'll have a quick lunch. If the staff at the courthouse isn't too busy, ask them for their recommendations.

Do the Advance Work

The more you do before leaving home, the more time you will have for in-depth research and visiting family sites on your trip. (See chapter three, Finding a Deed Without Using Vacation Time, for techniques.) **The better prepared you are, the more productive your on-site time will be.**

- Read FHL microfilm in your home community.
- Collect as many maps as possible (the more detailed the better). Use a highlighter or small colored sticky dots (available at office supply stores) to mark ancestral sites, the courthouse, the library, your motel, and restaurants.
- Use a three-ring binder to make a trip notebook. Include photocopies of pedigree charts and family groups sheets (don't forget collateral lines), a chronology, and a land chart (see chapter one, Why Use Land Records?). Make copies of the "family" areas of maps for the notebook, and also make photocopies of any photographs of houses, buildings, countryside, and cemeteries that you may have. Include copies, transcripts, or abstracts of any documents you have already found.
- The three-ring binder keeps everything in one place (pages won't blow away

or fall out, as they might from a file folder). It also provides a firm writing surface. Punch holes in both lined and plain paper to put in the front of the binder. Add one of those plastic zip school pouches that are punched to go in the binder. Include a pencil (for writing when around original documents, such as deed books), a pen, a yellow highlighter (I mark my route as I drive around the countryside—it makes it much easier to find my place on the map after peering at a road marker), and paper clips or a small stapler (so you can keep all the pages of each deed together—it's awful trying to sort them later if they get mixed up).

- Pack a small bag with other necessities: folding umbrella or disposable rain cape, parking-meter change, prepackaged moist towelettes, and some kind of emergency nonsticky snack (not chocolate—it melts).
- If possible, put the binder and necessity kit into an upright briefcase. The working facilities in some courthouses can be minimal. You may have to stand up and share counter space with the other visitors as you go through the indexes and deed books. Microfilm readers often don't have any working surface at them. Soft bags and briefcases with lids may be awkward to use, and there may not be room for a laptop computer.
- Take clothing that won't show dirt and dust—they are unavoidable in courthouses. Remember tissues and medication if dust bothers your sinuses.

YOU'RE THERE!

The typical courthouse visit begins with a long climb up the front steps. When you enter the front door, pause to let your eyes adjust to the gloom—and to catch your breath. Many courthouses have implemented security procedures, so be prepared to put all your belongings through airport-style x-ray equipment or to have them hand-searched.

Look for the building directory on the wall. Some large courthouses have an information counter. Deeds may be listed under Register of Deeds, or they may be in a court (if you did your homework, you'll know what office to look for). You should also look for the rest room. Although your necessities kit contains moistened towelettes, you will find it wiser to stop at the end of your visit and wash off the century-old dust that transferred itself from the deed books to your hands and clothing—and to clean the smudge off your face that you didn't even know was there until you saw it in the mirror.

When you get to the office, don't ask a clerk where the "old deeds" are. The clerk's definition of "old" is likely to be "1980s." Be specific. Ask, "Where are the indexes and the deeds for the mid-1800s?" Never tell the clerk about your family history. The staff's first priority is to perform their duties for the county. These duties lie in the present, not in the past.

A few county employees may have had bad experiences with rude genealogists or those who monopolized them with stories about their ancestors, but most are pleasant and helpful—just busy with their other tasks. A few may inquire if you're doing family history or ask what families you're researching. Keep your answer brief. Often the person will suggest that you also visit the local library or historical society or will tell you about a resource with which you were unfamiliar.

Before you leave the counter to head for the indexes, inquire about the photocopy rules. In some courthouses, the staff must make the copies (occasionally you must wait for the copies to be mailed to you). Don't assume that because the photocopier is in the public area that you're supposed to make your own copies. Usually, no matter who makes the copies, you keep track of the number of copies and pay at the end of the visit.

It's Time to Research

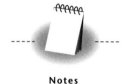

Notes

Take a few minutes to look around the area to which you've been directed. **Most land records are in large, heavy books, which are filed horizontally in racks around the walls and under counters.** The racks have rollers to make it easy to slide the volumes out. There should be one section of indexes and another section of deeds. We'll discuss indexes in detail on pages 58–67.

Look to see if there are smaller groups of volumes. Especially if you are working on, say, your great-grandfather's family at the beginning of the twentieth century, there may be separate volumes for records such as mortgages that you'll want to examine.

You may find that instead of heavy books, you will be reading microfilm or microfiche. If this is the case, let the staff person show you how to use it, as some systems have their own quirks. Ask about making photocopies and whether the material is to be retrieved and refiled by you or by the staff. Often the machines are reader-printers.

USING DEED INDEXES

The most difficult—and time consuming—part of deed research can be the indexes. The number of different types of indexes is amazing. What is even more amazing to many first-time users is that the indexes are rarely in alphabetical order. It may take a bit of time to get used to a particular system.

The reason indexes are so complex is that land records are so voluminous. There are many more volumes of deed books in a courthouse than there are will books. A variety of systems have been devised to aid in finding specific deeds relatively quickly.

Research Tip

You may find that the courthouse has a computerized deed index. However, **most of the computerized indexes do not extend into the distant past, so if the staff directs you to a computer, ask what time period the computer index covers.** Because some deeds were filed so long after they were written, it may still be a good idea to check the computer index, just in case.

Define the Problem

The discussion that follows focuses on finding the deeds for a single surname, but good research methods suggest that you will also want to look for records of collateral families.

Let's say we're looking for records about the family of James Kerr, who lived in Greene and Washington counties in Pennsylvania between the 1790s and

1840. His descendants lived in Greene County on into the twentieth century, and he also had a probable brother Archibald.

Greene County was formed from Washington County in 1796. James moved from Washington County to Greene County around the early 1820s. Land records are filed in the county in which the land lies, not in the county of residence, so there might be records in Washington County for James's land after the 1820s, if he had not disposed of all of his land before moving. Clearly, we will have to visit both courthouses before the research is complete. (Actually, both counties have been filmed and are also available as FHL microfilm, but the process to be followed is the same.)

Our immediate research goal is to find all the deeds related to the *family of James Kerr* in Greene County. **Do not limit your search to just the given name of your ancestor.** There may be several valuable and interesting deeds concerning your ancestor that are not indexed under his name. That is why your notebook contains not just a pedigree chart, but also family group sheets for the extended family.

Research Tip

How Many Indexes?

The first step in finding your ancestral-family deeds is to determine how many index volumes you will need to check. Most indexes have two groups.

- *Grantor indexes* are organized by the name of the person selling the land. They also may be called *direct indexes.*
- *Grantee indexes* are organized by the name of the person buying the land. They also may be called *indirect indexes.*

Greene County organizes its deed indexes separately by grantor and grantee. In other localities, there are, of course, several variations.

- For the earliest years of some colonial counties, it isn't uncommon to find a single index. In some, this may be because the terms *grantor* and *grantee* weren't appropriate since the index contained many types of records, not just deeds.
- Some indexes have a single list, with the words "to" and "from" between the names of the two parties.
- Some indexes have two lists but in a single volume, with the grantor/direct index on one page (or column) and the grantee/indirect index on the other page (or column).
- I know of at least one county that for its early deeds has only a grantee index. I had to read every page of the index, scanning the grantor column to find the rest of the entries for my ancestral families—and there were a lot of them.

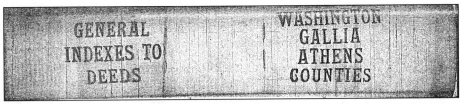

Figure 4-1 Look for special index volumes, such as this one in Meigs County, Ohio, listing deeds from the parent counties of Washington, Gallia, and Athens counties.

Once you've determined how many index series there are for grantor and grantee, you need to determine if there is more than one series for the time period of interest. Many indexes cover broad time periods, but as the volume eventually became unwieldy, a new series would begin. In Greene County, the first index series runs from 1796–1941.

Don't forget to look for special indexes. For example, in Meigs County, Ohio, the clerk made a special index to the deeds for land that lay within Meigs but were originally filed in the parent counties of Washington, Gallia, and Athens.

Finding the Volume

I'm never sure whether it is better to look at the grantor index or the grantee index first. Chronologically, your ancestor would appear first in the grantee index, when he made his first purchase of land (unless he received it by a grant). Grantee deeds may tell you his earliest date of residence in the area and maybe even where he came from. Grantor deeds, on the other hand, are those most likely to be filled with "good stuff" such as the name of the wife or the children (in the case of inheritance). In truth, you need to do both, so it really doesn't matter.

Pick a series and go to the first letter of the ancestral surname (in this case *K* for Kerr). The Greene County grantor index managed to fit all of the *K*s into a single volume, but that isn't true of other, more voluminous, letters. The next subdivision is by first letter of *given* name, so it may be necessary for you to pull two or more volumes to complete the family. (See figure 4-2.)

Carefully remove the volume from the rack. **Be forewarned—the volumes usually slide out smoothly, until you suddenly find yourself balancing a very heavy book.** It is almost impossible to avoid getting dirty, so wear practical clothes that don't show dirt. (Avoiding dust is one reason I am so much in favor of doing as much preliminary work with microfilm as I can. I use on-site time for unmicrofilmed records and to verify records that did not microfilm clearly.)

Warning

Finding the Name

When you place the index at your workspace, do not open it to the middle. Instead, open it to the front. If the index is a proprietary type (the county purchased preprinted volumes and pages for the system), there's usually an explanation and/or key at the front of each volume. If not, carefully study the first page of the volume. It is easier to figure out the system if you understand how it starts.

Look at the illustration of the cover of the Greene County index at left. Notice at the bottom the symbol of a key containing the letters *l-m-n-r-t,* with a patent notice beneath. This identifies the index as a *Russell index* (also called *key index* and *l-m-n-r-t index*). You've probably encountered the work of its inventor, Robert C. Russell, who developed the Soundex system. This is one of the most popular systems—and possibly the most confusing for the uninitiated—so we'll go through it in detail.

Figure 4-2 The Russell Index, recognizable from the key symbol, is organized by first letter of the surname.

There are distinct similarities between Soundex coding and the first steps to using the Russell index for deeds. We've already done the first three steps.

1. Choose grantor or grantee. (We chose grantor.)
2. Choose the right time period. (1796–1941)
3. Retrieve the volume(s) for the first letter of the surname. (*K*, given names *A–Z*.) (See figure 4-2.)
4. Write down the surname. (Kerr)
5. Strike out the first letter and all letters except *l, m, n, r,* and *t.* Also strike out any doubled letter. For Kerr, then, we are left with *R*. If you struck out all of the letters, as with *Law,* then your ancestor is classified as "Misc." and will be found at the bottom of the chart.
6. On the chart at the front of the volume, find the key letter in the column at the left. Next to the key letter is a long row of numbers: 140, 240, 340, and so on. (See figure 4-3.)
7. Look at the area just above the numbers, labeled "Given Name Initials and Section Number." We are most interested in *James* Kerr (we will, however, eventually check all given names to be sure we've found as many family-related documents as possible). Follow down the column headed "J," for *James,* until it meets the row for "R." The magic number is 940. (Names other than individuals, such as churches or banks, are classified in the right-most column under "Corps. Etc.") (See figure 4-3.)

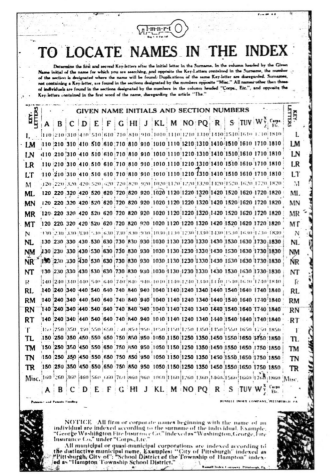

Figure 4-3 Key page from a Russell Index.

Figure 4-4 In the Russell Index for Greene County, Pennsylvania, each section begins with a listing of surnames in that section.

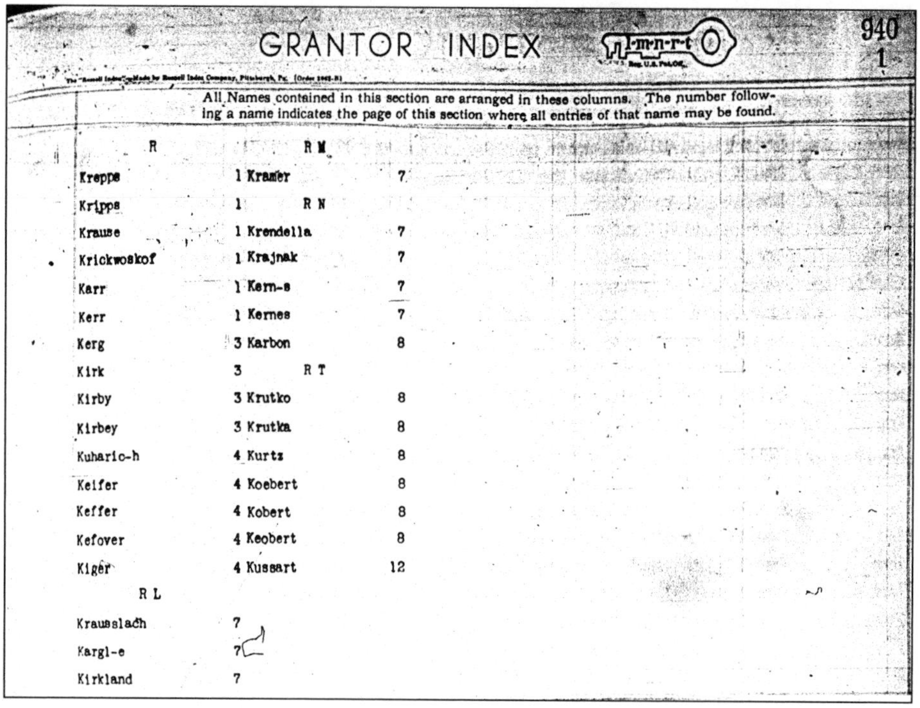
GRANTOR INDEX

940
1

All Names contained in this section are arranged in these columns. The number following a name indicates the page of this section where all entries of that name may be found.

R		R M	
Kreppe	1	Kramer	7
Kripps	1	R N	
Krause	1	Krendella	7
Krickwoskof	1	Krajnak	7
Karr	1	Kern-s	7
Kerr	1	Kernes	7
Kerg	3	Karbon	8
Kirk	3	R T	
Kirby	3	Krutko	8
Kirbey	3	Krutka	8
Kuharic-h	4	Kurtz	8
Keifer	4	Koebert	8
Keffer	4	Kobert	8
Kefover	4	Keobert	8
Kiger	4	Kussart	12
R L			
Krausslach	7		
Kargl-e	7		
Kirkland	7		

8. Go to section 940. (See figure 4-4.)
9. The initial page of each section contains an index to the surnames in that section. Here we learn that Kerr begins on page 940-1 (for given names beginning *J*, only).

For genealogists, one of the frustrations of the Russell system is that entries for the surname are not together. Because the system organizes the pages by first letter of the given name, rather than the key-code of the surname, the men with given name James are together (sections 910–960), but the Kerrs are spread throughout the volume (sections 140, 240, 340, . . . 1840). You will have to do a lot of page turning (or microfilm cranking) and keep a check-off list to be sure you've found all the entries for the Kerr family.

Finding the Entry

Within the surname in the Russell system, entries are arranged chronologically. This is true in almost any index system—once you finally get to the right page, entries are arranged chronologically. Beware, though, because they are arranged chronologically by date of recording, which may be much later than the date of the transaction. (See figure 4-5.)

In this example, there is a column for year of instrument. Some counties show the full date; a few show none. Always scan the index for at least several decades after the time of interest. Don't forget that the instrument may have been created many years after the primary event. For example, the deeds or quitclaims resolving land inherited in a will dated 1800 may not have been written until the mother died in 1825, thereby freeing up her dower interest, or maybe not even until 1840 when the heirs actually sold the land.

GRANTOR		GRANTEE	Year of Inst.	Date of Record Month Day Year		Recorded Vol.	Page	LOCATION AND AREA
Kripps	John	ux John Staggoner	1818	Oct 13 1818		4	91	Morris Tp 51 A 144 P
Krepps	John	ux Ezekiel Braden	1831	May 31 1834		7	429	Ten Mile Crk 133 A
Krepps	John	ux John Booze	1834	Nov 17 1835		7	499	Q C-Clarksvl 1 Lot
Krause	John	ux S R Huss	1890	Jun 13 1890		78	61	P of A
Krickwoskof	Jacob	ux Challen W Waychoff	1929	Apr 26 1929		344	272	Plan Town Site Dunkard Tp L 9-10 New Works
Kerr	Joseph	ux Aaron Jenkins	1796	Mar 23 1797		1	83	Nr Greensbg 1 Lot
Kerr	Joseph	ux George Yeager	1797	Jan 3 1798		1	218	Adj Greensbg Lot
Kerr	Joseph	ux William Williams	1796	Sep 5 1803		1	728	Adj Greensbg
Kerr	Joseph	al Christian Shryor	1807	Nov 24 1807		2	298	Greensbg 3 Lots
Karr	Jacob	ux Geo Graham	1841	Apr 7 1841		9	311	- - - 50 A
Kerr	Jane	con William Chisler	1858	Mar 7 1860		16	419	Cumb Tp 170 A 31 P
Karr	Jacob	ux James McNay	1842	Jan 21 1864		18	227	Richhill Tp 50 A
Kerr	John Morris	Wm A Shepherd	1864	Jan 5 1865		19	191	Asgnt Lease
Kerr	James K	al James B Henry al	1865	Apr 14 1865		19	593	Dunkard Tp 201 A 112 P
Kerr	James K & Atty	Border Oil Co By Trus	1865	Apr 26 1865		20	41	Lease-Dunkard Tp 2 A
Kerr	John Morris	William A Shepherd	1864	May 23 1865		20	112	Asgnt Lease

Figure 4-5 Each deed is listed chronologically within surname.

Other Indexing Systems

To some extent, the system used in a particular deed index is driven by the number of records. In areas and times in which there were not a tremendous number of deeds, the system could be quite simple, since it didn't take long to scan a column or two of names. As transactions became more numerous, systems became more complex. Eventually, they were also business opportunities for companies that sold preprinted forms for their system. **Some systems you may encounter:**

- Individual deed books usually have indexes for that book (at the front of the book, not the back), alphabetical by first letter of the surname. There may be separate columns for grantor and grantee indexes, or they may be merged, with "to" and "from" indicating whether buyer or seller. Individual book indexes are often skipped in microfilming.

- Once a county had more than a couple of deed books, it became impractical to pull out each volume to check the index. The simplest solution was to copy the individual indexes into a single volume. A section was begun for each initial surname letter, and then the entries were copied by volume. Therefore, under the letter *W*, one would find first the *W*-surname entries (chronologically by recording) for volume A, then the entries for volume B, and so on.

- As the number of deeds increased, the next most popular simple method was to organize the index by first letter of surname, and then by first letter of given name, with entries listed chronologically.

- Another commercial system first clumps together surnames beginning with certain two-letter combinations, then sorted by first letter of given name. Unlike the Russell system, this method kept the entries for a surname within a contiguous section of the index.

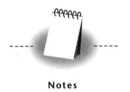

Notes

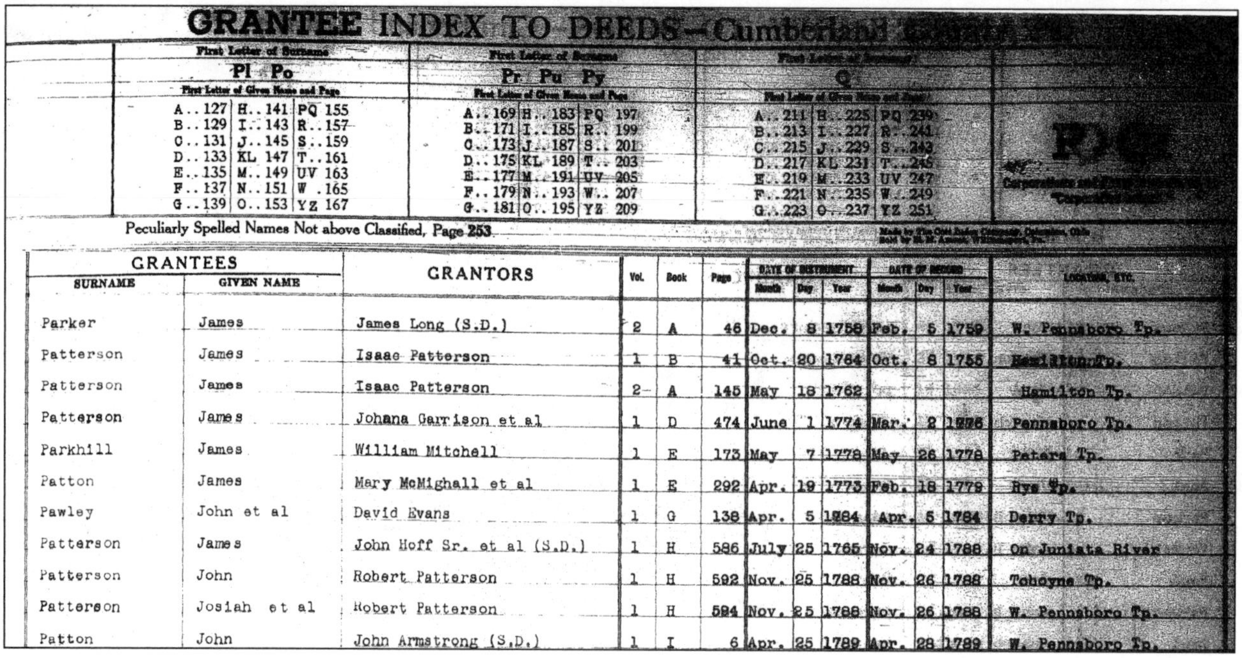

GRANTEE INDEX TO DEEDS—Cumberland County

First Letter of Surname: Pl Po			First Letter of Surname: Pr Pu Py			First Letter of Surname: Q		
A..127	H..141	PQ 155	A..169	H..183	PQ 197	A..211	H..225	PQ 239
B..129	I..143	R..157	B..171	I..185	R..199	B..213	I..227	R..241
C..131	J..145	S..159	C..173	J..187	S..201	C..215	J..229	S..243
D..133	KL 147	T..161	D..175	KL 189	T..203	D..217	KL 231	T..245
E..135	M..149	UV 163	E..177	M..191	UV 205	E..219	M..233	UV 247
F..137	N..151	W .165	F..179	N..193	W..207	F..221	N..235	W..249
G..139	O..153	YZ 167	G..181	O..195	YZ 209	G..223	O..237	YZ 251

Peculiarly Spelled Names Not above Classified, Page 253

GRANTEES Surname	Given Name	GRANTORS	Vol.	Book	Page	Date of Instrument Month	Day	Year	Date of Record Month	Day	Year	Location, etc.
Parker	James	James Long (S.D.)	2	A	46	Dec.	8	1758	Feb.	5	1759	W. Pennsboro Tp.
Patterson	James	Isaac Patterson	1	B	41	Oct.	20	1764	Oct.	8	1755	Hamilton Tp.
Patterson	James	Isaac Patterson	2	A	145	May	18	1762				Hamilton Tp.
Patterson	James	Johana Garrison et al	1	D	474	June	1	1774	Mar.	2	[illegible]	Pennsboro Tp.
Parkhill	James	William Mitchell	1	E	173	May	7	1778	May	26	1778	Peters Tp.
Patton	James	Mary McMighall et al	1	E	292	Apr.	19	1773	Feb.	18	1779	Rye Tp.
Pawley	John et al	David Evans	1	G	138	Apr.	5	1784	Apr.	5	1784	Derry Tp.
Patterson	James	John Hoff Sr. et al (S.D.)	1	H	586	July	25	1765	Nov.	24	1788	On Juniata River
Patterson	John	Robert Patterson	1	H	592	Nov.	25	1788	Nov.	26	1788	Tohoyne Tp.
Patterson	Josiah et al	Robert Patterson	1	H	594	Nov.	25	1788	Nov.	26	1788	W. Pennsboro Tp.
Patton	John	John Armstrong (S.D.)	1	I	6	Apr.	25	1789	Apr.	28	1789	W. Pennsboro Tp.

Figure 4-6 As seen by the key at the top of the page, this index is organized by the first two letters of the surname.

- My least favorite index was one that was organized by the first letter of the surname of the grantor—and then by the first letter of the surname of the grantee. Even if you know you want the deed when Thomas Williams sold his land, you still have to go through all of the *W*s. Fortunately, I've only found this used once.

There are a couple of wrinkles to watch for. Some indexes record a tremendous amount of information—so much information, in fact, that it may be recorded on two pages. This is especially true of indexes for deeds in public-land states, which often include the lengthy description for rectangular-survey parcels. (See figure 4-7.)

It isn't too difficult to follow the entry for George Law across two pages, since it was on the second line, but it can become more difficult lower on the page, especially if you are working from microfilm.

Most deed book series began with Book A. This means that they ran out of letters after *Z*. A few counties began again with AA, then BB, and eventually encountered the same problem. Some switched to numbers, so the books after *Z* are 1, 2, and so on. Still other counties began the new series with 1A (or A1), followed by 1B, and so on. Make sure that you carefully record the book, especially if there is potentially both a Book I and a Book 1.

Corporations, governments (and their representatives, such as the commissioners or sheriff), and other nonindividuals often are treated specially in the index. Large entities often have pages to themselves. These exceptions are usually noted at the front of the volume or initial letter.

Some letters are routinely combined. *I* and *J* were considered the same letter in earlier times, so if you are having trouble finding your *Isaac,* you might check the *J*s.

GRANTEES.	GRANTORS.	Instrument.	DATE.			Consideration.	Book.	Page.
			Month.	Date.	Year.			
Smith C. S. *etc*	Hugh Duffy	Mortg.	July	8	1856	600 00	*T*	503
Law George	John Conley	deed	" "	21	1856	200 00	*T*	534
Lanier August	H. Horine et al by Com	" "	12	1856	1500 00	*T*	537
Lanier John L. Com:	August Lanier	Mortg	"	12	1856	1350 00	*T*	543
Laufer Peter	Adam Klein	deed	"	31	1856	1050 00	*T*	555
Lanier August	William C. Moore	quitclm	Febuary	22	1855	40 00	*T*	556

DESCRIPTION OF PROPERTY.	WHEN FILED.		
N.½ S.E.¼ + S.E.¼ N.W.¼ S. 15. T. 3 S.R. 3 W. - 80 acres			
N.W.¼ N.W.¼ S. 23, + N.½ N.W.¼ S. 26. T. 4 S.R. 9 W. - 120 acres			
Claim No. 2623 Survey No. 697. - 400 acres			
Claim No. 2623 Survey No. 697. - 400 acres			
N.½ S.E.½ N.E.¼ S. 19, S.W.¼ N.W.¼ S. 31, + N.E.¼ S.E.¼ S. 30 T. 2 S. R. 9 W. 152 Feet			
Lot No. 6 in Col. 770 Sur. 65 in 18½ acre + lot No 6 in Col No. 769 Sur 482 - 21 acre			

Figure 4-7 Some index entries are two pages wide, especially in public-land states where full land descriptions are often included.

Analyzing the Entries

Most index entries provide a substantial amount of information. Almost all contain grantor, grantee, book, and page. Other elements you may find are date of recording, date of instrument, type of instrument, consideration (payment), and land description.

I've said earlier that you should collect (or at least make a note of) all deeds for your family. But what if you can't tell which entries for, say, Kerr belong to your family? Don't just skip quickly through the index looking for your ancestor's name. Examine each index entry for clues.

Focusing on the place description helps me clump together several given names (once I've collected all the index entries for all the given names of the surname). Just by analyzing the place, date, book-page references, and name groupings, in combination with what I already know about the family (and those who share the surname but are not my family), I can decide which deeds need to be examined and which do not. Then I can prioritize them. Notice that I even examine the book-page references. Deeds recorded on adjacent pages usually all refer to the same family.

In chapter two, Where Are the Records?, we discussed magic abbreviations such as *et ux., et al., est., admr., excr., QC,* and so on. To be honest, I almost always **make note of any such index entry for my surnames and examine every magic-word deed**, even when I'm almost positive that it isn't for my family. Why? Because those deeds may efficiently give me the names and relationships of a number of people who are not my family, saving me hours of time trying to sort out individuals of the same surname.

Research Tip

Managing the Information From the Index Entries

Because land records are voluminous and because you need to do whole-family research to benefit from them, the index entries alone can create an information-management problem. Your time is limited, so you want to accomplish as much as possible, but at the same time not shortchange yourself on future research by skipping index entries. A number of feasible techniques can help with this. The best choice may vary with the specific situation. I've used every one of these techniques at one time or another.

- Write the book and page numbers on a pad of paper, and then look up each one in the deed book. This works fine for a family for which there are fewer than a half dozen deeds recorded. It isn't as efficient otherwise.

- Photocopy all pertinent index pages. This works fine for a family for which there are not a tremendous number of index pages. If you have a family who shows up just once per page, this isn't the best method; however, if there are many entries on the page, not only will it save time, it will also help avoid potential transcription errors.

- Transcribe all family index entries into a laptop computer. This is what I do when I work from a microfilmed index at the Family History Library or at my local library. It takes a long time (sometimes hours), but I am then prepared for the long run with, in effect, a snapshot of my family's land transactions, even if I only have time to read a few critical deeds immediately. After I've entered everything, I sort the entries into book-page order. Then, when I check a deed in a specific deed book on microfilm or at a courthouse, I do all the deeds in that book, no matter where they were on the priority list. It saves time overall.

Tip

- **Courthouses often do not have good facilities for using a laptop,** lacking working space, a way to secure the laptop, and electrical outlets. I would not recommend taking a laptop along until after you've seen what's available.

- Try recording each index entry on a three-by-five-inch or five-by-seven-inch file card. Deed work can go more quickly if you work with a friend or relative. The file cards provide an efficient way to merge, sort, and divide the work. Put a star on the card for each "must read" deed. Mark each card for which the deed has been examined, with a special symbol if it was photocopied. You can make notes and abstracts on the backs of the cards.

Finding the Deed

Once you've mastered the index, finding the deeds themselves is relatively simple. The exception is in very early colonial records in which the system was not well organized. In that case, it can be difficult to figure out exactly where the correct volumes are.

There also can be problems if the deed books have been renumbered, which happened occasionally when the early system was outgrown or when copies were maintained at other jurisdictions or transferred and renumbered. Sometimes the index will use one volume-numbering system, while the books themselves have another system. Sometimes the numbering doesn't make sense, because it isn't systematic. Maryland would be a good example of this (or a bad example, depending on your perspective).

Having found the correct volume, you may have further difficulty finding the page. On microfilmed deed books, the page number is often obscured in the darkened corners of the page. Look for a page number that you can read, and then count. It's tedious, but it's the most efficient way.

If this fails, find the index entry for the deed currently displayed on the microfilm. The index will tell you what page you are on. Then count.

In very early deeds, you may encounter problems with "folio" numbering. In this case, a single number referred to two of what we would call pages. I have seen indexes in which the left and right pages were indexed under the number, and I have seen indexes in which the front and back of the page were indexed under the number. Often these volumes later had single-page numbers added. The problem is that you aren't always sure which system goes with the index you are using. You may have to check several places to find the desired deed.

When you still can't find the deed, you may have made a mistake in noting the volume or page number, or it may simply have been hard to read and you guessed wrong. It is also possible that the index itself has the wrong reference. Recheck the index. Remember that the index entries are in deed-book order. You may be able to determine immediately that 16:123 was really 10:123 because the index entry is between one for Book 9 and one for Book 12. Or, you may be able to see that 68:418 is quite likely 68:478 because it has the same grantor as the next line, which is for 68:480.

Once you've found the deed, there are a number of ways to record the information. See chapter eight, How to Record What You Find, to learn more.

FIVE

First Transfer—Getting Land Into the Hands of Individuals

A t one time, all the land in America was owned by a European monarchy, with a significant portion later belonging to Mexico. Eventually, much of it ended up in the hands of individuals like your ancestors and my ancestors.

First transfers to individuals varied over time. The process included several stages and different types of participants. This chapter offers a generic overview of that process. Transfers between individuals was discussed in chapter two, Where Are the Records?

There are, broadly speaking, four paths that were followed in getting land from the ownership of kings and into the hands of yeomen farmers (see "From Crown to Individual" on page 69). The model determines where we find the records. Be aware that there are many wrinkles and variations. Once you've identified a time and place of significance for your ancestor, you'll need to learn more about that specific case.

Land in almost all of the original thirteen colonies was granted in a variety of ways. As an example, Maine had some early proprietorships granted by the crown and others by Plymouth Colony. It also had towns that followed the New England model, several types of bounty or compensatory land, school land, land granted by the colony of Massachusetts (its original parent), and land granted by the state. (See table 5-1 on page 77.)

MODEL ONE: THE NEW ENGLAND SYSTEM

The earliest "settlers" in New England were not the Pilgrims or the Puritans, but the fishermen who frequented the northeast coast to profit from its well-stocked waters. Being seamen, they quickly noted another rich resource on shore—tall, straight timbers perfect for ship masts. Hence, the crown saw value in promoting permanent settlement in their far-off possession.

The best-known New England settlers were, of course, the Pilgrims and the Puritans. They both came for religious motivations and brought with them their

FROM CROWN TO INDIVIDUAL			
Model One New England	**Model Two Colonial**	**Model Three Proprietor**	**Model Four Federal**
crown	crown	crown	crown
⬇	⬇	⬇	⬇
colony	colony	(colony)	colony
⬇		⬇	
town/ proprietors		individual/ proprietor	
			⬇
			federal government
⬇	⬇	⬇	⬇
individual	individual	individual	individual

Note: After the Revolutionary War, colony land became state land.

understanding of how a community founded on religious principles should function. Their understanding of government was based on a consideration that civil functions were derived from religious principles. This ultimately determined the way that most land in New England was transferred into the hands of individuals.

The king granted charters initially to Plymouth Colony and Massachusetts Bay Colony, soon followed by New Haven Colony, Connecticut, and Rhode Island. The individuals administering the charter *planted* towns by giving the land for specified towns to *proprietors* for the town. As time went on, new towns were established in the same organized manner, either because the land was used up or because of political or religious friction. Thus, many of the early settlers in the new town came from the parent town.

The religious foundations of their town model said that community was more important than individuals. The New England system was designed for the common good. Therefore, these proprietors behaved in a way completely in variance with the behavior of proprietors in the colonies we'll consider on pages 70-77, such as New York, Maryland, Pennsylvania, Virginia, and Georgia.

The proprietors began by studying the land they had under their administration. They determined a good location for the town itself, the best pasture land, the best growing land, the marshland (which wasn't valueless—grass grown in the salt marshes provided an important food source for livestock), and so on. They determined how many families in the town were eligible for land by virtue of being approved residents. Then they had the town surveyed, subdividing each type of land into a sufficient number of portions for the families—or designating it as common land, to be used by all.

Their model went beyond dividing the land. They also specified land for common use—designating portions for roads, a burying ground, and communal grazing—and they allocated parcels for the church, the school, and future growth. This model will become important to us again as we look at chapter six, Public Lands.

Having planned the use of the land in a way designed to benefit the community, the proprietors distributed it communally. The settlers drew for their lots in what the records often called "the first division." Each family might get one town lot and one meadow lot or one swamp lot. Things weren't always exactly equal; sometimes the town leaders did get better or larger lots, and some towns determined the size of the lot based on the size of the family.

When the time came to dispose of additional land ("the second division"), it was once again an orderly, controlled process in which the land reserved for future growth was surveyed into lots and the drawing done according to the needs determined by the town leaders.

The interesting thing is that the lots were numbered, and the numbers were picked out of a hat, so to speak. In other words, the inhabitants didn't choose where they lived; that was determined by the luck of the draw. Thus, the adjoining owners in town weren't necessarily the adjoining owners of their cultivated land. Hence, we place less emphasis on immediate neighbors in New England than in the South.

The records of these first land transfers, from town to individual, are usually in the town record books. There should be an accompanying plat, identifying the location of each lot. However, many of the plats were probably large separate sheets and did not remain with the books. The lot numbers were the identifier for the property, so you can use a later map showing the lot numbers to identify your ancestor's lot.

Sources

MODEL TWO: THE COLONIAL GOVERNMENT SYSTEM

In the royal colonies of the South, much of the land passed from the crown to the administration of the colony in a fairly straightforward manner. For example, once the crown decided in 1623 that the Virginia Company of London was not doing a good job of achieving the goals the crown desired—settling Virginia with the intent of returning valuable products to England—it revoked their charter and instituted a system with a royal governor, a model that would be followed in other areas.

Land Sales

All colonies and proprietors eventually offered land for sale. The rules and costs varied over time, influenced in part by competition from other areas. The price might include a cost per acre, an annual *quitrent* (a remnant of the European feudal system), up-front processing fees, or any combination thereof.

Most of these areas followed the indiscriminate survey system, meaning that land was selected first and then it was settled. South Carolina and Georgia, however, both made some attempts at methodical surveys before offering land.

Grant Process

Grants or *patents* (the terms mean the same thing, but be sure to use the right term for your locality—Virginians are particularly touchy about this; they had patents during the colonial period and grants after, but the Northern Neck always had grants) had to be obtained from the capital. If buying from a proprietor, the man had to go to the office of the proprietor's agent. Sometimes individuals hired agents or issued powers of attorney to avoid making the lengthy trip twice. Eventually in some areas, agents were established closer to where the new land was available.

In general, the process was that an individual first established his right to acquire a certain number of acres, either by headright (see "Headrights" below) or purchase, and received a warrant. He stated exactly where the land was (in other words, it wasn't an open warrant). His warrant was recorded so as to (theoretically) prevent overlaps.

The warrant allowed him to hire—at his own cost—a surveyor (usually there was a designated surveyor for an area).

Once he had the survey in hand, he could return to the capital and—after making any required adjustments in fee based on the dissimilarity between the acreage of the warrant and that of the survey—would *mature* the warrant into a grant (or patent). Warrants and even surveys were negotiable instruments that could be *assigned* to other individuals.

In general, then, the broad process for the first transfer to an individual outside of New England was:

1. obtain right
2. survey
3. grant

Headrights

Virginia, the proprietorship of Maryland, parts of the Carolinas, Georgia, and the Republic of Texas used a headright system to distribute land to promote immigration.

Records of headright claims often provide information quite different from records of simple land purchase. For example, **the *headright* system in Virginia said that anyone settling in the colony had a right to fifty acres.** In practice, the person paying the costs of transport usually was considered to own the headright. If a man brought his wife and two children, he was eligible for 200 acres. If a plantation owner imported seven servants, paying for their passage, he was eligible for 350 acres. If a ship captain imported men and women who were sold as indentured servants, he could claim their headright. As a ship captain, he probably didn't want land and therefore sold the headright with the indenture or possibly to an individual who was buying up headrights.

Fifty acres wasn't a practical amount in Virginia, so it appears there was a brisk trade in headrights, allowing larger grants to men who hadn't participated personally in the importation. Other localities instituted restrictions, such as requiring claimants to appear personally and provide details, and there was less abuse of the system. North Carolina, for example, did not allow the sale of a headright until the person had been a resident for two years.

Headright claims may be found in court records or in land records. The Virginia patents, for example, give the names of the headright individuals and have now been published up to the Revolution. Thus, you can find the "immigrated by" date in land patents for a seventeenth-century Virginia ancestor who never owned land. There were, however, no records of immigration for the

\di'fin\ *vb*

Definitions

courts to compare to. Hence, there were many abuses, usually with individuals being claimed more than once.

Maryland found itself desperately needing settlers and instituted a headright system early. However, it failed to specify that the settler had to have come from England, thereby attracting some Virginia settlers (who might already have had a Virginia headright) into Maryland, especially on the eastern shore. The headright system operated only briefly in Maryland and the Carolinas, largely because of the abuses, and it died out in Virginia after the early 1700s. In spite of the earlier experiences, Georgia used the system when it was seeking settlers.

Land Lotteries

To encourage settlement in the western and northern portions of the state, Georgia held a series of land lotteries in 1805, 1807, 1820, 1821, 1827, 1832 (Cherokee), 1832 (Gold), and 1833 that were used to promote settlement in the western and northern portions of the state.

Each lottery created two lists—one of the eligible, one of the winners. However, eligibility lists do not survive for all counties for all lotteries. When they do, they can be very valuable. Consider the case of Lemuel E. Owen. He first appeared in Illinois on the 1820 census. In 1850 we learn that he was born about 1798 in Georgia.

Of all the land lotteries, that of 1807 had the most liberal terms. One draw was given to men over twenty-one, widowed or single women over twenty-one, a minor orphan with the father (or father and mother) dead, or to a family of orphans whose father was dead, but whose mother was living. Two draws were given to a married man with a wife and at least one child or to a family of orphans who had lost both parents. The only exclusions were for the winners of the 1805 drawing. Thus it is that I learn so much about Lemuel.

The eligibility list for Oglethorpe County survives and has been published. Carefully study any list. Do not just grab the information about your ancestor and ignore the rest. One portion of the list includes the following:

> 2 William Owen, Senior
> [*two names*]
> 1 Milley Owen, Widow
> 2 Lucy Owen, Lemuel Owen, Levie Owen, orphans of Obediah Owen, Deceased
> 1 Salley H. Owen, 21 years of age

The names are grouped together, strongly suggesting familial connections. Since Salley is listed immediately after the orphans, she might be their sister. However, she would have been born before about 1786, which makes quite a gap (Levi was born in Georgia in 1800, and Lucy married in 1813, suggesting a birth around 1792). Milley would seem to be a good candidate for the mother of the orphans of Obediah—except for the terms of the draw, which explicitly say that a family of orphans with the father dead but mother living only gets one draw.

The lists establish the name of the father of the three siblings and that Obediah died by 1807. Obediah does not appear on the 1790 tax list of Wilkes

County (the parent of Oglethorpe), but he is there in 1794, with no land, but next to William Owen on Long Creek. The 1800 Georgia census survives only for Oglethorpe; Obediah and presumed wife are 26 to 45, and their presumed daughter is under 10, hence Salley H. is not another daughter. We have, however, four "families" here to help with our future research.

Continuing our study of the lotteries, we find that Lemuel Owen of Putnam County had a successful draw in the 1821 lottery for land in Fayette County. Is this my Lemuel? No. We must always analyze land records in context with other records. Lemuel may seem an unusual name to us, but it was annoyingly popular in this time period. My Lemuel, as mentioned previously, was already in Illinois by 1820. This Lemuel married in Putnam in 1815 and raised a family in Georgia.

MODEL THREE: LARGE GRANTS AND PROPRIETORS

You probably remember reading in history class about Lord Baltimore and William Penn. The colonies of Maryland and Pennsylvania were direct grants to individuals, as was the Northern Neck of Virginia, granted to several proprietors but later associated with Lord Fairfax; the northern portion of North Carolina, granted to Earl Granville; and the Jersey proprietorships. In New York, proprietorships were usually referred to as *manors* (remember the feudal concept of landownership).

The land was, technically, the private property of the proprietor. He then sold parcels to individuals. Because he owned the land privately, the record of the transfer was private. However, in Maryland and Pennsylvania, the grants were enormous and soon became colonies, so a public record also is available, as is true with the Fairfax grants in Virginia.

There were smaller grants made to proprietors by the crown or by the administrators of the colony. In these cases, the transactions from proprietor to individual often were recorded as private records. Also, some proprietors, most notably in New York state, followed the European custom of renting or leasing the land, rather than selling it outright. These factors can be frustrating for genealogists. Some records, such as those for the Holland Land Company in New York and the Granville grants in North Carolina, are publicly available. Others, such as those for the Otego Patent, also in New York, aren't public and quite possibly don't survive.

The close of the Revolution brought concern to the many landholders who held their land by a right from a proprietorship, which usually held its authority from the crown. However, in almost all cases, states recognized that established settlement was a positive thing and accepted these landholders as the valid landowners.

Because recording a deed was at the option of the buyer, some cautious buyers had their patents recorded. More often, you'll find the grant mentioned in the chain of title when the first individual owner sold the land.

Look at the deed for Edward Halsey (spelling does not seem to have been the scribe's strong point).

> This Indenture made the twenty seventh day of September in the year of our Lord one thousand seven hundred and ninety 1790 between Edward Halsey of Otego Osago Township Montgomery County and State of New York and Hannah his wife of one part and Thomas Cartwright late of Varmont now of Otego in County and State afsd of the other part.

Notice that even the opening of the deed provides helpful information—the given name of Edward's wife (the *only* place this is ever mentioned) and, for Cartwright descendants, Thomas's state of origin.

> one hundred acres strict measure . . . which piece of Land is part of one thousand acres formerly belong to Samuel Alison which part was given unto the sd Edward Halsey and the same conve'd by Deed of Lece and Relece breeing date the seventeenth day of March one thousand seven hundred and seventy five, the same is a part of sixty nine thousand acres formerly granted unto the sd Saml Alison by Thomas Warton of the City of Phildelphia on the third day of Feabruary 1770 as by the sd patent record in the Secritarys Offics at New York in Libro Number 14 of Patents 535 which may appear by the former grants, and the sd Saml Alison by Deed of Leace and Releace to the said Edward Halsey his heirs and assigns, and the Lot hereby granted is a part of Lot No. 39.

The deed mentions Edward Halsey's 1775 grant as part of the chain of title, a section often found in deeds. Unfortunately, this 1775 grant does not appear to have been recorded.

It took some digging to figure out what those early records referred to (as has been mentioned, land records can contain confusing elements), but the investigation proved useful to learning more about Edward Halsey's life. Samuel Alinson was one of sixty-nine proprietors who patented sixty-nine thousand acres as the Otego patent. They took approximately one thousand acres each.

The grant to the proprietors had an interesting quirk (fortunately, I didn't have to read the New York patents; I found it printed in a book). The proprietors would lose the land unless

> . . . within three years next after the date of this our present grant [3 February 1770] settle on the said tract of land hereby granted, so many Families as shall amount to one Family for every thousand Acres . . . also within three years plant and effectually cultivate at the least three Acres for every fifty Acres . . . capable of cultivation . . .

Restrictions such as these were not uncommon in areas where the goal was getting inhabitants onto the land (often with the unstated intentions of pushing the Indians farther west and serving as a buffer). A single element of the metes-and-bounds description in Edward's deed tells us that he was one of those earliest settlers fulfilling that requirement and that he had lived in Otego two years before the date of his patent.

> . . . beginning at Beach tree by the west side of Otego Creek now dead and fallen down on Lot number 39 & 40 thence runing west fifty chain to a maple marked on three sides, then north twelve degrees East twenty chain

to a stak formley set up for a corner, thence East fifty chain to a Hemlock standing on the bank of Oteo [*sic*] Creek marked thus **E. H. 1773** thence down sd Creek to the place of beginning . . .

Some proprietorships first had the land surveyed into lots and then sold the land on a lot-by-lot basis. In the Otego patent above, each proprietor got a numbered lot, but how he divided that lot was his business.

Most proprietors, however, sold land described by *metes and bounds*. The individual chose the exact boundaries of the land he wished to obtain, and a survey was then done (the *indiscriminate-survey* system). The title transferred via patent, grant, or other instrument according to the survey description.

MODEL FOUR: FEDERAL LANDS

After the Revolutionary War, the states—sometimes reluctantly—relinquished their ungranted western lands to the federal government (see chapter six, Public Land). The majority of American land acquired by individuals was initially *public land* belonging to the federal government. The ultimate disposition of those public lands was

- one-third sold to settlers
- one-third given or sold to speculators, railroads, and so on (much of which was resold to settlers)
- one-third remained in public domain

The federal-land model most closely resembles that of New England. The land was surveyed before sale, marked out in townships, ranges, and sections. Portions were reserved for public purposes. As the survey for an area was completed, a land office was opened to sell land in the area, which often covered a significant portion of a state. Thus, our westward expansion occurred in a continual, but controlled, series of small waves as each new office opened, much like the settlement pattern in New England.

BIG CITIES AND SMALLER TOWNS

In the confined areas of cities and towns, the indiscriminate survey system obviously isn't practical. Most municipalities of any size are developed under a system of *subdivision*. This is similar to the process followed in New England, in which streets and public areas were designated in the survey and lots were sold by number (albeit with an underlying metes-and-bounds description). However, the buyer chose the lot he wanted.

The developer may have been an individual seeking profit, or a group of commissioners or trustees may have been designated to administer the sales, as for the town of Glasgow, Kentucky.

Deed 7 Jun 1800 from Haiden Trigg, Abel Hannon, William Welsh, John Cole, John Moss, John McFerran, John Matthews (trustees for town of Glasgow) to Rhody Fuell for $26: lot #25 in Glasgow, Barren County, Kentucky.

BOUNTY LAND

Colonies used land as rewards for public service (political patronage is not a new institution) and as incentive or payment, particularly for military service. In primarily agricultural America, military campaigns were significant disruptions in the planting and harvesting cycle. Some of the greatest damage of King Philip's War in New England in 1675 and 1676, for example, resulted not from the direct conflict, but from a missed growing season on the part of both the colonists and the Indians. This war also represented the first campaign in which land was used as bounty to reward for military service.

The Revolutionary War saw a major increase in the use of bounty land, with Virginia and North Carolina making significant use of the incentive at the state level, as did the federal government. Bounty land continued to be offered through federal-period conflicts, most notably the War of 1812.

However, because land was relatively cheap and available throughout the colonies (later states), military bounty land wasn't necessarily a strong inducement. When bounty was offered and accepted, the man who gave the military service often didn't settle the land. Instead, he assigned the scrip or warrant he had received for whatever cold, hard cash he could get from an agent who was buying and consolidating bounty-land rights.

Colonial and State Bounty Land

During the colonial period, bounty land was offered as inducement for service or as recompense for service, injury, or death during military conflicts, mostly with the Indians and the French.

During the Revolution, colonies continued the practice, especially as the conflict dragged on and they had little cash. The introduction to Bockstruck's *Revolutionary War Bounty Land Grants Awarded by State Governments* describes the practice of each colony and is recommended reading (don't just look for your ancestor's name).

Records related to any bounty land offered in the colonial period would be under the custody of the appropriate state, with the exception of the Virginia Military District warrants that were converted into land, which are in the possession of the National Archives. You will have to research the records to determine the location and best method of access.

Federal Bounty Land

The federal government began offering bounty land in 1776 as inducement for a man to enlist—and stay enlisted—during the Revolutionary War. It continued to issue bounty land for service through 1855. See "Bounty Land Warrant Records" in *Guide to Genealogical Research in the National Archives* for more information.

Remember that bounty land was not necessarily taken up by the man eligible for the bounty. Your ancestor might have been involved at either end of the process. He might have given service, received a bounty-land right, certificate, or warrant, and then sold (*assigned*) it to someone else. If that person was an agent, he in turn sold (*assigned*) it to the individual who wanted to settle the land. If this person was your ancestor, then he didn't necessarily have military service, even though he took up bounty land.

Warrants for the Revolutionary War and War of 1812 could be used only in specified areas. When it became clear that the amount of land was insufficient, new claimants received bounty-land scrip and existing warrants could be exchanged for scrip. Warrants and early scrip were for land in Arkansas, Illinois, Indiana, Michigan (the land was considered so undesirable that it was soon withdrawn), Missouri, and Ohio. In 1842 it became possible to redeem the scrip at any federal land office, prompting increased settlement in the other states.

When requesting a copy of a bounty-land warrant, you must provide the act of Congress, certificate number, and, for acts between 1847 and 1855, the acreage. There are name indexes for the Revolutionary War and the War of 1812. Use NATF 85 to order bounty-land warrant applications. Use NATF 80 to request a search for warrants from acts between 1847 and 1855. See

TABLE OF BOUNTY LAND		
Granted by	**Conflict**	**Location of Grants**
Massachusetts	King Phillip's War (1675–76)	7 Narrangansett Townships: Massachusetts (3), Maine (2), New Hampshire (2)
Virginia	Indian Wars (1701)	Virginia
crown	French and Indian War (1763)	various colonies
federal	Rev War—Continental line	U.S. Military District, Symmes Purchase, Ohio Company (Ohio)
federal	Rev War—Canadian refugees	Refugee Tract (Ohio)
Connecticut	Rev War—for claims, not service	Fire Lands (Ohio)
Maine	Rev War—from any colony	Maine
Massachusetts	Rev War	Maine
New York	Rev War	New York
Pennsylvania	Rev War	Pennsylvania "Donation Lands"
Maryland	Rev War	Maryland
Virginia	Rev War	south of the Green River (Kentucky); Virginia Military Tract (Ohio); Indiana
North Carolina	Rev War	Tennessee
South Carolina	Rev War	South Carolina
Georgia	Rev War	Georgia
federal	War of 1812	Arkansas; Illinois; Missouri
federal	Mexican War (1847)	any federal land office
Texas	Republic of Texas (1835–88)	Texas

Note: This is a partial list.
Bounty land offers usually had restrictions on who was eligible. Scrip for federal bounty land was eventually honored at any federal land office. Bounty land acts often were passed—and the warrants issued—many years after the conflict.

Table 5-1

<www.archives.gov> for more information. You can request form NATF 85 easily from the Web site. The form comes with instructions.

Bounty Land Resources

Bockstruck, Lloyd DeWitt. *Revolutionary War Bounty Land Grants: Awarded by State Governments.* Baltimore: Genealogical Publishing Co., 1996.

Christensen, Katheren. *Arkansas Military Bounty Grants (War of 1812).* n.p.: Arkansas Ancestors, 1971.

Miller, Thomas Lloyd. *Bounty and Donation Land Grants of Texas, 1835–1888.* Austin: University of Texas Press, 1967.

National Archives and Records Administration. *Guide to Genealogical Research in the National Archives.* 3d ed. Washington, D.C.: 2000. "Bounty Land Warrant Records," describes M804 *Revolutionary War Pension and Bounty-Land-Warrant Application Files* (2,670 rolls), M848 *War of 1812 Military Bounty Land Warrants* (14 rolls), and other sources.

National Genealogical Society. *Index of Revolutionary War Pension Applications in the National Archives.* Washington, D.C.: National Genealogical Society, 1976. Serves as index to bounty-land warrants, which are part of the M804 *Revolutionary War Pension and Bounty-Land-Warrant Application Files* series.

White, Virgil D. *Genealogical Abstracts of Revolutionary War Pension Files.* 4 vols. Waynesboro, Tenn.: National Historical Publishing Company, 1990–92.

SIX

Public Lands

I n the decades after the Revolution, the federal government acquired a large amount of land. Some was ceded by the states (in varying degrees of willingness), some was acquired through war or treaty, and some was purchased (the Louisiana Purchase literally doubled the size of the United States). In the early federal period, the government viewed land as its only source of revenue, so selling land was high on the agenda. To the Confederation, land equaled money. Land did not represent opportunity, nor was the Confederation concerned about expansion.

As the Confederation struggled with determining how to pay for its debts by selling its only asset—the western lands—the debate focused on the fundamental differences between the New England method of land settlement and that used elsewhere (see chapter five, First Transfer—Getting Land Into the Hands of Individuals). The root of the problem lay in the order of the steps in their processes:

- In New England: Survey first, then distribution.
- In the South: Selection first, survey second.

It was going to be necessary for each state to formally give up its ungranted western lands, but the states' regional experience shaped views of how the new federal lands should be disposed. For example, Connecticut's first cession offer, in 1780, stated that the township system should prevail in the lands ceded by her and that it should be

> laid out and surveyed in townships in regular form to a suitable number of settlers in such manner as will best promote the settlement and cultivation of the same.

Neither faction seemed to think that the other's method made sense. The New England influence was strong. The fact that conflicts arising from overlapping claims in metes-and-bounds surveys were clogging court systems in the South didn't speak well for the alternative.

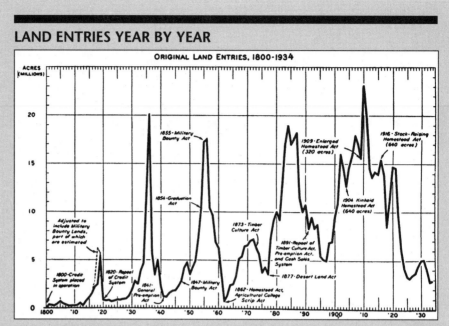

LAND ENTRIES YEAR BY YEAR

Prepared by the United States Department of Agriculture, Bureau of Agricultural Economics. *United States National Resources Board, Land Planning Committee, Report on Land Planning*, "Part 7: Certain Aspects of Land Problems and Government Land Policies" (Washington, 1935), 61.

In the preparation of this chart, all of the original land entries under the various laws were compiled, insofar as this was possible. This chart includes the following types of cash entries: Private cash entries, public auction sales, preemption entries, Indian land sales, timber and stone entries under the act of 1877, mineral land entries (small), coal land entries (small), abandoned military reservations, and miscellaneous sales. It also includes entries made with military warrants and various kinds of scrip. Original entries under the Homestead, Timber Culture, and Desert Land acts are included. It was not possible to secure data concerning all the land entered with scrip and military warrants, the amount not included in the chart being less than 3,000,000 acres, the absence of which does not materially affect the picture here presented. It should be pointed out that this chart is for original entries. A chart of final entries or one showing the amount of entries going to patent would be substantially different, as a large amount of homestead, timber culture, and desert land entries never were proved up. The chart does not include lands granted to railroads or states, nor certain small grants to individuals. Nor does it include Indian land sales prior to 1879, nor the sale of Indian allotments at any time.

Establishing the Public Land System

The *Ordinance of 1785* that defined the federal land system largely followed the New England model described previously. The land would be presurveyed. The ordinance also reserved four out of thirty-six townships to the federal government, and section 16 was reserved for schools. The advantages of the rectangular survey system were simple.

- No overlapping claims, because land descriptions were unique and explicit. Payson Jackson Treat commented that " . . . the security of title and the simplicity of conveyance were the two great contributions of the land surveys."
- Descriptions were simple and formulaic and were not dependent upon physical features.

Land sales under the Ordinance got off to a slow start. Land was to be sold at public auction for a minimum one dollar per acre. At the time, land in New York, Pennsylvania, Maine, Kentucky, and Tennessee was selling at or below one dollar per acre, so the Northwest Territory wasn't competitive in the marketplace. Surveying took longer than expected. The first sale was made in September 1787. Section lines hadn't been run; only corners were marked. But after 1796, all new land was surveyed as we know it today—except, of course, for the usual government inefficiencies.

- Money was not allocated for surveys.
- Some townships didn't have section lines run because they were supposed to be sold as complete townships, but later they were sold by section.
- Surveys were contracts let through government patronage.
- Settlers—a.k.a. *squatters*—were continually moving into new, unsurveyed territory seeking the best lands, sometimes resulting in *preemption claims* with metes-and-bounds descriptions that had to be resolved before sales could begin.

Sales of Public Land—Process

The steps in surveying and claiming land under the public-land system were:

1. Settle Indian claims.
2. Survey.
3. Announce land opening.
4. Settle preemption (private) claims.
5. Open land office and sell land.
6. Close land office.

The policy debates over public land (called the *public domain*) continued. Attempts to dispose of what by now was a massive amount of land under federal control prolonged the debates between wealthy speculators and the growing numbers of poor farmers, many with families. Senator Thomas Hart Benson of Missouri and Congressman Andrew Johnson of Tennessee promoted the interests of the small farmers. Laws gradually moved toward helping the small farmer. The ultimate goal of many, however, was to get the government to *give* farmers the land in small parcels—just enough to support a family. Southerners opposed giving land to impoverished settlers, assuming that they would be antislavery.

The controversies were well known to our ancestors. They were debated not only in Congress, but also in newspapers, frontier stores, saloons, and anywhere citizens met. The issues included large versus small sales, credit versus cash sales, antiforeigner sentiment, land for income versus expansion of settlement, preemption (squatting), fraud, free soil (formation of nonslave states), and free land (homesteading). Each shaped the public-land policy that determined how our ancestors acquired their land.

How Was Public Land Distributed?

Public land was distributed in a variety of ways. (See "Land Acts" on page 83 for a list of some of the acts legislating distribution.)

- resellers
- railroad, road, and canal companies
- Indian allotments
- states
- private claims
- preemption claims
- donation lands
- bounty-land warrant
- bounty-land scrip
- cash sales
- credit sales
- homestead
- timber-culture claims
- desert claims
- mineral claims
- timber and stone claims
- Kinkaid Act

Transfer to Individuals

The transfer of public land was dictated by a series of legislative acts. As with most legislation, each act had a specific goal—and numerous terms and restrictions designed to accomplish that goal. In reality the details (and sometimes the original goal) were not always practical, necessitating further legislation.

Each time a law was passed, a substantial number of land entries (intent to patent land) usually were made soon after (see chart in "Land Entries Year by Year" on page 80). For a variety of reasons, however, many entries did not mature ("prove up") to patents. In other words, a similar chart showing patents would have lower peaks and smoother valleys. However, migration into an area was highly reflective of the peaks of the chart. If your ancestor migrated at the time of one of the peaks, he was probably responding to the most recent land act.

Schools, Railroads, Favoritism, and the Common Good

Not all land was sold directly to individuals. **Some public land was transferred from the federal government to another government or to a company.** This land may then have been used to build a school or railroad—or it may have been sold to raise funds.

States received land for designated common good. Section 16 (or its equivalent) in every township was designated for education. This land did not have to be used for school buildings. It could be sold to raise funds for education.

Notes

LAND ACTS

Most people think of "homesteading" when they think of the original occupant of public land, but there were many other ways of acquiring the land. You may have heard that your ancestor "homesteaded" land, when in actuality he made a cash or credit purchase or acquired it under one of the other acts. Don't short-circuit your research by focusing solely on homestead records.

A number of special acts were passed to control the transfer of public land directly into the hands of individuals. Almost all of the acts were driven by special agendas or motives, ranging from the desire to establish more nonslave states to the need for governmental revenue to the ideal of an agrarian, family-based economy.

For example, the Homestead Act required citizenship or that a declaration of intent had been filed, hence encouraging aliens to become citizens. It also allowed Civil War veterans to count their service time against the residency requirement. There were eligibility criteria that allowed women to obtain land under the Homestead Act, too, and a few did so.

The variety of acts is testimony to the fact that not all land is created equal. Some acts were modified several times as flaws in the original theory emerged. Some acts required residency on the land and some did not.

- 1785 Land Ordinance, cash sales of whole townships (thirty-six square miles) alternating with sales of whole sections; minimum acreage was reduced in 1796, 1800, and 1832; repealed in 1891.

- 1800 Credit Sales, allowing four years to pay; popular but not very practical because many people couldn't keep up the payments; repealed in 1820.

- 1841 General Preemption Rights (many earlier, specific acts had been passed); repealed in 1891.

- 1842–1853 Donation Land, in Florida, Oregon/Washington, and New Mexico/Arizona.

- 1854 Graduation Act, reduced prices for less-desirable, still-vacant land; repealed in 1862.

- 1855 Military Bounty Land Act, reduced and generalized the requirements from earlier acts.

- 1862 Homestead Act, for 160 acres, enlarged to 320 acres in 1909; repealed in 1972.

- 1862 Agricultural Colleges Scrip Act, issued to states to be used to raise money for agricultural colleges; could be used like bounty-land scrip.

- 1866 Mineral Act, allowed patenting of mineral claims.

continued

- 1873 Timber Culture Act, for 160 acres (later 80 acres); repealed in 1891.

- 1877 Desert Land Act, for 640 acres in a dozen western states, which required irrigation.

- 1878 Timber and Stone Act, for 160 acres of land unfit for cultivation.

- 1894 Desert Reclamation.

- 1904 Kinkaid Act, a version of the Homestead Act, for 640 acres in western Nebraska.

- 1909 Enlarged Homestead Act, for 320 acres in seven western states.

- 1916 Stock-Raising Homestead Act, 640 acres.

Land-grant colleges, found in several states, were funded out of land donated for that purpose. The New England model is reflected in early areas, which also included land to support churches.

Sometimes the federal government turned lands over to the state that didn't fit into their land-marketing system because the lands were valued far below the standard rates, such as saline land or swampland, which the state then sold. The amount of land designated in this way was not necessarily insignificant. For example, approximately one-fourth of the land in Arkansas was sold as swampland, with records of first transfer being at the state level.

Land was sometimes given to states or to private corporations to finance major capital improvements such as roads, canals, river improvements, swamp or desert reclamation, and railroads. This means that the first transfer of land was from the government to a corporation, usually by a law. The second transfer was from the corporation to individuals. Hence, your ancestor could be the first settler on his land, but there would be no federal-level records for him.

The corporation records are private. If the company still exists, it may not be set up to search old records. Many records have been lost or destroyed, but a few survive and often have been donated to state archives. For example, both the Burlington and Missouri Railroad Company and the Union Pacific Railroad Company received land in Nebraska. The Union Pacific retained its records, but the Burlington Railroad records have been microfilmed by the Nebraska Historical Society, in cooperation with the Burlington Railroad and the Newberry Library. (See figures 6-2 and 6-3 on page 85.)

Private Claims and Preemptions

Before offering the land for sale, the government had first to deal with various claims from persons said to be previously settled on the land. The testimony presented to establish the right can provide genealogical and family information. Private claims generally refer to persons on land that was acquired from another government; preemptions generally refer to persons on federal land not yet opened for purchase.

RAILROADS

The railroads played several important roles in the development of the American West. As a mode of transportation they facilitated the move of settlers westward, particularly those arriving directly from Europe with few household possessions and no farm implements or livestock. The federal government gave the railroads massive amounts of land to encourage the building of tracks. These two factors prompted a third important role—in order to sell tickets and land, the railroads advertised the advantages of western settlement.

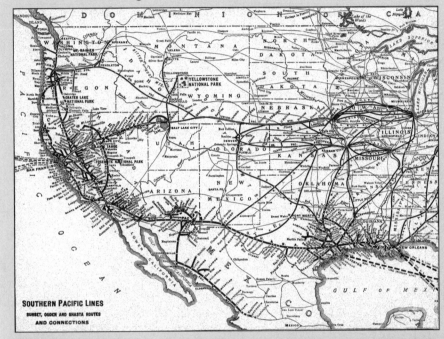

Figure 6-2 The railroads were a dramatic influence on the settlement of the American West, both as a transportation medium and because of the large amounts of land they offered for sale to individuals.

Figure 6-3 The railroads offered a peaceful vision of the agrarian countryside, as in this 1899 sketch.

When the federal government took over public-domain land, once it had made treaties with the Indians, it was necessary to clear the preemptions before the land could be opened for sale.

Many pioneers were squatters who had moved onto vacant land before the land was legally available for settlement. Their motives varied. They may have been the typical frontiersmen, moving when they could see the smoke from a neighboring cabin. Often they were well aware through the grapevine of potential land acts (although some never happened and others weren't passed for decades). They may have been participating in a form of speculation—gambling that they could get land on the basis of preemptive settlement, without having to pay for it. They may have been trying to stake out the best land before the office opened sales to everyone. They may have been living on land that belonged to nobody, in order to support themselves or their families, simply because it was the only option they could afford.

These preestablished claims in public-land states were, of course, in the form of metes-and-bounds descriptions. In a few areas, these original, irregular property lines were retained, but in most areas, the settler may have received credit for land—sometimes in approximately the same area and sometimes elsewhere.

The amount of land that was confirmed to private-land claimants varied widely by state. In most states, it was less than 1 percent of the land, but in others—particularly those with long-established French, Spanish, and Mexican control—the proportion was much higher, probably due to large original grants: New Mexico (30 percent), California (27 percent), Louisiana (13 percent), Florida (8 percent), Oregon (7 percent), Colorado (4 percent), Missouri (3 percent), and Mississippi (2 percent). Oregon's ranking is high because of the rumor mill that prompted families to move there before the 1850 *Donation Land Law* was passed.

Family historians who find a private claim in their ancestry should rejoice. By studying the social and historical background of the early settlements and reading the claim files, they may learn much about the lives and motivations of their ancestors.

Donation Lands

The Homestead Act wasn't passed until 1862, but several earlier acts offered attractive terms for land to encourage settlement in specific areas. These acts included such requirements as occupation, cultivation, construction of a dwelling, and being armed. **Researchers should be cautioned that statements made in applications may not always be fully truthful.** Also, if terms were beneficial for, say, married couples, researchers may find atypical marriage patterns with extremely young or (occasionally) much older brides. Land distributions generally considered to fall in this category are

Warning

- **Arkansas.** *Donation Law*, 24 May 1828. This was made to pacify settlers in the Lovely Purchase Donation Land, an area specified by the government to be given to the Cherokee Indians. There was significant abuse.
- **East Florida.** *Act for the Armed Occupation and Settlement of East Florida*, 4 August 1842. The head of household was required to be able to bear arms, so that the area might be more easily defended, if necessary.
- **Oregon.** *Donation Land Law*, 27 September 1850. This law was promoted by Midwesterners, particularly from Missouri, who were hungry for affordable land. Much migration occurred in anticipation before the law was passed. The law favored married couples. It was originally hoped

the law would be based on the size of a family, but as passed, rights were not given for children, but only for head of household and spouse. However, many single men claimed land, which included land in present-day Washington state. Settlers before 1 December 1850 received 320 acres; those after received half that amount.

- **New Mexico.** *Donation Law*, 22 July 1854. The least troublesome of the donation-land acts, land was awarded based on the federal survey system.

Note: The so-called Donation Lands in Pennsylvania were really a form of bounty land.

Homesteads

Ten percent of American land was homesteaded before the Public Land Management Act of 1972 effectively ended the process. The *Homestead Act of 1862* was finally passed following the secession of Southern states.

> *An Act—H.R. No. 125—To Secure Homesteads to Actual Settlers on the Public Domain.* Approved and signed May 20, 1862

It allowed an adult citizen—or intended citizen—to enter for up to 160 acres. He had to improve the property by building a dwelling, planting and cultivating crops, and remaining on the land for five years. He could buy the residency requirement early if he could come up with the cash or scrip.

If these obligations were met, the homesteader paid six dollars, and the property was his. Unfortunately, for many this didn't happen—only 40 percent of homestead applicants completed the process. Thus, if your ancestor was in the right place at the right time but didn't have land, you may still want to check the tract books for his name and follow up in the case files.

As a practical matter, 160 acres was insufficient to support a family in much of the prairie lands that were available for homesteading. Some families did well enough to buy additional parcels or to qualify under other programs for additional land. Others found the goal desirable, but the task impossible, and canceled their claims. Some moved on, seeking a more workable piece of land.

For those of us doing research on poor, migrating, frontier families, understanding where the land was located, when it was settled, and the reason and mechanism through which it was acquired can be crucial.

Fulfilling Requirements

Perhaps nothing conveys more to us about our ancestors' driving desire for land than contemplating the details of the requirements they had to fulfill to get and keep their land. Many didn't succeed. Considerably more than half of the entries for homestead, timber, and desert lands didn't make it through to patent.

Ferdinand Augustus Halsey was typical in that he tried to acquire land in more than one way—and was unable to hang on to all of it. The tract book for Township 14 North Range 7 West shows two entries for Ferdinand in section 4, in Merrick County, Nebraska. Deed books and court records supply the rest of the information.

THE FIRST HOMESTEAD

Shortly after midnight on 1 January 1863, Daniel Freeman, a Union scout from Iowa, registered a 160-acre homestead in Gage County, Nebraska. This claim, west of the town of Beatrice, is recognized as the first homestead and is now the site of Homestead National Monument. Daniel immediately returned to his unit, leaving his wife, Agnes, to fulfill the homestead requirements!

Important

In May of 1879, two years after arriving in Nebraska from Ohio, Ferdinand began the land-acquisition process on a timber-culture claim of 160 acres under the *Timber Culture Acts of 1873, 1874, and 1878.*

The terms of this act give us an idea of what our ancestors went through to get land. Unlike homesteads, timber-culture claims did not require residency on the land. Individuals could file a timber-culture claim even if they had land under the Homestead Act. Many settlers undoubtedly saw this as a way to acquire land to pass on to their children. It meant, though, that they had to work two pieces of property, fulfilling the requirements on both.

Ferdinand, however, did not have a homestead claim, so he built a sod house on the claim (a *soddy* to the locals), in which the family lived. Sod houses were substantial buildings, not small huts. His daughter Dot described it as forty-eight feet by twenty feet. Planting trees made sense, as the nearest source of wood at the time was forty miles away.

Land under a timber claim was worked in five-acre increments. The first year the land had to be broken. This was no small task for land covered by virgin prairie grass, whose tough, interwoven roots were a daunting opponent for plow, mule, and man. In the second year, the five acres had to be cultivated, and in the third year, trees were to be planted. Not just a few trees—13,500 trees on the five acres! Ferdinand planted cottonwood and ash. Each year an additional five acres was brought into the cycle. Thus, by the fourth year, the farmer was breaking five acres of prairie, cultivating five acres, planting 13,500 trees, and nurturing the trees he'd planted the year before—in addition to working on his homestead claim, if he had one.

For the claim to mature at the end of eight years, one-fourth of the trees on ten acres had to survive (the claimant needed to prove 6,750 closely planted, thriving trees), but extensions were given for the common prairie perils of drought and insects. Both locusts and grasshoppers hit the Halsey claim during these years.

For More Info

If your ancestor was working land, you can learn even more about the family's activities by looking at agricultural censuses. (See Kathleen W. Hinckley's *Your Guide to the Federal Census.*) One was taken in Nebraska in 1885, when the Halseys had been on the claim for six years. It shows that during the year they had mowed 40 acres of grass, harvested 110 acres of hay, raised 20 acres of Indian corn and 3 acres of potatoes, and cared for 17 milch cows (all of which dropped calves and from which they churned 900 pounds of butter), 12 other head of cattle, 25 swine, and 14 poultry (which produced 80 dozen eggs). Clearly, it required a family working together to achieve this while also planting 13,500 trees.

Ferdinand managed to fulfill the requirements for the tree claim. On 10 May 1887—eight years and one week after starting the process—he got the final certificate. He received the patent in 1892.

On the day the final claim was filed, Ferdinand purchased another eighty acres east of the timber claim for two thousand dollars.

A few months later, in August of 1887, he entered a homestead on eighty acres in the same section, but six months later the entry was relinquished.

Ferdinand (my black-sheep ancestor) was soon overextended. In 1891 he and his wife, Lorania, mortgaged the timber-claim land; in 1892 they mortgaged the purchased land. Today the land is no longer in the family. Ironically, subsequent farmers have reversed the process by cutting the trees Ferdinand planted and putting the land into crops. Only a few shrubby trees near the former location of the soddy remain.

DISPOSITION

Although we think of public land as going directly to individuals, as you can see in the following chart, less than half went directly to individuals, about a quarter went to governments or corporations (some of which was then sold to individuals), and more than a quarter of the public domain remained government property. This chart is based on government figures as of 1924, but the federal land distributed since that time is minimal in comparison.

	Millions of acres	
Homestead, timber culture, desert land reclamation	256	
Cash and credit sales	220	
Military bounty land	68	
Swamp-land	64	
Individuals		**608**
Railroads, canals, wagon roads	137	
Education	99	
Grants to states and miscellaneous	79	
Special purpose		**315**
Remaining public domain land	186	
National parks, monuments, forest reserves	170	
Mineral and power reserves	48	
Indian reservations	36	
Timber and stone	35	
Government		**474**
Total public land		**1,399**

THE RECORDS

The federal government created and maintained the records of first transfer of public-domain lands. Since this is the government, you shouldn't be surprised to learn that not only did they create a variety of records, they often created them in duplicate and triplicate. Your ancestor may have received a copy of his patent, but the government kept a duplicate. Thus, the Bureau of Land Management (BLM) states on its Web site that it holds the "duplicate original survey plats and field notes" for sixteen states (but does not consider that to be an oxymoron!). Each copy went to a different office, which often made additional notes.

The types of records created included books for survey field notes, surveys, and each type of transfer. They kept records of each transfer organized geographically (tract books). They kept files of depositions, claims, applications, and loose papers (land-entry case files). They kept copies of the patents.

Eventually, 362 land offices were created. They are listed under each state in Appendix A: Locality Reference, with the year each was created. As each land office closed, the books for that office were usually moved to the office that had jurisdiction over the remaining vacant land administered from the old office. Eventually, most of the records from the land offices were turned over to the National Archives and Record Administration (NARA) and the General Land Office (GLO) or Bureau of Land Management (BLM).

The federal government did not maintain any records about transfers of land subsequent to the first transfer out of their hands. Those are found at the local level, usually the county (see Appendix A: Locality Reference).

In addition to the records discussed below, there were other groups of records, such as credit sales. **Refer to "Land Records" in** *Guide to Genealogical Research in the National Archives* **for information on additional record types.**

Printed Source

Field Survey Notes and Survey Plats

If you happen to have an ancestor who was in the public domain *really* early (before he was supposed to be), you may find his residence identified in field survey notes or in survey plats, both of which are in the custody of the appropriate BLM office. Occasionally, the surveys include sketches. Some of them have been microfilmed. (See figure 6-4.)

Figure 6-4 George Bumgardner, Deputy Surveyor, made notes describing the geology, soil, trees, waterways, and structures that he found as he made measurements and set quarter-section posts in Pottawattamie County, Iowa.

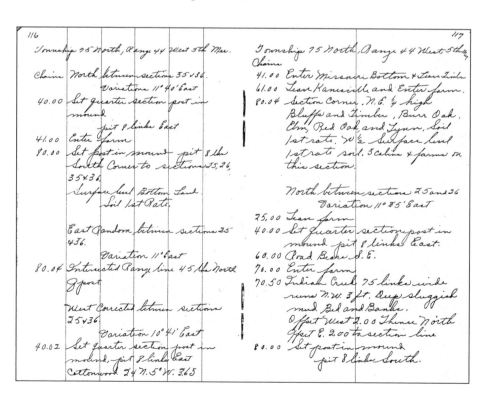

Tract Books

Tract books are the best place to begin your search for a complete land description, which you will need before you can order any additional information. There is more than one copy of the tract books (one for each governmental unit that needed to keep track of what land had been granted and what land had not). These were working documents, so they are not precisely identical.

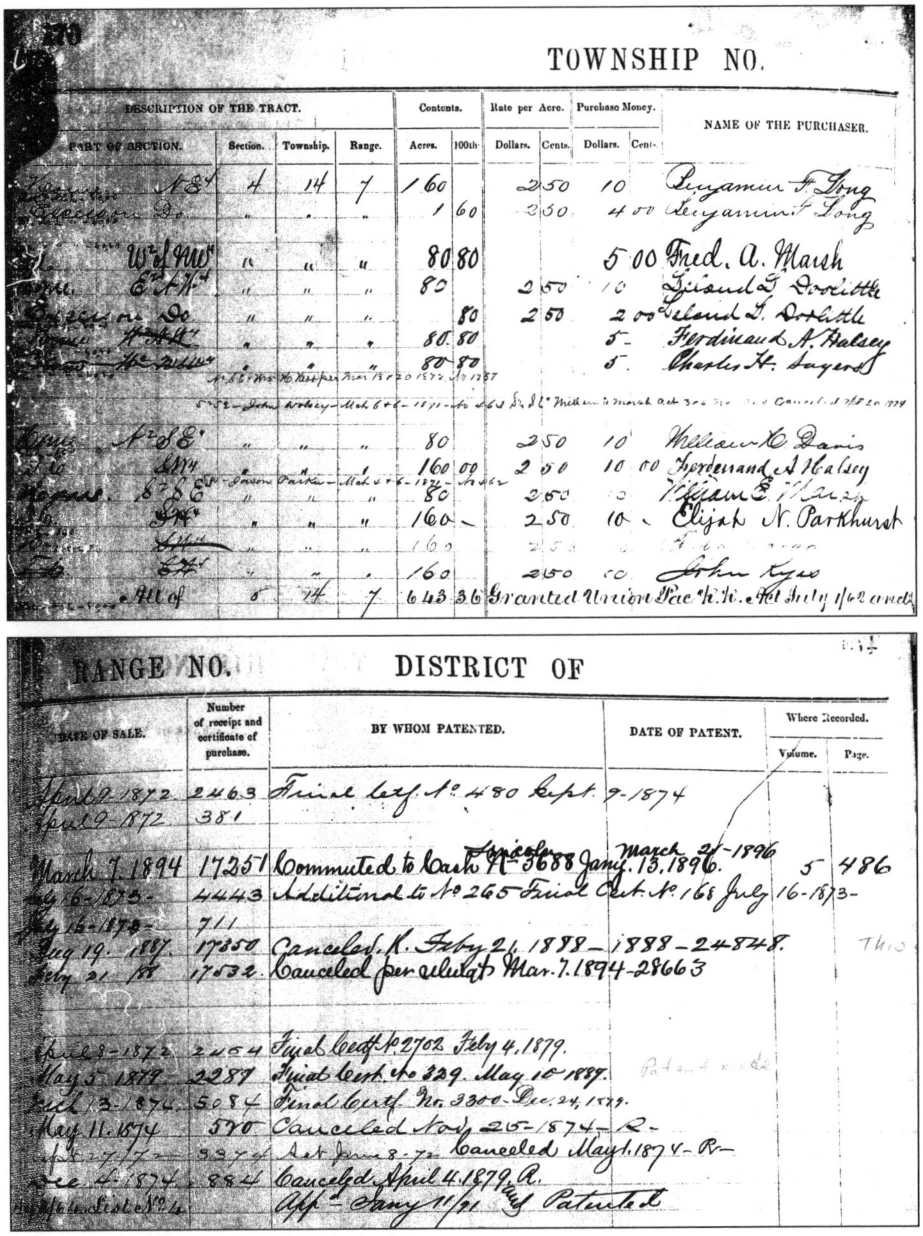

Figure 6-5 The information in the tract books is the key to ordering case files, particularly for land entries that were canceled. They also provide the names of other early settlers.

The central copy of tract books for the Eastern States is in custody of the BLM; for the Western States, they are held by NARA (see chart in "Bureau of Land Management Records and Web Site" on page 95). To determine the location of the tract books for your area of interest, consult several of the sources listed at the end of this chapter and in Appendix A: Locality Reference.

In addition to the copy belonging to the federal government, there is often a copy at the regional NARA branch of or in the state archives. This is usually the copy originally held by the individual land office. Some tract books (3,907 according to my catalog) are available on microfilm loan through the Family History Library. Others have been filmed by the states and may be available through them. (See figure 6-5.)

Land-Entry Case Files

The land-entry case files for homestead applications contain up to thirty million individual items, therefore NARA, which has custody, is not planning to microfilm them. Homestead National Monument of America, located in Beatrice, Nebraska, has received funding to investigate and plan for the acquisition of homestead records. If they are able to proceed with the project, it will be a massive effort and take a very long time, but it is a project from which genealogists will benefit greatly. Watch for announcements in the genealogical press.

Land-entry case files may contain family information and detailed information about settling the land. Expect to find government paperwork. When you request a case file, read every word of every page. You never know where an interesting piece of information might be.

Important

In general, to request land-entry case files, you must know the *full* **legal description of the land to obtain application files.** In addition to township, range, and section, this includes the office from which it was issued (consult E. Wade Hone's *Land & Property Research in the United States* for helpful maps), the act under which it was issued, and the date of issue (see "Land Records" and "Cartographic Records" in *Guide to Genealogical Research in the National Archives*). The tract books are the best place to locate this information.

An entry file was created even when a homestead or other claim did not mature (about half did not). Files for which patents were issued are at NARA. Files for entries that were relinquished were maintained but are in a variety of places. NARA maintains the entry files for the Eastern States. Use NATF 84 to request a land-entry case file. (Use the main inquire form at <www.archives.gov> to order NATF 84.) Files for the Western States are not centralized; the locations for those that have been transferred isn't always clear—be patient. Begin by contacting the appropriate BLM office (see Appendix A: Locality Reference).

Figure 6-6 The relinquishment for the homestead entry for Ferdinand Halsey gives no reasons, but contains his original signature.

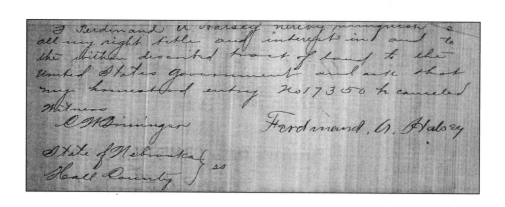

> State of Nebraska \ S.S.
> Merrick County \
>
>   I Ferdinand A. Halsey of Archer
> Merrick County Nebraska being first duly sworn
> depose & say that I am an American born Citizen and
> was born Meigs County Ohio on the 24th day of September
> AD 1842 and that I am the identical Ferdinand A.
> Halsey who made Timber Claim Entry & Proof on the
> SW¼ of Sec. 4 Township 14 Range 7 Merrick County
> Nebraska.   x   Ferdinand, A. Halsey
>
>
> Subscribed & sworn to before me J.R. Mason.
> a Notary Public in & for Merrick County Nebraska
> this 30th day of September 1891

Figure 6-7 The application for a timber-culture entry made by Ferdinand Halsey gives his exact date of birth and his county of birth in Ohio, plus an original signature.

Final Certificates and Patents

If your ancestor managed to fulfill all the requirements for the land, he received a numbered final certificate indicating that he had convinced the appropriate office that he had done so. Based on this, the patent could be issued.

Beginning in 1908, *serial patents* were issued for all public-land states chronologically from the main General Land Office in Washington, DC. These are available on the BLM Web site. Pre-1908 patents for the Eastern States are also on the Web site. Patents for the Western States are held by NARA. (See page 94.)

Bureau of Land Management Records and Web Site

The BLM has custody of most of the records relating to the transfer of property from the federal government to individuals. The Eastern States office has been aggressive about making many of its records electronically available to the public. Because the patents are available online for all but three states, earlier published works listing names are not included here. However, they are worth seeking out, especially for information in the introductions.

The BLM Web site <www.glorecords.blm.gov> lets you search in a variety of ways and access approximately two million federal land patents issued between 1820 and 1908. You can even order a copy of the patent as maintained by the office on either plain or parchment paper. They maintain survey plats and field notes for many states, which are not on the Web site.

The Eastern States office has all public-land patents after 1 July 1908. For Western land patents before 1 July 1908, contact the BLM State Office (see Appendix A: Locality Reference).

Internet Source

Figure 6-8 The BLM Web site provides an index to Eastern States land patents through 1908 and is adding post-1908 serial land patents (all states).

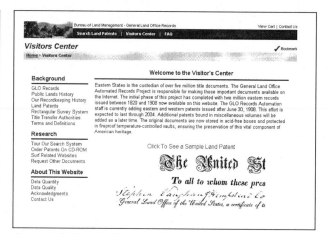

Figure 6-9 Visitor's Center. When you visit the BLM Web site, be sure to explore the valuable information provided in the Visitor's Center and FAQ section (Frequently-Asked Questions).

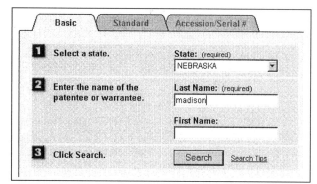

Figure 6-10 Land Patent Search. Enter the state and surname (given name optional) on the easy-to-use search screen. Remember, the Web site does not have pre-1908 records for Western States.

Figure 6-11 Results List. A list of names matching your search criteria is displayed. We are interested in Hans P. Madison, but may want to investigate James C. Madison, who also patented land in Garden County, to see if he is a relative.

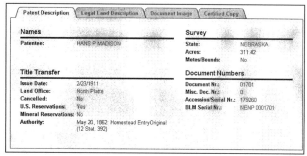

Figure 6-12 Land Patent Details. When you click on the name you want to view, the basic information for the specific patent is displayed.

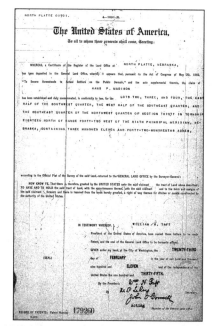

Figure 6-13 You can view, print, and order a reproduction of your ancestor's land patent.

	Eastern State	Western State	Patents on Web site	Survey plats, field notes
Serial patents, all states			post-1908 2,068,953	
Miscellaneous			643,000	
			Pre-1908	
Alabama	✓		260,000	orig BLM-ES
Alaska		✓		dupl BLM-ES
Arizona		✓		dupl BLM-ES
Arkansas	✓		157,000	orig BLM-ES
California		✓		dupl BLM-ES
Colorado		✓		dupl BLM-ES
Florida	✓		56,000	orig BLM-ES
Idaho		✓		dupl BLM-ES
Illinois	✓		247,000	orig NARA
Indiana	✓		188,000	orig NARA
Iowa	✓		145,000	orig NARA
Kansas		✓		orig NARA
Louisiana	✓		82,000	orig BLM-ES
Michigan	✓		167,000	orig BLM-ES
Minnesota	✓		167,000	orig BLM-ES
Mississippi	✓		169,000	orig BLM-ES
Missouri	✓		307,000	orig NARA
Montana		✓		dupl BLM-ES
Nebraska		✓		dupl BLM-ES
Nevada		✓		dupl BLM-ES
New Mexico		✓		dupl BLM-ES
North Dakota		✓		dupl BLM-ES
Ohio	✓		98,000	orig NARA
Oklahoma		✓		orig BLM-ES
Oregon		✓		orig BLM-ES
South Dakota		✓		dupl BLM-ES
Utah		✓		orig BLM-ES
Washington		✓		orig BLM-ES
Wisconsin	✓		188,000	orig BLM-ES
Wyoming		✓		orig BLM-ES

RESOURCES

Bureau of Land Management (BLM)—Eastern States, General Land Office (GLO) Records Automation. <www.glorecords.blm.gov> GLO Records Access Staff, Bureau of Land Management—Eastern States, 7450 Boston Blvd., Springfield, VA 22153-3121.

Carstensen, Vernon, ed. *The Public Lands: Studies in the History of the Public Domain.* Madison: University of Wisconsin Press, 1963. Essays on many aspects of public lands.

Dick, Everett. *The Lure of the Land: A Social History of the Public Lands From the Articles of Confederation to the New Deal.* Lincoln: University of Nebraska Press, 1970.

Gates, Paul W. *History of Public Land Law Development.* Washington, D.C.: U.S. Government Printing Office, 1968.

Hibbard, Benjamin Horace. *A History of the Public Land Policies.* New York: Macmillan and Co., 1924.

Hinckley, Kathleen W. *Your Guide to the Federal Census.* Cincinnati: Betterway Books, 2002.

Hone, E. Wade. *Land and Property Research in the United States.* Salt Lake City: Ancestry Inc., 1997. Extensive charts and maps on public land.

Lainhart, Ann S. *State Census Records.* Baltimore: Genealogical Publishing Co., Inc., 1992. Lists territorial and state censuses, published abstracts, and availability.

National Archives and Records Administration. *Guide to Genealogical Research in the National Archives.* 3d ed. Washington, D.C.: 2000. "Land Records" discusses the extensive records created by the public-land process. "Cartographic Records" describes the maps in the General Land Office, including T1234 *Township Plats of Selected States* (sixty-nine rolls).

Olsen, Pamelia Schwannecke. "Loopholes in the Homestead Acts or How One Man Could Claim Three Separate Homesteads and Own 480 Acres." *Heritage Quest* 24: 9.

Robbins, Roy M. *Our Landed Heritage: The Public Domain, 1776–1936.* Lincoln: University of Nebraska Press, 1962.

Stephenson, George M. *The Political History of the Public Lands From 1840 to 1862; From Preemption to Homestead.* New York: Russell & Russell, 1917, reissued, 1967.

Szucs, Loretto Dennis, and Sandra Hargreaves Luebking. *The Archives.* Salt Lake City: Ancestry Inc., 1988.

Treat, Payson Jackson. *The National Land System, 1785–1820.* New York: Russell & Russell, 1910, reissued, 1967.

HANS MADSEN AND HIS LAND

The case of Hans Madsen illustrates the search for land records of the many European immigrants who flocked to the farmland of the Midwest. By inter-weaving land records with other genealogical records, we gain a much more complete understanding of our ancestors' lives.

Hans Madsen, his wife Caroline Larsen, and their children Hans Peter and Kirstine left Copenhagen, Denmark, on 3 April 1878. Books and movies have popular-ized the immigrant experience as beginning in New York City. But for Hans, as for many other Europeans, especially Scandinavians, it meant heading straight for farm country. He told the emigration official in Copenhagen that he was going to "Council Bluffs, Ia." He may have been following relatives, friends, or neighbors—or like many immigrants, he may have been drawn by the advertis-ing of a railroad company seeking buyers for its land and laborers to build its tracks.

Hans and Lena lived in Council Bluffs while they got oriented and another child was born. They moved to the country on 29 June 1880. I know this because they were enumerated twice on the census. On the 28th, they were living on James Street in Council Bluffs. Hans was a laborer. The following day, they were out in Hazel Dell Township and Hans had achieved a goal—he was now a farmer.

At the time I worked on this family, the deeds for Pottawattamie County were not at the Family History Library. I had to go to the county. I finally found a parking space, got the correct change for the meter, discovered I was at the wrong building, and trudged through the light rain to the deed office. The records were microfilmed but used a type of reader I'd never encountered be-fore. There are several lessons here.

- The Family History Library and appropriate state archives or state library are constantly acquiring new films that you may be able to access from your own community. Check first; don't rely on old information. If I were making this search today, I wouldn't have to get wet.

- Use the Internet to determine what office the records are in and what building the office is in. Check to see if older records are stored in a different location.

- Scope out parking in advance. Many genealogical and governmental organi-zations provide parking information on their Web sites. Just in case, take a variety of change. (Six quarters are useless for a meter that only takes dimes, as I found to my chagrin at another courthouse recently.)

- Take a small umbrella or emergency rain cape with you everywhere.

- Never tell the staff you know how to use a microfilm reader until you're sure you know how to use *this* microfilm reader, but don't take up more of the staff's time than is absolutely necessary.

continued

I found several deeds in the records. Hans didn't have enough money to buy land when they made the move in 1880 and was probably working for another farmer. He acquired land at the end of 1881, but it would be 1884 before there was a record.

Deed on Contract. The Chicago, Rock Island & Pacific Railway Co. to H. Madson. Filed Nov 19th 1884 At 12 oclock M.

Whereas, heretofore, to wit: On the 13th day of December A.D. 1881, the Chicago, Rock Island & Pacific Railway Company made and entered into an agreement with Hans Madson of the county of Pottawattamie & State of Iowa, wherein the said Railway Company, in consideration of the principal sum of four hundred and forty dollars, thereafter to be paid to the said Railway Company, and for other considerations, agree to convey to the said Hans Madson . . . the northeast quarter of the northwest quarter of section 32 in township 77 north range 42 west, containing forty acres . . . and whereas the principal sum as aforesaid has been fully paid . . . the said Chicago, Rock Island & Pacific Railway Company . . . does hereby grant . . . 15 November 1884.

Even if Hans had not migrated in response to a railroad company ad, he did respond to their sale offer, possibly because he liked the land they possessed, possibly because the financing terms were attractive. He would have been the first individual owner of the land, but there is no federal-level record, because this—like much land across the Midwest—was granted to companies who were then expected to build railroads, canals, and so forth. These companies sold the lands to individuals. The railroad kept records of the payments, which may survive, but as private, not public, records.

Notice the legal description—range 42, township 77 (see chapter twelve, Public-Land Survey System). Why such large numbers? Is there an error? Land in Iowa was surveyed from the 5th Principal Meridian. This meridian ran north-south through the easternmost part of Iowa, which is why Hans's land at the western end of the state was in Range 42 West. The baseline for the 5th Principal Meridian lies far to the south, cutting Arkansas in half horizontally, hence the large township number of Township 77 North.

While Hans was paying for the land, he and Lena had another daughter, Marie Karol, but Lena died. On 26 June 1883, Hans married Christine (Fredricksen) Christiansen, a widow with a three-month-old son, Jens Christian, whose husband had died of typhoid fever while she was pregnant. Hans was still paying for the land when their first son, Franklin C., was born.

Forty acres is not a lot of land for farming, but on 26 May 1885, Hans and Christina sold a piece of it.

Warranty Deed. Hans Madson to District Township of Neola, filed 26 Sep. A.D. 1885 at 7½ o'clock AM.

Hans Madson and Christina Madson his wife of Pottawattamie . . . for $65 . . . one acre of land in the northwest corner of the northwest quarter of section 32 township 77 range 42 west of the 5th P.M. 26 May 1885.

The time of filing—"7½ o'clock AM"—reminds us that our ancestors and their governments didn't always use the language as we do—and that they started work earlier each day! Notice also that we are not told *why* the township bought the land. Transfers of title are about property, not people. This deed, unlike the previous one, is on a preprinted form. It's easy to skim forms like this, giving inadequate attention to the information.

Notice that this land description varies somewhat in form from the earlier deed. It mentions the northwest *corner* of the northwest quarter, which makes sense, since it's just one acre. Mentally, you should fix this tiny parcel in the upper left corner of section 32. Although it gives a direction modifier to the range (west), it does not do so to the township, and it abbreviates *Principal Meridian* as "P.M." (the previous deed didn't even mention the meridian). These omissions are common for county-level records. In Pottawattamie County, *everything* is surveyed from the 5th Principal Meridian; *all* townships are north; *all* ranges are west. The omissions were fine for them, but you may have to consult a map or scan other deeds to learn the system so that you will know if two pieces of property (and their resident owners) were right next door or several miles apart (see chapter twelve, Public-Land Survey System).

Even though they had only owned the land free and clear for three years, Hans and Christine sold it in 1887 twice.

Hans Madson and wife to Frank Spencer [Filed 22 August 1887]
Hans Madson and Christine his wife of Pottawattamie [for] $1600 to Frank Spencer . . . the west ½ of the northwest ¼ of section 32 in township 77 range 42 of the 5th P.M. excepting the school house lot of one acre in the north west corner of said above described land. Subject however to one mortgage of $700 executed June 2d 1884 and due June 2d 1889 with interest and which mortgage the said Frank Spencer hereby assumes and agrees to pay . . . 10 August 1887.

From this deed we learn that the one acre sold above was for a schoolhouse. Although section 16 was reserved as school lands, there was no obligation for a school to be placed there (although it was conveniently located in the middle of the section). Usually most or all of the land was sold; sometimes the school was located elsewhere. Surely Hans and Christine with their family of his four, her one, and their one were pleased to have the school so near. We learn that they'd mortgaged half the railroad land for five years for seven hundred dollars, probably using much of the money to purchase the land, but they cleared (at least on paper) nine hundred dollars by the sale. We do not learn to whom the land was mortgaged.

continued

Hans Madson and wife to Jens Madson [Filed 20 August 1887]
     Hans Madson and Christine his wife of Pottawattamie [for] $900 to Jens Madson . . . NE^4 NW^4 32 • 77 • 42 • 40 acres . . . subject to a mortgage of $450 which the grantee herein assumes and agrees to pay . . . 20 August 1887.

Jens Madson does not seem to be a relative. This deed is baffling (as are many deeds related to mortgages). The shorthand for the land description is clear; so clear, in fact, that we know right away that this deed also includes the land sold to Frank Spencer. Presumably the conflict was resolved, but in the meantime, between August 1887 and February 1888, Hans, Christine, and their eight children (two more daughters had been born) moved to the sand hills of western Nebraska.

Why would anyone leave the relatively green farms of Iowa for that arid wasteland? (The township was called "Alkali," if that makes the visual any clearer.) The answer is "Land!" Rumors were circulating that the federal government would pass legislation allowing homesteads of 640 acres in those inhospitable lands. However, the federal government is the federal government; they didn't pass the Kinkaid Act until 1904 (and then questionable transactions by large ranchers claimed almost all of the arable land).

Hans called himself a "Kinkaider," but he wasn't. He was one of many settlers through the entire history of America's westward movement who migrated *in anticipation* of favorable settlement terms. He did something else that was common to the settlement process; he moved with kinfolk. Not *his* family, *Christine's* family. She was one of six sisters who survived childhood, four of whom came to America. Christine's sister Petrea and Petrea's husband lived with them on the homestead in Alkali before settling on their own land.

Claiming public land could be difficult. Depending on the particular act, the applicant had to make payments, break ground, raise crops, plant trees, and/or build a house. Many claims didn't mature to patent when the applicant found the terms impossible to fulfill. Furthermore, only one entry could be made under each act, so there was only one chance to succeed (although the restriction doesn't seem to have been rigidly enforced). The tract books for the area tell us that Hans entered and canceled on several parcels of land in 1900 and 1901.

Even with the auxiliary job of postmaster, Hans was not able to make a go of it in western Nebraska and eventually made plans to return to Iowa. Five more children had been born in the Sand Hills, including my grandmother, Veola. When Hans and Christine left, not all of their children went with them—another typical situation. Hans's eldest daughter had died in 1899 and was buried in Antelope Valley; his eldest son and second daughter had both married and would remain with their spouses, as would Petrea's family, on farms near Oshkosh in what was then Deuel County and is now Garden County.

Hans and his family returned to Council Bluffs and started over again.

> Lars Jensen & wife to Hans Madsen [filed] 22 December 1901. Lars Jensen and wife Mary to Hans Madsen of Pottawattamie for $10,000 the east ½ of the southeast ¼ and the northwest ¼ of the southeast ¼ and the north ½ of the southwest ¼ of section 32 township 77 north range 43 west of the 5th P.M. . . . possession to be give 1 March 1902 . . . Hans Madsen to pay taxes for 1901. 24 December 1901.

By 1910 they had moved again, settling in Merrick County, in central Nebraska, where they would live out the rest of their days.

Notice how much the story of the lives of Hans and Christine and their children is really about land. Moves were motivated by land. Every move was prompted by optimism and hope, although the reality wasn't always there. The daily activities of farming were about making the land profitable; they were a family activity, with sons joining the father as they grew up. Surely, making payments or fulfilling homestead requirements was never far from their minds. Knowing where they lived can help us find other family members—those who came before and those they left behind.

SEVEN

What's in a Deed?

lthough it may not be apparent at first glance, deeds are organized into Predictable Parts:

- Preface
- Parties
- Payment
- Property
- Provenance
- Postlude
- Process

I can hear some of my colleagues fussing at my alliterative descriptions, "but that's not what it's called." The point is, they would have recognized immediately what I was referring to, which emphasizes the predictability of the structure. It won't be long before you, too, will be able to recognize the parts of a deed. Let's look at them in more detail.

PREFACE

In the margin you may find the clerk's index notation about the deed. Don't skip this. It may provide helpful information. Sometimes it is as simple as the names "Smith to Jones" or "Samuel Smith to Jeremiah Jones." Even this information can be helpful if the names are a bit difficult to read in the body of the deed, which is often true on microfilm copies. Smith and Jones may be pretty easy for you to guess at, but I've spent quite a bit of time squinting at the microfilm reader trying to decide if a name is Moore or Moses, Huwit or Hamel.

The clerk's index often tells you what type of instrument it is—deed, mortgage, quitclaim, agreement, or so on. Because it can be awfully confusing trying to decide this from the body of the deed, especially when you are getting started, this can be helpful.

The most common opening for a deed is "This Indenture. . . ." It is frequently written in larger letters. **The term *indenture* derives from the original format of the document.** The agreement was written twice on the same sheet of paper, and then the copies were cut apart with a curvy or jagged line to prevent forgery. Some people think of jack-o-lantern teeth (dentures) to help them remember this term. In theory, an indenture implies that both parties maintained a subsequent interest in the transaction (hence the duplicate copies), but eventually the term came to apply to ordinary deeds, even if they weren't written with the two copies and jagged cut.

At this point, the text may continue "made this . . ." and be followed by a date. This is the one thing about deed structure that isn't predictable. Well, it is predictable—the date is either near the beginning or end of the deed, but the placement seems to be determined by the custom of the scribe.

The date is normally written out in words.

> This Indenture made this ninth day of November one thousand Eight hundred and Eleven . . .

The wording may be more involved.

> This Indenture made this twenty third day of May Anno Domine one Thousand Seven Hundred & Ninety Two & in the Sixteenth Year of America Independence . . .

The latter phrase is a form of stating the date in *regnal years*. On American deeds, the numeric year is also given, so you don't need to convert, but statements such as the following are a strong reminder that in colonial America, we were part of England.

> This Indenture made the first day of the third month called May in the year of our Lord according to the English account One thousand Seven hundred & five, and in the fourth year of the reign of Queen Ann over England . . .

\di'fin\ *vb*

Definitions

HOW TO READ A DEED

We need to digress briefly to discuss exactly how one should read a deed. Our modern tendency is to look for the "important stuff," such as names and dates and amounts, which we recognize as containing capital letters and numbers. That wasn't true of our ancestors' handwriting. You don't have to read many deeds to realize that capitalization seems to be completely random and that the important numbers usually are written out as words (which is good, because it can often be difficult to interpret a single digit accurately).

So how do you read a deed? You *read* it. You read *every word* of it. Once you understand all the parts and what each part might contain, you will be able to skim certain parts more quickly, but you will never skip them. A simple little phrase—or lack of one—buried in a section of typical boilerplate language could be important to understanding the deed and even to proving a family relationship.

Reminder

PARTIES

The parties to a deed are, in general terminology, referred to as the *grantor* **and the** *grantee.* However, you will never see these terms in deeds. Instead, the parties are referred to as the *party of the first part* and the *party of the second part.* There may even be a *party of the third part* for instruments such as mortgages, bonds, and agreements. This is why I think my alliterative description is more accurate than the "correct" terminology of *grantor* and *grantee.*

This section can be incredibly valuable genealogically. It was not at all uncommon for there to be several men of the same name in the area. Hence, various identifiers (which I call *markers*) often were added to the names of the parties to make clear which John Jones was meant. Additionally, this section contains statements of relationships. Watch especially for the following markers:

- place of residence
- occupation
- seniority
- name of wife
- positions such as executor, administrator, guardian, trustee
- names of deceased persons
- statement of heirship or relationship

In some areas and times, the clerks favored using occupation as the identifier. In other areas or times, the clerks separated men by stating the township in which they lived.

The most interesting marker I have seen was used for German families in southeastern Pennsylvania in the nineteenth century. The limited naming pool, created by the practice of naming children for the sponsor of the same sex, meant that by the third generation there could be numerous men of the same name and similar ages, all farmers. The clerks came up with an interesting

SENIORITY IDENTIFIERS

If you are just beginning to research in older records, you may not realize that terminology such as *junior, senior, III, the elder, the younger,* and so on did not imply a familial relationship. Furthermore, they were usually (but not always) fluid, with the designation changing as the number of men of the same name varied in the community.

The terms generally implied chronological age. Thus, if there were two men named John Jones, aged sixty-five and thirty-five, they were designated, respectively, as John Jones senior and John Jones junior. If John Jones "senior" died, leaving just one John Jones, the identifiers became unnecessary. If, instead, a third John Jones, aged fifty-five, moved into town, then John Jones junior would have been demoted to John Jones III, and the new guy in town would become John Jones junior.

marker. I couldn't understand why I was seeing German men with middle initials in deeds. The practice of the first name given to a son usually being an honorary christening name and the second name (what we would think of as the middle name) being the "real" name, meant that they couldn't have middle initials.

In other words, the child christened as "Johan Georg Boyer" was known as George Boyer as an adult, so how could he be George M. Boyer in a deed? It was baffling. I eventually determined that the clerks were adding the first letter of the maiden name of the mother as a "middle initial." Thus, George M. Boyer was the Johan Georg Boyer christened as the son of Henry Boyer and Susanna Miller, whereas George H. Boyer was the Johan Georg Boyer christened as the son of John Boyer and Margret Hoff. Imagine establishing parentage based on a middle initial in a deed!

WOMEN

Wives are not usually named as *grantees,* since property was owned by the husband; however, they sometimes are named. If you find such a deed, examine other deeds in that deed book. It may simply be a local custom. If not, there may be some significance, such as the property belongs to her family. It still wasn't necessary to name her, but if the couple was buying out the interest of other heirs, the scribe may have preferred to include her name.

On the other hand, the wife should have been named as a *grantor* in any area in which dower rights were recognized, but she often was neglected until later in the recorded documents (see "Postlude" on page 108, "Signatures" on page 110, and "Dower Release" on page 114).

In the earliest records, women acting alone were rarely found in deeds. However, as time went on, they appear more and more often. Usually it was because they had sole possession of the land due to inheritance, death of a husband, or desertion, but eventually women became more active as land purchasers.

Avoid reading too much into the terms *single woman* or *spinster* in a deed. They seem to have been used to mean "doesn't have a husband to do this for her." Her real status may have been widowed, divorced, or abandoned.

You must study many examples in an area before coming to such a conclusion. John T. Humphrey has observed that for the Welsh in Pennsylvania and Germans in New York, you are more apt to find the "middle initial" representing the patronymic—the first letter of the father's given name.

Let's look at some examples of the parties named in deeds.

Important

[Merrick County, Nebraska, 1929, preprinted form] . . . Lorna M. Sprague, a single person of the County of Merrick and State of Nebraska, . . . unto Frank Gregg and Eva M. Gregg, husband and wife of the County of Merrick and State of Nebraska . . .

[Christian County, Kentucky, 1811.] . . . Between Thomas Alman and

Mary his wife of the County of Knox in the Indiana Territory of the one part and Elisha Riston of the County of Christian & State of Kentucky of the other part . . .

[Chester County, South Carolina, 1796] . . . between Ralph McFadden of Chester County District of Pinckney & State of So Carolina of the one part & John Barr of the County District & State aforesaid of the other part . . .

[York County, Pennsylvania, 1835] . . . Henry B. Hoff and Michael B. Hoff, executors of the will of Michael Hoff of Heidelburg dec'd to George Gitt of Hanover . . .

[Sussex County, Delaware, 1705] . . . Between William Fisher of the County of Sussex upon Delaware Bay Cordwayner of the one part and Yeates Conwill of Lewes in the afsd county of Sussex planter and Rebecca his wife daughter of sd William Fisher of the other part, . . .

[Essex County, Massachusetts, 1678] . . . I Richard Huchenson of salem in the county of Essex in New England . . . my daughter Mary, wife of Thomas Hale Junr of Newbery in the aforesd county. I the above said Richard Huchenson . . . unto my son in law Thomas Hale . . .

PAYMENT

Definitions

The term generally used for payment is *consideration*. It is another unfamiliar term if you're just beginning, but unlike *grantor* and *grantee,* you will encounter this one in deeds, usually in the phrase "in consideration of the sum . . . " or "and for other valuable considerations." A sum of money isn't always specified. If it is not, do not automatically assume that this is a deed of gift or that there is a special connection between the grantor and the grantee. Some people just wanted to keep their financial business to themselves (and from the tax assessor). We gave several examples of *deeds of gift* and *maintenance agreements* in "Find Statements of Relationships" in Why Use Land Records? on page 12, which you may want to review.

The payment usually is found immediately after the names of the parties. Sometimes the payment information is found between the names of the two parties.

There was no uniform system of currency until the U.S. Treasury was established after the Revolutionary War. Prior to that time, each colony issued its own currency (and sometimes changed its currency), and English money was accepted in most colonies. Notice the different ways in which the money is described in these three deeds from Worcester County, Massachusetts, in the mid-eighteenth century. At this time, Massachusetts was having a great deal of trouble with its currency system and had both "old tenor" money and "new tenor" money.

Nathaniel Farnsworth of Harvard husbandman for £69 good passable bills of credit ["of the old Tenor" in margin] to Andrew Harper of Harvard yeoman

William Harper of Harvard husbandman for 33 pounds to John Parke of Harvard husbandman

Andrew Harper of Harvard husbandman for £40 old tenor to Wm
Harper of Harvard labourer
William Harper of Harvard labourer for £6 lawfull money to Benajah
Davenport of Harvard husbandman

The deed may contain wording indicating that the consideration has already
been received. There may be a separate acknowledgment of receipt following
the signatures (see "Receipts" on page 112).

> [Goochland County, Virginia, 1764.] . . . I Edward Houtchen of Goochland
> County for Divers good causes, but more Especially for the Love and good
> will, favour and Affection, which I have and do bear towards my loving
> Son Francis Houtchen & also for and in consideration of five Shillings cur-
> rant Money of Virginia, *in hand paid to me before the Sealing and delivery
> hereof,* . . .

PROPERTY

The next section is a description of the property. This should include the acreage
and the political jurisdiction (at least the county, and possibly the township). In
public-land states it is given by the rectangular survey coordinates (see chapter
twelve, Public-Land Survey System). In subdivisions it is given by lot and block
number. In state-land states, it has several elements, including waterways, adjoining landowners, and a metes-and-bounds description (see chapter eleven,
Metes-and-Bounds Land Platting). In New England, you may find lot numbers;
in northern New England, you may even find the terminology of *township* and
range.

**Deeds often convey more than one parcel of land. This is easy to miss if you don't
carefully examine the property description.**

Metes-and-bounds land descriptions are easy to find. They begin with the
word "Beginning," usually written extra large. They often seem to go on forever. Don't skip over them, however; they can be very important.

Usually the land description was copied verbatim from the deed by which
the seller had purchased the land. Sometimes the names of adjoining landowners
were not updated, hence giving names of persons who were long dead. In other
instances, the description may contain information that is especially helpful if
you are descended from the neighbor, as in "adjoining land of Thomas Terry's
heirs" or "by the line of William Wilson, formerly Stephen Smith."

Sometimes the general land description with acreage precedes the metes-
and-bounds description, which is easy to locate. Other times it follows the
description, so you may have to wade through lots of text. Make sure you don't
get bogged down and forget to record it.

The detailed property description, whether in rectangular coordinates or in
metes and bounds, can be the most tedious to record. It is the place where errors
are most likely to occur. You can find suggestions for recording the information
you find in chapter eight, How to Record What You Find.

Research Tip

PROVENANCE

In state-land states, particularly in earlier time periods, you will often—but, alas, not always—find a detailed description of how the grantor acquired the property. It may continue with a description of how the preceding landowner acquired the property, continuing all the way back to the patent or grant to the first individual landowner. This is called the *chain of title*, and it can provide valuable information for your genealogical research, especially when inherited land is involved.

In public-land states, because the land was described explicitly and unambiguously by the rectangular survey description, it was often unimportant to provide this kind of information. A title search could be done easily in the deed books or tract books. Therefore, we rarely see chain-of-title information outside of state-land states.

POSTLUDE

Following the long and tedious description of the land is an equally long and tedious section of legalese. I think my choice to call this section the postlude was prompted in part by the "ta-dum ta-dum ta-dum" rhythm of the phrases. Don't let this put your mind into sleep mode. Important special circumstances may be described in this section. Many legal terms unfamiliar to the layperson are used. Appendix C: Glossary provides both a definition and a discussion of the meaning of such terms as *fee simple, hereditaments, improvements, assigns, feoffment, tenement, manor,* and *messuage,* so we won't go into them here.

The restrictions that make what seems to be an ordinary deed into a mortgage, bond, or agreement are found in the postlude. Since these are not absolute transfers of land, the conditions for fulfilling or terminating the agreement are stated. For example, the postlude is where you would find the description of the care required for elderly parents if the child is to receive the land. Payment terms for mortgages will be found here, also. A variety of restrictions on sale and use of the land may be found here. Watch especially for family-related information such as preservation of a cemetery or provisions for an elderly couple or the widow.

> [Goochland County, Virginia, 1764.] . . . only that I desire by these presents that my Loving Wife Hannah Houtchen, shall and may have Quite and peaceable Possession During her natural Life on the aforesaid Plantation and tract of Land with out any interuption . . .

The postlude is where the date of the instrument is found, if it wasn't at the beginning. You almost always find one or more repetitions of the names of the grantor(s) and grantee(s). Examine them carefully. They may be slightly different from what was given at the beginning. The spelling may be different. Sometimes the name is completely different, perhaps "Simon Smith" instead of "Solomon Smith" (you will have to determine which name is scribal error). Very often, this seems to be the point at which the scribe suddenly realized that there was a wife involved and added her name.

PROCESS

You'll understand this area of a recorded deed better if we first discuss the process of transferring land and making it a matter of record. There are several steps, which in a straightforward transaction would look like this:

1. The seller agrees to sell land to the buyer.
2. The buyer pays the seller.
3. They engage someone to write the deed.
4. The seller takes the deed to the courthouse, where he swears that he sold the land to the buyer.
5. If dower release is required, the seller's wife must swear that she agreed to sell the land.
6. The clerk records the deed.
7. The deed is given to the buyer.

As a result, the final sections of a deed are descriptive of this process. These many small sections may include the following elements:

- witnesses
- signatures
- acknowledgment of receipt of payment
- acknowledgment or proving of deed
- dower release
- recording information
- delivery information
- release (for mortgage or other agreements)

Witnesses

The purpose of the witnesses on a deed was so that if the seller of the land could not go into court to acknowledge that he sold the land, then the witnesses could say that they saw him sign the deed (see "Acknowledged or Proved" on page 112). The most common reasons that the witnesses were needed were that the seller had died; was old, infirm, or ill; or had moved away—although in some localities it seems to be routine that witnesses proved the deed.

Not all deeds have witnesses. Look at step number three above. It says that *somebody* wrote out the deed. It was almost never the buyer or the seller. It was not necessarily a lawyer. Often the county clerk (or someone close to him) had a business writing out the deeds right at the courthouse (or at the house of the clerk). In this case, it would be pointless to get witnesses, since the seller could acknowledge the deed then and there in front of the clerk. I've seen a number of deed books in which almost no deed has witnesses.

Often the scribe was a local justice of the peace who had learned to write deeds (probably based mostly on copying from existing deeds). The scribe usually had in hand the deed by which the buyer purchased the land, so he simply copied most of it. In this case, you may see the name of the scribe or justice of the peace as a witness, usually the first witness.

There has been a nasty, erroneous bit of "helpful" information circulating in genealogical newsletters for years stating that the first witness is related to the seller

Warning

and the second witness is related to the buyer, or some variation thereof. It is definitely erroneous. Furthermore, it is nasty because it can easily mislead the unwary into incorrect assumptions. In the previous discussion, we've already seen that a deed can have no witnesses or that one of the names may well be that of the scribe. Common sense tells us that the requirement for a witness is pretty simple—he or she had to be in the room when the seller signed the deed. That person *could* be a relative of the seller or the buyer—or of the scribe! (Can't you picture the local justice of the peace hollering at his wife, "Honey, can you come here for a minute and witness this deed?")

You may be able to determine that the witnesses are not connected personally to the buyer or seller. I find it helpful to look at the process information on this and adjacent deeds in the deed book. If you find one of the witnesses of your deed as a witness in other deeds, or named as a justice of the peace or clerk in an acknowledgment or dower release, then he is probably not related to the parties.

The fact that someone is a witness can tell you several important things. The person was alive on that date. Thus, it is useful to read deeds for your ancestors' siblings. You may be able to state that your ancestor died after the date on which he witnessed a deed for his brother. Published abstracts are invaluable in helping you locate this type of information.

While women rarely bought or sold land, they did witness deeds. Sometimes the witnesses were husband and wife. It won't say so, but if John Jones and Libby Jones witness a deed together, the deed was probably signed in a private home (if it were done at a public place, one of the men there would probably have witnessed), so Libby is almost surely connected to John in some way.

You may find the teenagers in a household as witnesses. Under English common law, boys could be witnesses at fourteen, girls at twelve.

Note the language above the signatures. If any of the witnesses "affirmed," they were probably Quaker, since Quakers don't swear oaths.

In some areas, the witnesses may have been customary to assure that the seller had signed the deed as his own free will. Some jurisdictions had requirements on how many witnesses were required or on how many were required to prove a deed (see "Acknowledged or Proved" on page 112).

Signatures

It's amazing how often the signatures contain names that are not in the deed, usually those of spouses. When this is the case, be certain to note who was named in the deed and who merely signed.

Soon after beginning their research, genealogists learn that the signatures on documents in deed books were not written by their ancestors. They also are told that if their ancestor signed with a mark, then they should note "signed with a mark." This conventional wisdom implies that signatures and marks are therefore not very useful as evidence. I believe, however, that in some cases they can be very powerful pieces of evidence.

Our general impression when we begin research is usually that if our ancestor couldn't sign his name then he made a simple x. However, many people who couldn't write made a more distinctive mark. It may have been a circle, a squiggle, or a combination of lines. Often it was one or more initial letters of the

Notes

signer's name. Many clerks (perhaps even most clerks) "copied" the mark into the deed book. With Thomas Almond of Louisa County, Virginia, we see typical variety. His usual mark appears to be an "A" with significant crosspieces, although he signed two documents with a "TA" mark. In a few instances, the clerk simply noted the mark as an "**x**" or "+."

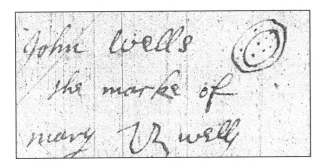

Figure 7-1 The marks of John and Mary Wells in this deed show interesting variety.

One of the delights of doing research in the earliest records in a colony is stumbling across the marks—actually more like pictographs—of Indians as they sold land to the early settlers.

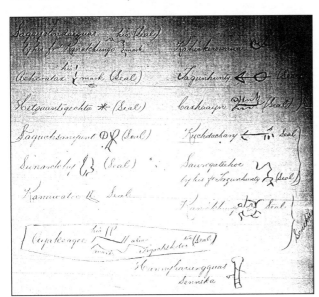

Figure 7-2 These marks, made in the 1740s by Indians selling their land in Pennsylvania, are delightful finds in early deed books.

When it comes to signatures, clerks seemed to have attempted to "copy" a signature only when it was distinctive or unusual, as seen with the signature of Robert Dougherty.

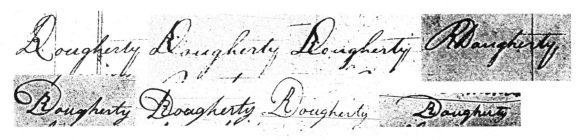

Figure 7-3 The clerk copied the distinctive signature of Robert Dougherty in the Barren County, Kentucky, deed books.

This custom has special benefit when it comes to early German ancestry. Because the handwriting was gothic rather than cursive, the clerk was unable to determine what the letters in the signature really were, so he usually "copied" it.

Always transcribe the signature exactly as rendered in the deed book. It may help you realize that the man who signed his name as "Wm. A. Smith" was a different man from the one who signed his name "William Smith," who is your ancestor.

Receipts

In many deed books, you will find an acknowledgment of receipt of payment. It may have been incorporated into the body of the deed, instead, and therefore covered by the signature to the deed, or there may not be an explicit acknowledgment.

> [South Carolina Chester District, 1792.] Received of John Barr twenty one Guineas I say received by me.
>
> his
> William X McCammon
> mark

There may be an additional statement of land transfer.

> [Goochland County, Virginia, 1747.] Receive'd on the Day of the Date of the within written Indenture of the within named Josias Payne Twenty five Pounds Currant Money it being the Consideration Money within mentioned Recd by me.
>
> his
> Edward E Houchins
> mark

> [Goochland County, Virginia, 1747.] Memorandum. That on the Day of the Date of the within written Indenture full and peacable Possession and Seizin of the within mention'd Premises with the Appurtenances was had and taken by me the within named Edward Houchin and by me given and Delivered unto the within Named Josias Payne As Witness my hand.
>
> his
> Edward E Houchins
> mark

Pay careful attention to the date of the receipt (if there is one). It tells you where your ancestor was on that date, which may not be the same as the date of the deed or the date of the acknowledgment of the deed.

Acknowledged or Proved

The general practice in most localities was that the seller of the deed appeared before an official—usually the clerk, but sometimes a justice of the peace—and stated that he had executed the deed.

ALIAS KILLIAN KREEK

The facsimile signatures for Killian Kreek, recorded in deed books in three different counties by three different clerks, allow us to determine that it was the same man in Pittsylvania County, Virginia; Barren County, Kentucky; Warren County, Kentucky; and Gibson County, Indiana. The "signatures" are noteworthy for several reasons.

- They bear no resemblance to the clerk's writing and are different from the way in which each clerk wrote Killian's name within the document.

- The signatures are similar, although not identical, as if the clerks had attempted to duplicate them.

- The gothic letterforms make it obvious that Killian was of German origin.

- The letters are "off" just enough from the real gothic forms to indicate that they aren't actual signatures.

- Taken in aggregate, they indicate he signed his name "Killian Kriek."

In April 1783, Killian Kreek sold it in two parcels in Pittsylvania County, Virginia. William Tunstall, the clerk of Pittsylvania, recorded Killian's "signature" three times for each of the deeds.

Killian mortgaged a third piece of land; the mortgage was recorded by Tunstall in July 1784.

William Logan was the clerk of Barren County, Kentucky, in 1799 when Killian sold a small parcel of land. Both Killian and his wife Margarett signed the deed, and the "signatures" of both are recorded. They are strikingly similar, both in gothic script. Either Margarett was of German origin also—or Killian signed her name for her.

Killian lived near the border of Barren and Warren Counties in Kentucky and owned land in both counties. It is in Warren County that we find the most interesting document of all. In 1817, "Killian Creek of the State of Endani State [sic] and County of Gibson" sold his last piece of land in Kentucky. Jonathan Hobson, clerk of Warren County, like William Tunstall and William Logan before him, carefully attempted to replicate Killian's signature.

The deed was proved by the witnesses six day after it was made. The wording is interesting, in that Hobson openly acknowledges the problem with the gothic signature of "Killion Creek," identifying it as an alias, once again attempting (not very successfully) to trace the curves.

[Pittsylvania County, Virginia, 1779.] At a Court held for Pittsylvania County the 25th day of February 1779. The within indenture together with the Memorandum of Livery and Seizen and Receipt hereon indorsed was acknowledged by the within named Hugh Reynalds to be his lawfull acts and deed and ordered to be recorded by the court.

Hugh Reynolds

[Barren County, Fourt [sic] October County Court 1799.] This Indenture was acknowledged by the within named Killian Kreek a party thereto to be his act and Deed & was ordered to be Recorded.

Attest W. Logan Cl.

When the seller did not (or could not) appear before an official to acknowledge a deed, the witnesses had to appear to say that they had seen him sign the deed. Therefore, when a deed is proved by the witnesses rather than acknowledged by the seller, you should seriously consider the possibility that the seller is dead, very ill, or has moved.

[Warren County, Kentucky, 1817, from "Killian Creek of the State of Endani State [sic] and County of Gibson."] I as Clerk of the County Court for said county do certify that this Indenture between Killion Creek (alias Killian Kreek) and Harden Camp was this day proven before me in my office by the oath of Aquilas Greer & Thomas Bridges to be the act and deed of the said Killion (they being subscribing witnesses thereto) & that I have recorded said indenture with this certificate as required by law. Witness my hand this 26th day of May 1817.

Jona[than] Hobson

[Chester County, Pinckney District, deed dated 1796.] Issac McFadden appeared & made oath that he seen Ralph McFadden Esqr Sign, Seal & deliver the within Deed unto John Barr Junr for the purposes therin contained & that he saw William Lyles Sign it as a Witness with himself. Sworn to before me this 31 December 1807.

Note that, as always in genealogy, there are exceptions. Some clerks may have used the word "acknowledge" rather than "prove" for witnesses. In some localities (notably South Carolina and parts of North Carolina without a strong Virginia influence), the custom was that deeds were proved rather than acknowledged, even when the seller was right there.

[Chester County, South Carolina, 1787 mortgage against personal property.] At a Court Continued and held by Adjournment for Chester County the third Day of October one Thousand seven hundred & eighty Seven, The Within Bill of Sale from Mary Hambleton to John McGlamory was proved in open Court by the Oaths of Daniel Cooke & Thos White Witnesses thereto & ordered to be Recorded.

Dower Release

When a man sold property (but not when he bought it), in many places his wife had to give a dower release of her lifetime interest in the property. This interest, also called *widow's thirds*, was supposed to maintain her and her children in event of her husband's death. If there's no wife's name in a time and place when dower was observed (look at other deeds in the book), this is a clue that she may have died.

The practice is not archaic. Nor is human nature. When my husband and I met with the attorney and the couple from whom we bought our house, the lawyer said, "I'm supposed to ask the husband to leave the room and ask the wife if she does this of her own free will, but I've never thought if he intimidated her that a door would make a bit of difference."

The term "dower" rarely appears in the release. Sometimes the dower release is recorded within the acknowledgment, so read carefully.

> [Louisa County, Virginia, 1774.] At a Court held for Louisa County on Monday the 10th Day of October 1774. This deed was this Day in open Court acknowledged by Thomas Almand and Anne his wife to be their act and Deed (*the said Anne being first privily Examined as the Law Directs*) and ordered to be Recorded.
>
> Teste [*no name*]

> [Greene County, Pennsylvania, 1842.] The 29th day of october AD one thousand eight hundred And forty two Personally appeared before me the subscriber one of the justices of the peace in and for the County aforesaid the within named Margaret Kerr John Wiley and Sarah his wife Samuel Murdock & Emily his wife Ann Eliza Kerr & Benjamin Groomes & Isabella his wife and acknowledged the forgoing indenture to be their and each of there [*sic*] acts and deeds and desired the Same as such might be recorded according to law *they the said Sarah Emily & Isabella being of lawful age separately and apart from their Said Husbands by me examined and the full Contents of the said Indenture unto them made known whereupon they did declare that they did voluntarily and of their own free will and accord seal and As there act and deed deliver the same without any coercion or Compulsion of their said Husbands whatever.*
> witness my hand and Seal the day and year above written.
>
> George Haver J.P.

Recording Information

The final element of the process section indicates when the deed was recorded. As we have discussed, this was not necessarily when the deed was made. The buyer may have had no funds remaining with which to pay for the recording. He really wouldn't feel a need to have the deed recorded until he sold the land.

If land stayed in the family, the recording may actually be several generations—and many decades—later.

Releases

Mortgages and other types of agreements are found in deed books. If the person borrowing the money repaid it, then the person making the loan often came into the courthouse to acknowledge that fact. This way the property would be free of encumbrance and could be sold.

This release might be found in one of several places:

- in a section following the deed
- in the margin
- elsewhere in the deed book
- in a block of space next to the deed, left for the release

Often the release was never recorded, so don't assume that your ancestor lost the land if you do not find a release.

One of the most interesting things about releases is that often they were actually signed, even written entirely by the mortgage holder. In other words, he—or she—came into the courthouse and physically wrote in the deed book. So it is possible that you will find an original signature in a deed book.

Thus, on two occasions, in 1869 and 1873, we find that Tamar (Weston) Law, "the undersigned Admx & Legatee of George Law decd hereby acknowledge full satisfaction of this mortgage and cancel the same." The notation was made in the margin of the Monroe County, Illinois, deed book, next to the mortgage—and both times it was signed by Tamar.

The genealogist must always be cautious in evaluating whether such a signature is original or a facsimile. Two important factors to consider are a letter-by-letter comparison with the clerk's handwriting and the weight of the ink.

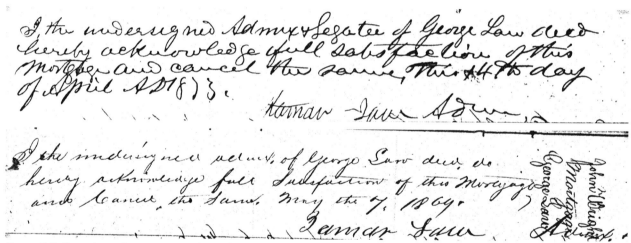

Figure 7-9 Sometimes the mortgage releases found in the margins of deed books contain original signatures.

EIGHT

How to Record What You Find

O nce you've found an ancestral deed, you want to be certain that you obtain all of the information in it. There are a variety of ways you can do this. However, when you are just beginning with land records, I strongly advise you to follow the procedures below. It would be a real shame if you spent another five years looking for information on your ancestors that was in the first deed you found, but you missed it because you didn't record the information properly.

STEP 1. Make a photocopy. Remember to copy the process information at the end of the document (see chapter seven, What's in a Deed?).

STEP 2. Make an extra photocopy of your ancestor's deed—and also make

Step By Step

WHAT IS BOILERPLATE LANGUAGE?

Boilerplate language is any wording that occurs typically in most deeds in your time and place. It is the legal and process language that helps assure that the transfer is final and cannot be challenged successfully in court. A genealogist/ attorney friend of mine assured me that every single word is there not because the scribe charged by the word (as I have heard from genealogical lecturers), but because some deed that didn't have that wording permitted a lawsuit.

How do you determine what is boilerplate language? By reading other deeds in the same book—the more the better. If you can recite the next phrase without looking at the page, it's probably boilerplate.

All too often, researchers focus only on the deeds concerning their own ancestor and do not read any others. This can be a big pitfall. I have observed that such researchers often try to read meanings into phrases that simply aren't there. Because they don't realize that a particular phrase occurs in almost every other deed, they think it means something special about their ancestors.

photocopies of the deed that precedes and the deed that follows your ancestor's deed.

STEP 3. Sit at a quiet table with good lighting. Keep this book at hand so you can refer to chapter seven, What's in a Deed?, and Appendix C: Glossary.

STEP 4. Read the two deeds that you copied that did not belong to your ancestor. This will start to give you a feel for boilerplate language.

STEP 5. Read your ancestor's deed. Using one of the photocopies (this is why you made several), cross out the boilerplate wording with a colored pen. Refer to the other two deeds you copied and Appendix C: Glossary in this book for help.

Figure 8-1 Make a photocopy of the deed and draw a line through all pieces of boilerplate text.

This indenture made the first day of the third month called May in the year of our Lord according to the English account One thousand seven hundred & five, and in the fourth year of the reign of Queen Ann over England. Between William Fisher of the County of Sussex upon Delaware Bay Cordwayner of the one part and Yeates Conwill of Lewes in the afsd county of Sussex planter and Rebecca his wife daughter of sd William Fisher of the other part, Witnesseth for & in consideration of the great love & affection that the sd William Fisher hath for his sd son in law Yeates Conwill & Rebecca his the sd William only daughter, do give

STEP 6. You may feel like you are done now, having isolated the "good stuff," but I recommend that you record that information in text form on your computer. Believe me, you do not want to have to reread the original deed every time you need information, especially as your research expands and your collection of deed photocopies grows.

Almost all experienced researchers find using preprinted abstract forms or computer templates to be inadvisable, even dangerous. As you have been reading this book, you probably noticed how often I used the phrases "in some places," "at some times," "often," "sometimes," "usually," and so on. Each deed has its own little differences. It is unwise to try to fit square, triangular, or hexagonal pegs into round holes.

Fortunately, there is an easy format, which I call an *extract*, that allows you to capture all the information efficiently.

EXTRACTING A DEED

I like to give each of my extracts a title. The exact wording may vary, but usually it identifies grantor, grantee, year, and place. It often states the number of acres and location of the land.

Begin your extract with a full citation of where you found the deed. If you don't do this at the very beginning, you will forget. (I have lots of experience in the forgetting department.)

Sample of Extract

Use ellipses points where you are omitting text, quotes to emphasize a literal transcription, [*sic*] where necessary, and square brackets for editorial comments.

William Fisher to Yeates Conwell deed of gift, 3 May 1705, 100 acres between Broad Creek & Prime Hooke, Sussex County, Delaware

Sussex County Deeds F6:149. [FHL #6,626.]

This indenture . . . "first day of the third month called May" [indicates he is a Quaker] . . . 1705 . . . Between William Fisher of the County of Sussex upon Delaware Bay Cordwayner [*sic*] of the one part and Yeates Conwill of Lewes in the af[ore]s[ai]d county of Sussex planter and Rebecca his wife daughter of s[ai]d William Fisher of the other part, . . . for . . . the great love & affection that the s[ai]d William Fisher hath for his s[ai]d son in law Yeates Conwill & Rebecca his the s[ai]d William['s] only daughter, do give . . .

HINTS FOR READING OLD HANDWRITING

Transcribe your ancestor's deed word for word. There is absolutely no better way for you to become comfortable with old handwriting and boilerplate language than to have to read all the letters in the little, unimportant words. Very often these are words that you know. When you are comfortable with the letterforms in familiar words, you will be much less likely to make errors in reading a letter in an important word—such as a proper name. Many a genealogist has been tripped up reading an old, upside-down (backward) *e* as an *o* in a surname, simply because he or she thought it wasn't important to bother to read—and become familiar with—little words like *the, and, to,* and *his.*

Because I transcribed a lot of deeds when I got my first personal computer, I learned a lot more about land records, terminology, and handwriting than I would have otherwise. I didn't always get it right. Many of the examples in this book were copied from those early abstracts I made—and I've had to correct some errors that occurred because I hadn't yet learned much of the terminology and become comfortable with old handwriting.

If you're having trouble with a particular script, try slowly *copying* or *tracing* the words, mimicking the clerk's handwriting. You'll soon get the rhythm of his writing and become comfortable with his letterforms so that you can read them easily.

You can use the typed copy to continue with step 5 on page 118.

TRANSCRIPTION CONVENTIONS

Several conventions that we use in recording deeds tell us efficiently and accurately how much of what we have recorded is in the deed—and how much of the deed we have recorded.

Quotation Marks

Anything found within quotation marks is taken literally from the deed. There is a lot of discussion about just how literal is literal when it comes to capitalization, punctuation, superscripts, and certain special characters such as the long *s* (often seen in a double *ss*), *ff* (for *F*), the thorn (looks like a *y* but is interpreted as *th*), and the "per" (a distinctive *p* that means "per," "par," "pre," and so on).

Most beginners find it safest to transcribe letters the way they look, simply because they haven't had enough experience in reading old handwriting to be confident they are making the correct "translation." They can always interpret from the "looks like" to the "really," but if they transcribe erroneously, they have no clues to let them know that they may have made an error.

Square Brackets

The editorial "I said this" square brackets are the most useful thing in recording deeds. Any time something is in square brackets, whether within quotation marks or not, it means that you, personally, are speaking and that the text is not in the document. Square brackets are powerful simply because they are so flexible.

- Use them when you want to add helpful information, such as "adjoining Thomas Smith's land [he was married to John's sister Martha]."

- Use them to comment on the physical characteristics of the document, such as "[ink blot obscures first two letters]."

- Use them when you fill in letters that aren't included in the document or are not fully visible, such as "to the s[ai]d Phill[ip] [tightly bound]."

[*Sic*]

Sometimes—actually, often—words in deeds aren't spelled the way we spell them today. But it is also easy to make typos. Therefore, we often indicate when a word is misspelled in the original, using [*sic*]. If an entire document is horrifically spelled, then we usually just make a note to that effect and don't try to handle it word by word.

We also use [*sic*] when facts in a document seem incorrect. For example, if the year of a deed is *after* the year of recording, we would probably look to see when nearby deeds were recorded, determine which one is in error, and put [*sic*] following the incorrect year. When, for example, the seller's wife is named "Mary" at the beginning of a deed and "Martha" in the dower release, and we have no external evidence to determine the correct name, we would put [*sic*] after both names.

Ellipsis Points

Use *ellipsis points* to indicate that you have omitted words from text. The left-out words are called an *ellipsis*. In extracting deeds, we have ample use for ellipsis points because there is so much boilerplate.

NINE

Records of Residence

T his chapter discusses two types of records that are records of *residence*. They may be related to landownership, but they do not require land-ownership. However, they let us discover some of the same information that we're looking for through land records. Using tax lists and city directories, we can anchor our ancestors in the neighborhoods in which they lived, and even uncover family relationships.

TAX RECORDS

Tax records vary significantly from place to place and from time to time. They often do not survive at all, which is disappointing because they were usually created annually. Thus, **they are more likely to show changes in family circumstances such as moves and deaths than are any other class of record.**

You will need to explore whether or not tax records are available for the time and place of your interest. I begin with the Family History Library Catalog. See "The Family History Library Catalog" in Finding a Deed Without Using Vacation Time on page 42 for instructions. "Tax Records," like "Land Records," is a category in the catalog.

Taxes were levied on land, personal property (including such things as farm animals, vehicles, business licenses, and occupations, and luxury items such as watches and pianos), and individuals (a poll tax). Sometimes tax lists combine these three types of taxes. Sometimes there were up to three separate lists.

In "My Ancestor Had Siblings—Joint Ownership" in Where Are the Records? on page 23, we looked at a 1796 deed from Jacob and Michael, two of the sons of Johannes Buch (Book/Books), selling the land their father had left them in his will. That will was written 27 April 1779 and probated 10 June 1786, so we don't know when in that time period Jacob died. On the 1782 tax list, the first one for Washington County, Pennsylvania, we find "Margrett Book" (she was the widow of Johannes) being taxed. Thus, we know that Johannes was dead by that year, even though his estate was not probated until

Notes

four years later. We also learn from the tax lists that in addition to the land, Margaret's holdings included several horses and cattle, sheep—and a still!

Tax lists often can destroy a theory about an ancestor. In "Land Lotteries" in First Transfer—Getting Land Into the Hands of Individuals on page 72, we learned from the Georgia land lottery of 1807 that Lemuel E. Owen was an orphan of Obediah Owen. Obediah was on the 1794 tax list of Wilkes County, with no land. Family researchers have suggested that Lemuel's mother was Dicey Toombs, whom Obediah had married in Halifax County, Virginia, on 21 December 1788.

I was looking for someone entirely different on the Halifax tax rolls when I spotted Obediah. I exclaimed (aloud, I must confess, much to the amusement of nearby patrons at the archives), "You can't be here, you're in Georgia." I read the tax rolls year by year for Halifax and neighboring Pittsylvania County. I discovered that there was more than one Obediah, but they were easy to separate as I noted that each appeared in a different location, each apparently surrounded by his immediate family (father, brothers, sons). The bad news came when the Obediah of 1786–1801 turned into "Obediah est" (Obediah['s] est[ate]) in 1802–1803, followed by Dicey in 1804–1809, who was succeeded by Obed (surely Obediah Jr.) beginning in 1810.

Clearly, my Obediah was on the tax lists in Georgia in 1794 when the Obediah who was married to Dicey was residing continuously in Halifax. Needless to say, I had to remove Dicey from my pedigree.

In public-land states, tax lists are usually organized by township and range, therefore you can learn where your ancestor lived—and his neighbors—even if he didn't own land.

The 1798 Direct Tax

Most taxes were levied by the colony or state and were collected at the county or local jurisdiction. However, one tax that was levied by the federal government is closely related to land. It can help us learn fascinating details about our ancestors. It is sometimes called the "windowpane tax" because the building descriptions included counts of the number of windows and the total number of windowpanes.

Unfortunately, only the rolls for Pennsylvania survive at the federal level. Partial rolls survive for Connecticut, Delaware, District of Columbia, Maine, Maryland, Massachusetts, New Hampshire, Rhode Island, Tennessee, and Vermont (see "Miscellaneous Records" in *Guide to Genealogical Research in the National Archives*).

In 1798 Richard Gregg lived in a 1½-story log house that was only twenty feet by ten feet. It had three windows, with a total of nineteen lights (panes). The kitchen was almost as large as the house, at fourteen feet by twelve feet. As a farmer, Richard had invested most of his construction effort on buildings related to running the farm. His barn was almost four times as big as the house, at forty feet by eighteen feet. His property also contained a thirty-by-twenty-two-foot stone mill house (a grist mill for grinding corn and other grain) and a sawmill.

URBANITES AND CITY DIRECTORIES

Records of land transfers in cities are generally found at the county level but may be described by lot and block. You may find the survey plat underlying that description in the city tax office.

Few people in big cities owned their own homes. Most were renters. Many were highly mobile, moving often from one rented room or house to another. **However, we can track our urban ancestors using city directories.** Whether he rented or owned his property, your ancestor was likely to attend a church in the neighborhood, buy goods at a store in the neighborhood, and be buried at a cemetery in the neighborhood. Spouses usually came from the neighborhood. Neighborhoods in large cities had distinctive personalities that may tell you more about your ancestor. City directories help us zoom in on our ancestors' neighborhoods quickly. Often the city directory will indicate if an ancestor owned or rented.

In "Establish Earlier or Later Residences" in Why Use Land Records? on page 8, we learned that the widow Tamar Law had moved from Illinois to Milwaukee, Wisconsin, where I found a state death certificate for her, which said (erroneously, as it turned out), that she was buried in Milwaukee. Searching the death index for the surname, I also located a death certificate for her son James William Law. His certificate gave the name of the cemetery where he was buried. A call to the cemetery produced the information that Tamar was not buried at that cemetery; however, when the nice person in the office mentioned others buried in the same plot, I recognized the names of several Illinois neighbors.

With this information, I was able to use city directories to learn more about Tamar's move to Milwaukee and about other family members and friends.

I followed the families of Kirkham, Law, and Wright (the surnames from the cemetery plot) for four decades—and I transcribed many more entries than those shown here. Like tax records, these entries reflect subtle year-by-year changes. We see variances in occupation, we see how often the people moved, and we can identify the part of town in which they lived.

Notice how easy it would have been to lose critical information if I had skipped even a single year. I was able to connect individuals of different surnames when I found them residing together at the same address. More importantly (and what you don't see here), is that I was able to eliminate individuals with the same surnames as possible family connections through the same process.

Through the city directories, I learned that Tamar came to live with John S. Wright, lake captain, in 1882. This helped me determine that Tamar's daughter Mary was married to him. Notice that in this directory, the name of the husband was provided for widows. (See figures 9-1 on page 124 and 9-2 on page 125.)

Early city directories contained verbal descriptions of the locations of streets. Later on, the directories included wonderfully detailed maps. Most of the addresses are southwest of downtown Milwaukee, but Bay View is much farther south along the lakeshore. On a trip to Milwaukee, I planned to see each house in which Tamar lived. The first thing I discovered was that I couldn't find all

Printed Source

Milwaukee City Directories

1861	Wright, John S., sailor, h e s Lake n Ontario
1862	Kirkham, Jas., mason, h 288 Van Buren
	Wright, John S., sailor, h e s Lake n Ontario
1863	Kirkum — mason, h 288 Van Buren
1865	Wright, John S., sailor, r. 248 Washington
1866–67	Kirkham, James, mason, r. 543 Van Buren
	Wright, John, sailor, r. 347 Oregon
1867	Kirkhan, James, mason, r. 231 Knapp
1868–69	Kirkham, James, mason, res. 638 Van Buren
1869–70	Kirkham, James, mason, res. 761 Jackson
	Wright, John, sailor, bds. 128 Reed
1870–71	Wright, John, sailor, res. 280 Walker
1871–72	Kirkham, James, mason, res. 184 Lynn
	Wright, John, sailor, res. 280 Walker
1872–73	Kirkham, James, mason, res. 184 Lyon
	Law, James W. apprentice, bds, 748 Cass
	Wright, John S., sailor, res. 748 Cass
1873–74	Kirkham, James, mason, res. 184 Lyon
	Wright, John, sailor, res. 419 Cedar
	Wright, John S., captain, res. 748 Cass
1874–75	Kirkham, James, architect, res. 6th ave bet. Scott and Madison
	Wright, John, sailor, res. 629 Cedar
1875–76	Kirkham, James, mason, res. 382 Clinton
	Law, James, stonecutter, bds. 382 Clinton
1876–77	Kirkham, James, stone-cutter, res. 474 Washington
	Law, James, stone-cutter, bds. 116 3d
1877–78	Kirkham, James, stone-contractor, res. 474 Washington
	Wright, John, captain, 584 Reed
1878	Kirkham, James, carpenter, res. 474 Washington
	Law, James, stone-cutter, bds. 353 Clinton
	Wright, John S., captain, 353 Clinton
1879	Kirkham, James, mason, res. 474 Washington
	Wright, John S., lake-captain, res. 353 Clinton
1880	Kirkham, James, mason, res. 474 Washington
	Wright, John S., captain, res. 351 Clinton
1881	Wright, John S., captain, res. e. s. Erie, nr. Ontario, Bay View
1882	Law James W., stonecutter, r. 280 Walker
	Law Tamar (wid. George), r. e. s. Erie, 5 s. Ontario, Bay View
	Wright, John S., lake captain, r. e. s. Erie, 5 s. Ontario, Bay View
1883	Kirkham, James, mason, r. 707 Hill
	Law James W., stonecutter, r. 280 Walker
	Wright, John S., lake captain, r. 90 5th

1884	Kirkham, James, contractor, r. 123 5th
	Law, James W., stonecutter, r. 280 Walker
1885	Kirkham, James, building contractor, r. 123 5th
	Law, James W., stonecutter, r. 280 Walker
1886	Kirkham, James, contractor, r. 123 5th
	Law, James W., stonecutter, r. 280 Walker
1887	Kirkham, James, contractor, r. 123 5th
	Law, James W., stone-cutter, r. 280 Walker
1888	Kirkham, James, contractor, r. 616 Sycamore
1889	Kirkham, James, supt., r. 616 Sycamore
	Law, James W., stone-cutter, 461 Murray av.
1890	Kirkham, James, supt., r. 373 13th
	Law, James W., stonectr, 487 Walker av
	Wright, John S., capt., h. r. 474 Mineral
1891	Kirkham, James, mason-insp., h. 410 11th
	Law, James Wm., stonectr, h. 474 Mineral
	Law, Tama (wid. George), h. r. 474 Mineral
	Wright, John S., capt., h. r. 474 Mineral
1892	Kirkham, James, died May 29, 1892
	Law, James Wm., stonectr, h. 474 Mineral
	Law, Tama (wid. George), h. 514 Greenbush
	Wright, John S., captain, h. 514 Greenbush
1893	Law, James Wm., stonectr, h. 474 Mineral
	Law, Tamar (wid. Geo.), h. 514 Greenbush
	Wright, John S., capt., h. 514 Greenbush
1894	Kirkham, Mary (wid. James) h. 746 2d
	Law, James W., stonectr, h. 474 Mineral
	Wright, John S., sailor, h. 514 Greenbush
1895	Kirkham, Mary (wid. James) h. 746 2d.
	Law, James Wm., stonectr, h. 3112 Mt. Vernon
	Law, Tamar (wid. Geo.), h. 514 Greenbush
	Wright, John S., capt., h. 514 Greenbush
1896	Kirkham, Mary A. (wid. James) h. 746 2d.
	Law, James W., died June 30, '95
	Law, Tamar A. (wid. Geo.), h. 514 Greenbush
	Wright, John S., sailor, h. 514 Greenbush
1897	Kirkham, Mary A. (wid. James) h. 746 2d.
	Law, Melinda (wid. James) h. 3112 Mt. Vernon av.
	Law, Tamar A. (wid. George) h. 514 Greenbush
	Wright, John S., lake capt., h. 514 Greenbush
1898	Kirkham, Mary A. (wid. James) h. 746 2d.
	Law, Melinda (37) died Dec. 28, '97
	Law, Tamar (wid. George), h. 1916 Prairie
	Wright, John S., capt., h. 1916 Prairie
1899	Kirkham, Mary (wid. James) h. 746 2d.
	Law, Tamar (79) died Feb. 1, '99.
	Wright, John S., sailor, h. 1916 Prairie
1900	Kirkham, Mary (wid. James) h. 216 Lee

Figure 9-1 By reading the city directories year by year, we can learn much about where our ancestors lived and with whom, their occupations, and even information about spouses and deaths.

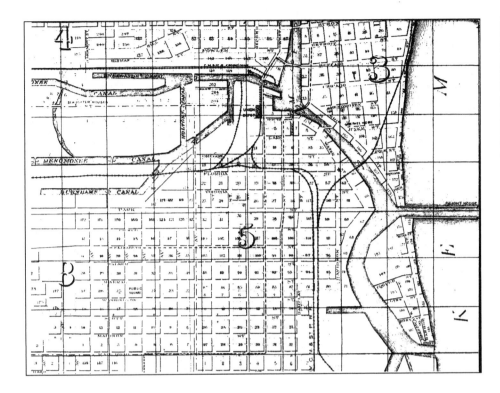

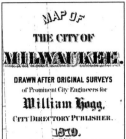

Figure 9-2 Most city directories contained excellent, detailed maps.

of the street names on my modern map. I compared an old map from the city directory with the modern map. The streets had been renamed between the beginning and end of the twentieth century! Reed had become Second, Greenbush had become Fourth, First had become Sixth, and so on.

Having mastered the street shifts, I set out to look for the dwellings. Unfortunately, it turned out that the numbering system for the houses had also changed, so I was only able to get a feel for the neighborhood. But that in itself is valuable. A visit to Bay View helped me realize that John S. Wright had been hauling either fuel or raw material for the rolling mill established there in 1868. The workers' humble housing had been replaced by family homes in the early twentieth century, but the wind off of Lake Erie was just as cold as it was in the 1880s when Tamar resided in her son-in-law's household.

Most early city directories have been microfilmed or microfiched. Check with libraries and archives to locate copies for your ancestral city.

TEN

Maps, Atlases, and Gazetteers

Sources

M aps, atlases, and gazetteers are the indispensable companions to land records. As you read deeds and patents and as you plat land, you will find yourself repeatedly consulting these invaluable aids.

- Maps come in a wide variety of types. **Of particular interest to genealogists are old maps, county highway maps, tax maps, Sanborn fire insurance maps, and USGS (United States Geological Survey) topographic maps, all of which are discussed in greater detail on the following pages.**

- Atlases aren't simply collections of maps. They typically include demographic, geologic, and social data, and they may have little of interest to researchers seeking land records for their ancestors. Historical atlases, on the other hand, may provide helpful information. In particular, state atlases may show county formations, early roads and waterways, and settlement patterns. A number of historical atlases are listed in "Resources" starting on page 132.

- Gazetteers and place-name guides can help you focus your efforts in the right area. If you are baffled by a place reference in a letter, an obituary, or a land record, turn to these sources. For genealogists, older is better, as we often are seeking place names that have long since disappeared from modern maps. Fortunately, many older gazetteers have been reprinted and are available to us. A number of these publications are listed in "Resources." Additionally, the Geographic Names Information System (see "Resources") is a great help in locating place names. Check out the category **Names-Geographical** in the Family History Library Catalog for publications on your area of interest (usually under the state).

TYPES OF MAPS

I love maps, really love them. I somehow do not feel I have connected with my ancestors until I can visualize their environment. I want to know where the roads went, which way the creek flowed, how far it was to church, school, cemetery, and courthouse. Maps provide those answers for me.

- Old maps often can be found in town and county histories. Several publishers have reproduced volumes with old maps, and The Gold Bug specializes in reproductions of old maps (see "Resources"). Maps may still be in the custody of towns and counties, but it may require a personal visit to obtain them. Check out the categories **Maps, Maps-Bibliography,** and **History-Maps** in the Family History Library Catalog. For many counties there are commercially produced atlases and maps, showing the property and homes of the residents.

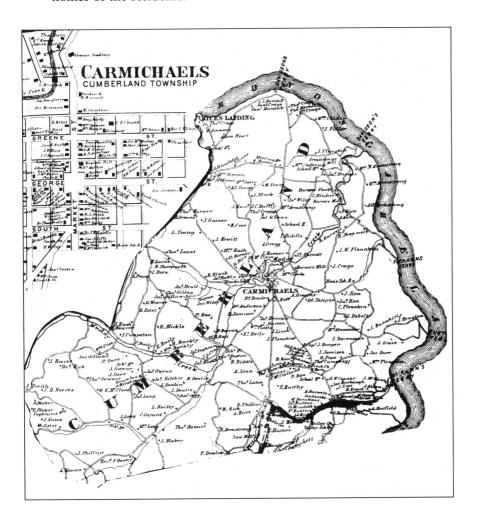

Figure 10-1 The home of A. Gregg (Alford Gregg) is immediately below the *A* in Cumberland. This is the property surveyed for James Kerr and quitclaimed by his widows and heirs discussed elsewhere in this book.

- Counties often maintained maps showing the plats of land and their owners. These may go back to the original patents. Tax maps are created by the county taxing agency to be certain they aren't missing anyone when they send out property-tax bills each year. In public-land states, maps are often bound in a booklet, one page for each township. In state-land states, they are more likely to be loose maps. In either case, the maps are usually moderately priced. They will be maintained by the tax or revenue office, not by the registrar of deeds. Some localities have started putting this information on the Internet.

Figure 10-2 Parcel number 17 is the James Kerr-Alford Gregg land, which is difficult to see because it is small and there were several boundary adjustments made to it.

- County highway maps (engineering maps) are wonderful. They usually are maintained by the state department in charge of infrastructure such as roads and bridges. They show roads (including those dusty dirt and gravel roads ignored on other maps) and waterways (a bridge is required when a road crosses a waterway). They often show churches and cemeteries (I guess because the same department is in charge of the signs we see along paved roads pointing the way to Pisgah Church or Mt. Tabor Cemetery). County maps often come in two sizes, an 8½-by-11-inch size that's perfect for filing with your research and a larger size that's easier to read. I always order one of each (they're usually nominally priced). Consult Allen's *Where to Write for County Maps*. DeLorme prints atlases of county maps for some states.

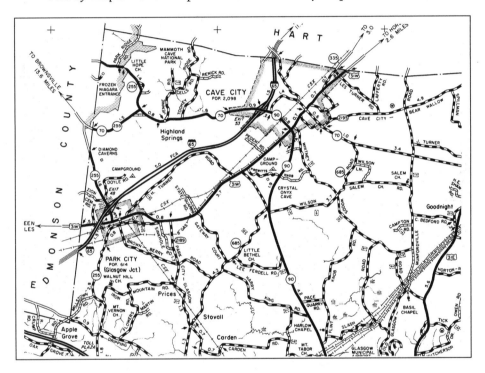

Figure 10-3 Kentucky's detailed county highway maps show the churches and cemeteries around Mammoth Cave. There are few long, running streams in this area, because the water tends to go into the caves below.

- Sanborn fire insurance maps are an important resource for studying urban property. **Some Sanborn Maps are available on microfilm.** Unfortunately, the microfilm does not reproduce the color on the maps that provided some of the information keys. According to the Library of Congress Web site,

  . . . the fire insurance map is probably the single most important record of urban growth and development in the United States during the past one hundred years. It contains data used in estimating the potential risk for urban structures and includes such information as their construction material, height, and function as well as the location of lot lines. The Sanborn Map Company has been the dominant American publisher of fire insurance maps and atlases for over seventy years. Founded by D. A. Sanborn in 1867, the firm has issued and periodically updated detailed plans of 12,000 American cities and towns.

- USGS topographic (quadrangle) maps are truly my favorite maps. They have so much information that they must use color to show it all. Not

Microfilm Source

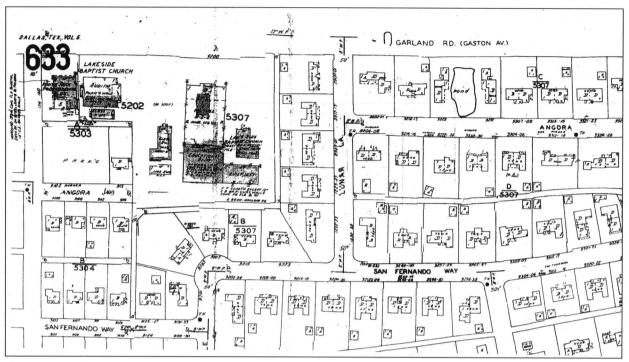

Figure 10-4 Sanborn fire insurance maps show homes, businesses, and other buildings in both large cities and small towns.

only do they include contour and geographic information, they also include some man-made features. Thus, houses, barns, private roads, cemeteries, churches, and fence boundaries may all be included. They are so wonderful that they deserve greater discussion (see "USGS Topographic Quadrangle Maps" below).

- DeLorme produces less-detailed topographic atlases (one-fourth the size of the USGS maps) for all states except Florida, Michigan, and Ohio. They do not include as many details as the USGS maps do, but they generally include cemeteries and churches. I usually buy the DeLorme atlas for the state in which I'm interested at a bookstore (the major chains carry them and can order other states if your state isn't in stock). Once I've identified the locality in which my ancestor lived, I order the USGS quadrangle map. DeLorme also produces several versions of map software.

- Many maps, including old maps and the USGS maps, are available online. Check the Maps, Gazetteers, and Geographical Information category on Cyndi's List <www.cyndislist.com> to get you started.

USGS Topographic Quadrangle Maps

The most popular of the USGS United States Geological Survey maps with genealogists are the topographic maps. Of these, the 7.5-minute quadrangle maps are the most popular size. At a scale of 1:24,000, each large sheet covers an area a bit over 6.3 miles by 8.6 miles.

You can learn a lot about your ancestors' environment by studying the map. Color and symbols are used to describe the land (ask for the "Topographic Map Symbols" booklet when ordering your map). Brown contour lines show the

Tip

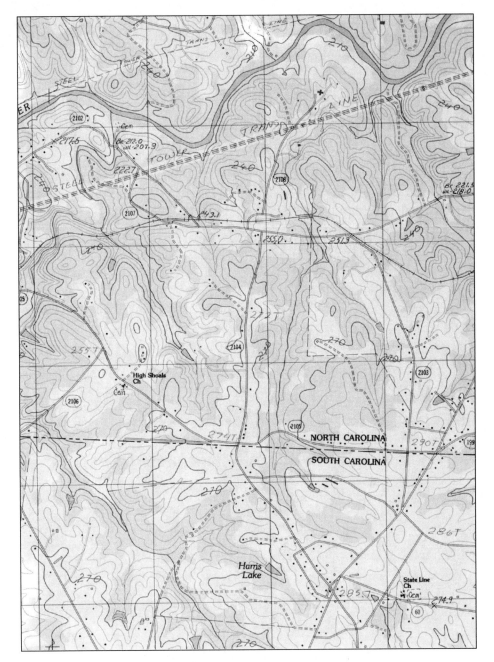

Figure 10-5 USGS Quadrangle maps are independent of political boundaries. This map spans the North Carolina-South Carolina border, giving us a truer picture of the land surrounding our ancestor's homes.

shape of the terrain, black indicates man-made features, red marks the public-land survey lines (section, township, range), purple indicates features observed only from the air, green indicates vegetation, and blue is for water. Combinations of color, symbols, and line style indicate swampland, fence and field lines, intermittent streams, woodland, scrub, orchards, vineyards, quarries, tidal areas, rice fields, and dozens of other features.

To order a USGS map, begin with the state index to identify the appropriate quadrangle map (they have names, not numbers, and are not necessarily the name of the town on the map). The quickest way to access an index map is to go to the USGS Web site at <http://mapping.usgs.gov> and use the MapFinder feature under "General Information, Indexes, and Catalogs." Enter the state and a town

TOPOGRAPHIC MAPS AND CONTOUR LINES

Topographic maps have a feature that you can't find on road maps. Contour lines let you see how hilly or flat your ancestor's farm was. A *contour line* is a continuous line at a single altitude (which is indicated). A hill, for example, would be apparent on the map from the ring of contour lines surrounding the summit. If the contour lines on one side of the hill are closer together than those on the other side, then that is the steeper side of the hill. USGS chooses an interval between the contour lines that is appropriate for the map. Contour lines in moutainous regions may be at one-hundred-foot intervals, while those near the seashore may be at ten–foot intervals.

near where your ancestor lived. The index map appears, centered on the town. There is enough detail with towns and waterways that you should be able to identify the correct map. (Actually, Murphy's Law of USGS maps says that your ancestor's land will always lie near the edge of a quadrangle, requiring that you order two maps to get a complete picture of his neighborhood.)

When you click on one of the quadrangles, it is added to your shopping cart. Ain't technology grand? (I cleared a nice amount of space in my file cabinet when I discovered I no longer needed my pile of USGS indexes.) You can also order by more traditional methods (see "Resources").

You'll learn more about using the USGS maps when you plat your ancestor's land (see chapter eleven, Metes-and-Bounds Land Platting, and chapter twelve, Public-Land Survey System).

RESOURCES

Allen, Desmond Walls. *Where to Write for County Maps*. 3d ed. Bryant, Ark.: Research Associates, 1998.

Andriot, Jay. *Township Atlas of the United States*. McLean, Va.: Documents Index, 1991. Earlier editions by John L. Andriot. McLean, Va.: Andriot Associates, 1979, 1987.

AniMap Plus software from The Gold Bug, P.O. Box 588, Alamo, CA 94507. <www.goldbug.com> Shows changing county boundaries over time.

Cyndi's List. <www.cyndislist.com>, created by Cyndi Howells, is a good starting point for finding maps online.

DeLorme. <www.delorme.com>, for map software.

Geographic Names Information System (GNIS). <http://geonames.usgs.gov> GNIS was developed by USGS in cooperation with the U.S. Board on Geographic Names. The database contains a variety of name types, including physical features, political features, and man-made features. It also tells you which USGS quadrangle map to order! This is a government database, so you also can find it on other Internet sites and distributed with genealogy software.

The Gold Bug, P.O. Box 588, Alamo, CA 94507. <www.goldbug.com> A good source for old maps on paper and CD-ROM.

List of Post Offices in the United States. This reference was published regularly by the Government Printing Office in the latter part of the nineteenth century. Several have been reprinted by Theron Wierenga, Holland, Mich.

Makower, Joel, ed. *The Map Catalog: Every Kind of Map and Chart on Earth and Even Some Above It.* 3d ed. New York: Vintage Books, 1992.

Map Express, P.O. Box 280445, Lakewood, CO 80228. (800) MAP-0039; (800) 627-0039. Twenty-four-hour fax: (303) 969-8195. <www.mapexp .com> Fast commercial service for USGS maps.

National Archives and Records Service. *Guide to Genealogical Research in the National Archives.* 3d ed. Washington, D.C.: 2000. "Cartographic Records" describes the maps in the General Land Office, including T1234 *Township Plats of Selected States* (sixty-nine rolls).

Schiffman, Carol Mehr. "Geographic Tools: Maps, Atlases, and Gazetteers." In *Printed Sources: A Guide to Published Genealogical Records* edited by Kory L. Meyerink. Salt Lake City: Ancestry Inc., 1996.

Thorndale, William, and William Dollarhide. *Map Guide to the U.S. Federal Censuses, 1790–1920.* Baltimore: Genealogical Publishing Co., Inc., 1987. Absolutely necessary to ensure that you are looking in the right locality and to identify other likely localities.

USGS Western Distribution Branch, P.O. Box 25286, Federal Center, Denver, CO 80225. (800) USA-MAPS; (800) 872-6277; eight to four on weekdays. Government source for USGS quadrangle maps (7.5-minute scale). Use the index online at <http://mapping.usgs.gov> to identify the quadrangle name, and then order the map.

BY LOCALITY

The following atlases and gazetteers are by no means all that are available but are the ones that I have examined. Because many of the maps, atlases, and gazetteers we seek are old, availability will vary widely from one library to another.

Alabama   public-land state

Foscue, Virginia O. *Place Names in Alabama.* Tuscaloosa: University of Alabama, 1989.

Long, John H., ed., and Peggy Tuck Sinko, comp. *Alabama Atlas of Historical County Boundaries.* New York: Charles Scribner's Sons, 1996.

Remington, W. Craig, and Thomas J. Kallsen. *The Historical Atlas of Alabama.* Tuscaloosa: University of Alabama, 2d ed., 1999.

Alaska   public-land state

Schorr, Alan Edward, ed. *Alaska Place Names.* 2d ed. Juneau: University of Alaska, 1980.

Arizona   public-land state

Barnes, Will C., rev. by Byrd H. Granger. *Arizona Place Names*. Tucson: University of Arizona Press, 1960.

Walker, Henry P., and Don Bufkin. *Historical Atlas of Arizona*. Norman: University of Oklahoma Press, 1979.

California   public-land state

Gudde, Erwin G. *California Place Names*. Berkeley: University of California Press, 1969.

Colorado   public-land state

Elliott, Donald R., comp., and Doris L. (Salmen) Elliott, ed. *Place Names of Colorado*. Denver: Colorado Council of Genealogical Societies, Inc., 1999.

Connecticut   original colony

Long, John H., ed., and Gordon DenBoer and John H. Long, comp. *Connecticut, Maine, Massachusetts, Rhode Island Atlas of Historical County Boundaries*. New York: Simon and Schuster, 1994.

Delaware   original colony

Long, John H., ed. and comp. *Delaware, Maryland, District of Columbia Atlas of Historical County Boundaries*. New York: Charles Scribner's Sons, Simon and Schuster Macmillan, 1996.

District of Columbia

Long, John H., ed. and comp. *Delaware, Maryland, District of Columbia Atlas of Historical County Boundaries*. New York: Charles Scribner's Sons, Simon and Schuster Macmillan, 1996.

Florida   public-land state

Long, John H., ed., and Peggy Tuck Sinko and Kathryn Ford Thorn, comp. *Florida Atlas of Historical County Boundaries*. New York: Charles Scribner's Sons, 1997.

Illinois   public-land state

Long, John H., ed., and Gordon DenBoer, comp. *Illinois Atlas of Historical County Boundaries*. New York: Charles Scribner's Sons, 1997.

Indiana   public-land state

Illustrated Historical Atlas of the State of Indiana. Chicago: Baskin, Forster & Company, 1876; reprinted as *Maps of Indiana Counties in 1876*. n.p.: Indiana Historical Society, 1968.

Long, John H., ed., and Peggy Tuck Sinko, comp. *Indiana Atlas of Historical County Boundaries*. New York: Charles Scribner's Sons, 1996.

Iowa   **public-land state**

Long, John H., ed., and Gordon DenBoer, comp. *Iowa Atlas of Historical County Boundaries*. New York: Charles Scribner's Sons, 1998.

Kansas   **public-land state**

Official State Atlas of Kansas. Philadelphia: L.H. Everts & Co., 1887; reprinted Kansas Council of Genealogical Societies, 1982.

Socolofsky, Homer E., and Huber Self. *Historical Atlas of Kansas*. Norman: University of Oklahoma Press, 1988.

Kentucky   **state-land state**

Clark, Thomas D. *Historic Maps of Kentucky*. Lexington: University Press of Kentucky, 1979.

Long, John H., ed., and Gordon DenBoer, comp. *Kentucky Atlas of Historical County Boundaries*. New York: Charles Scribner's Sons, 1995.

Rennick, Robert M. *Kentucky Place Names*. Lexington: University Press of Kentucky, 1984.

Maine   **state-land state**

Long, John H., ed., and Gordon DenBoer and John H. Long, comp. *Connecticut, Maine, Massachusetts, Rhode Island Atlas of Historical County Boundaries*. New York: Simon and Schuster, 1994.

Morris, Gerald E., ed, *The Maine Bicentennial Atlas*. Portland: Maine Historical Society, 1976.

Old Maps of . . . Maine. Series by county, reproducing maps from latter half of nineteenth century. Fryeburg: Saco Valley Printing, 1980s.

Rutherford, Phillip R. *The Dictionary of Maine Place-Names*. Freeport: Bond Wheelwright Company, 1970.

Maryland   **original colony**

Long, John H., ed. and comp. *Delaware, Maryland, District of Columbia Atlas of Historical County Boundaries*. New York: Charles Scribner's Sons, Simon and Schuster Macmillan, 1996.

Massachusetts   **original colony**

Davis, Charlotte Pease. *Directory of Massachusetts Place Names*. Lexington: Bay State News, 1987.

Denis, Michael J. *Massachusetts Towns and Counties*. Oakland, Me.: Danbury House Books, 1984.

Galvin, William Francis. *Historical Data Relating to Counties, Cities, and Towns in Massachusetts*. 5th ed. Boston: New England Historic Genealogical Society, 1997.

Krieger, Alex, and David Cobb, eds. *Mapping Boston*. Cambridge: Massachusetts Institute of Technology, 1999.

Long, John H., ed., and Gordon DenBoer and John H. Long, comp. *Connecticut, Maine, Massachusetts, Rhode Island Atlas of Historical County Boundaries*. New York: Simon and Schuster, 1994.

Old Maps of Northeastern Essex County, Massachusetts and *Old Maps of Southern Essex County, Massachusetts.* Reproducing 1880s maps. Fryeburg: Saco Valley Printing, 1982, 1984.

Michigan   public-land state

Long, John H., ed., and Peggy Tuck Sinko, comp. *Michigan Atlas of Historical County Boundaries.* New York: Charles Scribner's Sons, 1997.

Minnesota   public-land state

Bakeman, Mary Hawker. *Minnesota Land Owner Maps and Directories.* Brooklyn Park, Minn.: Park Genealogical Books, 1994.

Long, John H., ed., and Gordon DenBoer, comp. *Minnesota Atlas of Historical County Boundaries.* New York: Charles Scribner's Sons, 2000.

Mississippi   public-land state

Long, John H., ed., and Peggy Tuck Sinko, comp. *Mississippi Atlas of Historical County Boundaries.* New York: Charles Scribner's Sons, 1993.

Montana   public-land state

Richards, Dennis Lee. *Montana's Genealogical and Local History Records.* Detroit: Gale Research, 1981. See chapter sixteen, "Land Records."

Nevada   public-land state

Carlson, Helen S. *Nevada Place Names.* Reno: University of Nevada Press, 1974.

New Hampshire   original colony

Long, John H., ed., and Gordon DenBoer, comp., with George E. Goodridge Jr. *New Hampshire and Vermont Atlas of Historical County Boundaries.* New York: Simon and Schuster, 1993.

Merrill, Eliphalet, and Phinehas Merrill. *Gazetteer of the State of New Hampshire.* Exeter: Norris & Co., 1817; reprinted Bowie, Md.: Heritage Books, 1987.

Old Maps of . . . New Hampshire. Series by county, reproducing 1892 cadastral maps. Fryeburg: Saco Valley Printing, 1980s.

New Mexico   public-land state

Beck, Warren A., and Ynez D. Haase. *Historical Atlas of New Mexico.* Norman: University of Oklahoma Press, 1969.

Pearce, T.M. *New Mexico Place Names.* Albuquerque: University of New Mexico Press, 1965.

New York   original colony

French, J.H. *Gazetteer of the State of New York.* Syracuse; the author, 1860; reprinted Baltimore: Genealogical Publishing Company, 1983.

Long, John H., ed., and Kathryn Ford Thorne, comp. *New York Atlas of Historical County Boundaries.* New York: Charles Scribner's Sons, 1993.

Spafford, Horatio Gates. *Gazetteer of the State of New York*. Albany: B.D. Packard, 1824; reprinted by Interlaken: Heart of the Lakes Publishing, 1981.

North Carolina   original colony

Clark, David Sanders. *Index to Maps of North Carolina in Books and Periodicals*. Fayetteville: the author, 1976.

Long, John H., ed., and Gordon DenBoer, comp. *North Carolina Atlas of Historical County Boundaries*. New York: Charles Scribner's Sons, 1998.

Ohio   public-land state

Long, John H., ed., and Peggy Tuck Sinko, comp. *Ohio Atlas of Historical County Boundaries*. New York: Charles Scribner's Sons, 1998.

Oklahoma   public-land state

Morris, John W., and Edwin C. McReynolds. *Historical Atlas of Oklahoma*. Norman: University of Oklahoma Press, 1965.

Shirk, George H. *Oklahoma Place Names*. Norman: University of Oklahoma Press, 1974.

Oregon   public-land state

McArthur, Lewis A. *Oregon Geographic Names*. Portland: Oregon Historical Society, 1974.

Pennsylvania   original colony

Gordon, Thomas F. *A Gazetteer of the State of Pennsylvania*. Philadelphia: T. Belknap, 1832; reprinted New Orleans: Polyanthos, 1975.

Long, John H., ed., and Gordon DenBoer, comp. *Pennsylvania Atlas of Historical County Boundaries*. New York: Charles Scribner's Sons, Simon and Schuster Macmillan, 1996.

Rhode Island   original colony

Long, John H., ed., and Gordon DenBoer and John H. Long, comp. *Connecticut, Maine, Massachusetts, Rhode Island Atlas of Historical County Boundaries*. New York: Simon and Schuster, 1994.

South Carolina   original colony

Long, John H., ed., and Gordon DenBoer and Kathryn Ford Thorne, comp. *South Carolina Atlas of Historical County Boundaries*. New York: Charles Scribner's Sons, 1997.

Mills, Robert. *Mills' Atlas: Atlas of the State of South Carolina, 1825*. Reprinted Easley, S.C.: Southern Historical Press, 1980.

Tennessee   state-land state

Fullerton, Ralph O. *Place Names of Tennessee*. Nashville: State of Tennessee, 1974.

Long, John H., ed., and Peggy Tuck Sinko, comp. *Tennessee Atlas of Historical County Boundaries*. New York: Charles Scribner's Sons, 2000.

Texas   state-land state

Day, James M., and Ann B. Dunlap, comps. *Map Collection of the Texas State Archives, 1527–1900*. Austin: Texas State Library, 1962.

Stephens, A. Ray, and William M. Holmes. *Historical Atlas of Texas*. Norman: University of Oklahoma Press, 1989.

Vermont   state-land state

Long, John H., ed., and Gordon DenBoer, comp., with George E. Goodridge Jr. *New Hampshire and Vermont Atlas of Historical County Boundaries*. New York: Simon and Schuster, 1993.

Virginia   original colony

Doran, Michael F. *Atlas of County Boundary Changes in Virginia, 1634–1895*. Athens, Georgia: Iberian Publishing, 1987.

Wisconsin   public-land state

Gard, Robert E., and L.G. Sorden. *Romance of Wisconsin Place Names*. New York: Wisconsin House, 1968.

Long, John H., ed., and Gordon DenBoer, comp. *Wisconsin Atlas of Historical County Boundaries*. New York: Charles Scribner's Sons, 1997.

"Wisconsin Post Offices 1821–1917." *Wisconsin State Genealogical Society Newsletter*. Published alphabetically between 1971 and 1985.

ELEVEN

Metes-and-Bounds Land Platting

I n the original thirteen colonies, Hawaii, and Texas, the crown gave land either to the colony itself or to a major proprietor, who then transferred the title to individuals. **These states, plus those in which they granted land, are known as** *state-land states,* **because land remaining ungranted at the time of the Revolution ended up in the hands of the states, rather than the federal government.**

\di'fin\ *vb*

Definitions

STATE-LAND STATES

- Connecticut
- Delaware
- Georgia
- Hawaii
- Kentucky
- Maine
- Maryland
- Massachusetts
- New Hampshire
- New Jersey

- New York
- North Carolina
- Pennsylvania
- Rhode Island
- South Carolina
- Tennessee
- Texas
- Vermont
- Virginia
- West Virginia

State-land states use the *indiscriminate-survey system,* so-called because the land was chosen indiscriminately (independently) of the survey system. We generally call this the *metes-and-bounds* system. This isn't totally correct, because a traditional *metes-and-bounds* description would not give distance and direction, but would simply name neighbors and describe corners. However, for convenience we use the term broadly.

The first time you see a metes-and-bounds description in a deed, it will probably look like a run-on jumble to you.

> [Louisa County, Virginia, Peter McAllaster to Thomas Allmon, 1769, 100 acres] . . . Land situate, lying, and being on Branches of Christophers Run and Tomerhawk Creek, in the sd parish of Trinity and County of Louisa containing by Estimation One Hundred Acres, be the same more or less and Bounded thus. Viz, Beginning at Elizabeth Hesters corner of several marked pines thence in this line North Forty two degrees West one hundred and seventy nine poles to the sd Eliz[abet]h Hesters corner several pines, Thence North fifty degrees East one hundred and four poles to a corner of several pines, thence south forty two degees East one hundred and thirty six poles to a corner of several pines, thence south twenty seven degrees west one hundred and eight poles to the beginning. . . .

The first part of the description provides you with a general location of the land, possibly identifying the township, the waterways, and the acreage (which may instead follow the detailed description). When a waterway is mentioned, it doesn't necessarily mean that your ancestor's land lies on that waterway. It means that your ancestor's land is on the drainage system of that waterway. If you've ever visited the Continental Divide, your guide probably told you that if you spit to the west, it would eventually end up in the Pacific Ocean, and if you spit to the east, it would eventually end up in the Atlantic Ocean. This drainage area is what is meant in the general description (but on a much smaller scale, of course).

Notes

The descriptions of the boundaries of the land begin with the word "Beginning." They are generally referred to as *calls*. Calls are of two types—*corners* and *lines*—which alternate. The first call, "Beginning at" is always a corner. The last call, "thence to the beginning," always returns us full circle.

Let's take another look at the description of the land that Thomas Allmon is purchasing, but this time we'll try to identify the corners, which I've marked with a ◉, and the lines, which I've marked with a →.

- ◉ Beginning at Elizabeth Hesters corner of several marked pines.
- → thence in this line North Forty two degrees West one hundred and seventy nine poles
- ◉ to the sd Eliz[abet]h Hesters corner several pines,
- → Thence North fifty degrees East one hundred and four poles
- ◉ to a corner of several pines,
- → thence south forty two degrees East one hundred and thirty six poles
- ◉ to a corner of several pines,
- → thence south twenty seven degrees west one hundred and eight poles
- ◉ to the beginning.

It's much easier to see if we organize it like this, isn't it? But we can do even more. A *corner* may have several components, all of which you should note when abstracting.

- the marker indicating a corner ("a chestnut oak," "several pines," "stakes," "markers")
- other geographical features ("on the side of a hill," "near a small run," "at the mouth of a creek")
- the names of other landowners whose land also includes that corner

Likewise, a *line* may have several components, all of which you should note when abstracting.
- the direction ("North thirty degrees east")
- the distance ("thirty poles," "130 feet")
- other descriptions ("up the meanders of the creek," "along the court house road")
- the name of the landowner whose land shares that line

Let's take another look at those lines and corners, and see what elements we can isolate.

◉ Beginning at Elizabeth Hesters corner	[neighbor]
of several marked pines	[marker]
→ thence in this line	[neighbor]
North Forty two degrees West	[direction]
one hundred and seventy nine poles	[distance]
◉ to the sd Eliz[abet]h Hesters corner	[neighbor]
several pines,	[marker]
→ Thence North fifty degrees East	[direction]
one hundred and four poles	[distance]
◉ to a corner of several pines,	[marker]
→ thence south forty two degrees East	[direction]
one hundred and thirty six poles	[distance]
◉ to a corner of several pines,	[marker]
→ thence south twenty seven degrees west	[direction]
one hundred and eight poles	[distance]
◉ to the beginning.	

I guess we know what the most common tree in the area is, don't we? We were lucky in this deed. All of the lines have both a direction and a distance. You may encounter deeds where this is not true. We usually call a line without both a *meander*—even if there isn't any water involved. If your deed has only one meander, you can still plat it (see "Problems" on page 148).

I like to abstract the calls into a form like this one. On page 150, you'll find a full-page blank version of this form that you may photocopy to use with your own deeds. (See figure 11-1 on page 142.)

PLATTING

Land platting is simply a way of retracing on paper the steps followed by the original surveyor on the land. Think of yourself as literally retracing his steps, and the task should be easy.

\di'fin\ *vb*

Definitions

Grantor: *Peter McAllaster*

Grantee: *Thomas Allmon*

Acreage: *100 acres Trinity Parish, Louisa County*

Waterways: *Christophers Run and Tomerhawk Creek*

Citation: *Louisa County, Virginia, Deeds D ½:160–61*

Scale: *USGS (1:24000); divide poles by 4.8 to get mm*

	Corner markers	Neighbors	Direction	Distance	mm
corner	Beginning at: *several marked pines*	*Elizabeth Hesters*			
line		*her line*	*N42W*	*179 poles*	*37*
corner	*several pines*	*Elizabeth Hesters*			
line			*N50E*	*104 poles*	*22*
corner	*several pines*				
line			*S42E*	*136 poles*	*28*
corner	*several pines*				
line			*S27W*	*108 poles*	*23*
corner	to the beginning				

Thumbnail sketch:

Figure 11-1 Example of completed form for abstracting calls.

Surveying

The surveyor had only a few simple tools. They improved over time, but generally speaking, the surveyor had a tool to measure direction and a tool to measure distance. The tools were costly, so as improved versions appeared, it was often a long time before they came into common use.

- Distance was usually measured with a Gunter's chain. It was four poles (sixty-six feet) long and had one hundred straight links, each pair connected with three small roundish links. Dangling indicators (like on a charm bracelet) marked important subdivisions. The chain is heavy, and in New England, which has smaller pieces of land, a half chain was sometimes used.

- A variety of different instruments were used to determine direction. The rough terrain of the colonial landscape, plus the fact that magnetic north and true north were not the same often led to significant errors in direction, even more so than in distance.

- Acreage was calculated primarily using tables and charts. These were based on four-sided, generally rectangular, parcels. Since early tracts were rarely this shape (except in New England), the acreage could be significantly different from that indicated in the deed. Often there is a later deed mentioning a new survey and resultant corrected acreage.

MEASUREMENTS

Most of the terms we find for distance in deeds derive from the tools used by the surveyor. The basic measurements of distance—*pole, rod,* and *perch*—are the same, 16½ feet. A *link* is less than 8 inches.

A pole is 4.8 millimeters on a USGS map; a link is less than a fifth of a millimeter, so we ignore links in platting. A perch also was commonly used as a measurement of area, so in Pennsylvania, we often see the area given as, say, "44 acres 75 perches."

You may find other measurements used, such as *chains, varas,* and *furlongs.* You'll find all the conversion equivalents you'll need in *Merriam-Webster's New Collegiate Dictionary.* See "Scale" on page 149 for instructions on calculating scale.

Supplies

You'll need a few basic supplies, all of which you can obtain at a local drug store, grocery store, or office-supply store.

- *Protractor or surveyor's compass.* Remember the half-circle protractor you used in trigonometry? That's what we're talking about. They still use them in school, so you'll be able to get one anywhere that parents shop for school supplies. Hold the protractor with the straight edge vertical, not horizontal. Notice that the numbering begins with 0° at the top (north) and bottom (south), and increases to 90° at the outside of the curve (east or west). Most continue on to 180°, but in land platting we don't encounter degrees greater than 90°.

  If you plan to do much land platting, you may want to purchase a surveyor's compass (see "Resources" on page 148). This is a specially designed round protractor (even though it's called a compass) that you will have to order. Do not purchase one of the round protractors found in office-supply stores; they have just one 0° and go to 360°, so they aren't compatible (without subtraction) with the directions you will find in deeds.

- Ruler marked in millimeters. Once again, you'll be able to find this supply anywhere that parents shop for school supplies. The short six-inch kind is usually sufficient for your needs (unless you had very wealthy ancestors buying very large tracts of land).
- Graph paper. The size and type of the graph paper isn't important. You are not using it for measurement but only to keep the compass aligned exactly north-south. If you have time to shop, though, I prefer what is usually called "engineering paper," which has four or five light-blue lines per inch, all of which are the same weight.
- Sharp pencil and eraser (a mechanical pencil is fine).
- A simple calculator.

STEP BY STEP

Step By Step

Platting a deed isn't difficult with the simplified instructions below. Mostly it's a matter of paying attention to what you're doing. I've provided hints for the most common errors that I see students making in my classes.

STEP 1. Make a photocopy or transcript of the deed.

STEP 2. Identify each element of the calls. I find it useful to use the following conventions:

- Underline the lines (direction, distance, and adjoining owners).
- Circle the corners (include neighbors).
- Use a wavy line for meanders or other indefinite calls.

Land situate, lying, and being on Branches of Christophers Run and Tomerhawk Creek, in the sd parish of Trinity and County of Louisa containing by Estimation One Hundred Acres, be the same more or less and Bounded thus. Viz, Beginning at Elizabeth Hesters corner of several marked pines thence in this line North Forty two degrees West one hundred and seventy nine poles to the sd Eliz[abet]h Hesters corner several pines, Thence North Fifty degrees East one hundred and Four poles to a corner of several pines, thence south Forty two degrees East one hundred and thirty six poles to a corner of several pines, thence south twenty seven degrees west one hundred and eight poles to the beginning

Figure 11-2 It will be easier to keep track of the calls if you circle the words that describe a corner and underline the words that describe a line.

STEP 3. Abstract the calls into a tabular format (see page 142 for a completed form and page 150 for a blank form that you can copy for personal use). Check off each line and corner on the photocopy as you abstract it. One of the most common problems is skipping or repeating all or part of a call. If you are doing many plats, you might want to use a uniform system of abbreviations for common trees: *RO* for "red oak," *WO* for "white oak," *P* for "pine," *H* for "hickory," and so on.

STEP 4. Convert all distances into the drawing distance at the same time, and write them on the form. (For poles/rods/perches, divide by 4.8 to use a standard USGS quadrangle map. See "scale" on page 149, if not USGS scale.) Make a thumbnail sketch on the form. This helps you plan where to place the point on the paper, and it serves as a visual quick-check as you plat.

STEP 5. Draw a solid dot (point) on your graph paper, and mark it "the beginning." This helps avoid the common mistake of starting the second line at the beginning instead of the end of the first line.

STEP 6. Place the center of your round surveyor's compass (or semicircular protractor) on top of the point, with north at the top. Align the direction of the grid on the compass/protractor with the direction of the grid on the graph paper. If you are using a semicircular protractor, the straight side should be vertical and the round side should be toward the east or west direction of the call.

STEP 7. Place your finger at the first direction named in the call (almost always north or south).

STEP 8. Beginning at the 0°, move your finger *toward* the second direction named (almost always east or west). Stop when you come to the number of

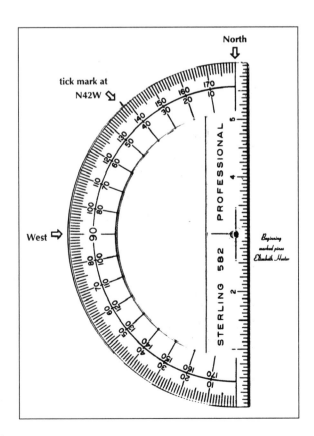

Figure 11-3 Platting the direction (not to scale).

degrees given in the deed, and make a small tick mark. (A tick mark is a slender line going in the direction of the call. By making it a line, you are less likely to get confused and choose the wrong mark in the next step.)

STEP 9. Place the 0 millimeter of your ruler on the beginning point, and align the edge of the ruler with the tick mark. All rulers have extra space at the end so that the 0 cannot wear away; make sure that you put the 0 at the point, not the end of the ruler.

STEP 10. Measure along the ruler the distance shown. The numbering on the millimeter side is in centimeters. Thus, 10 millimeters is at the 1, 20 millimeters is at the 2, and so on. Make a dot at the distance point, and draw the line. You can rotate your paper so that you are looking squarely at the edge of the ruler. This helps considerably with the accuracy of your platting.

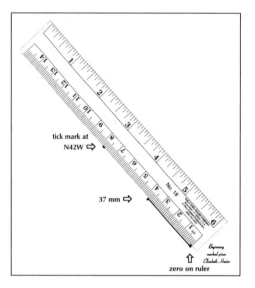

Figure 11-4 Platting the direction (not to scale).

STEP 11. Label the line you have drawn and the new point. Draw an arrow to show the direction you are "walking." Erase the tick mark to avoid future confusion. Check off the distance and direction on your abstract, so you won't repeat or skip a number.

STEP 12. Place the center of the compass on the *new* point, and repeat steps 6 through 11.

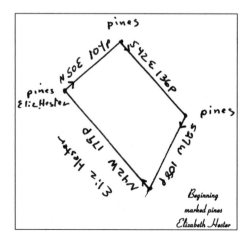

Figure 11-5 Final plat (USGS scale 1:24,000).

LOCATING YOUR ANCESTOR'S LAND

Once you've finished platting your ancestor's deed, you'll want to figure out exactly where your ancestor lived. There are two techniques you can use to do this.

Plat and Plug

Some plats have distinctive shapes. If you can find all the property in the region already platted and "matched up," you may be able simply to plug your plat into place. (However, it is possible that subdivisions of the land may make it difficult for you to recognize where your piece fits.) There are two time periods for which you might be able to locate such a map.

- **Current owners.** Modern-day (the term is used loosely, it can be decades ago) plat or tract maps may exist at the county level. Taxing entities, county surveyors, and other public entities may have created comprehensive plat maps showing the current owner in order to ease their public duties. The maps may be large vellum maps, they may be bound in books, or they may be on computer.

- **Patents.** Again, entities from the granting body to the surveyor may have found it useful to have such a reference work, especially during the granting process. These are more likely to be at a state level, but many counties also have copies. Additionally, many genealogists are participating in grant-platting projects to create such maps today. Check the DeedMapper Web site (see "Resources" on page 148) for current projects.

Building a Neighborhood

To place a deed on a map, you need what I call a "thumbtack"—some feature named as a corner on a deed that you can also find on a map, such as a crossroads, a bridge, or the mouth of a creek. Search for deeds adjoining parcels, looking for better geographic identifiers in their plats. If that is unsuccessful, continue to broaden the search to the parcels that adjoin the adjoining parcels in ever-widening circles. Look in two types of records.

Tip

- **Deeds.** This is usually our first attack. We search deed books for the names of neighbors. If the deed books have been abstracted and properly indexed, we can search for the names of waterways. However, it may be difficult to locate enough deeds.

- **Patents.** Any piece of property can be granted (transferred from government to individual) only one time (although it may have been entered or surveyed more than once). The granting entity had to keep the process organized, so often every tract is clearly identified as being on a particular waterway or part of some specific larger tract. Often it is easier to plat the grants, and then try and match your parcel to a patent or part of a patent.

It is easier to place a cluster of deeds on a map than it is to place a single deed, so look for those neighbors.

Tip

Remember that features such as public roads were usually run *between* property lines, not *through* them. Likewise, old property boundaries may be preserved in today's fence lines. On USGS quadrangle maps, these are marked with a dashed line and often make it easier than you would think to place a cluster of deeds.

PROBLEMS
Closure Errors

If you don't arrive back at the beginning, recheck your work. I find it most efficient to first check all the distances and then check all the angles. Don't just say "never mind, this is good enough." It will be helpful for future plats if you figure out what you did wrong in this one. Don't worry if things still don't quite "match up." Early surveying equipment was primitive, and the techniques were designed for flat, rectangular plots.

"Missing" Lines

Sometimes you will not have an explicit direction and/or distance for a line. This may be a meander ("thence along the meanders of the creek"), a partial ("60 poles along said road")—or where a mouse munched the deed book ("Thence North 3 [mouse munching] 9 poles"). **You can still plat the property if there is only one meandering line.**

Step By Step

STEP 1. Begin platting at the corner *after* the missing line.

STEP 2. When you come to the "thence to the beginning" corner, continue platting with the beginning corner.

STEP 3. When you come to the meander (it will be the only line left), draw a wavy or dotted line to indicate that it is a meander.

COMPUTER SOFTWARE

Computer software can help with the mechanical aspects of platting a deed (see "Resources"). It is, however, advisable to go through the full process by hand several times to better understand the basics of the software.

RESOURCES

C-Thru® Ruler Company, 6 Britton Drive, Bloomfield, CT 06002. (800) 243-8419. <www.cthruruler.com> Manufactures a circular land measure compass (A-26) and a clear six-inch ruler with millimeter markings (#18).

DeedMapper 3.0 for Windows. Land-platting software developed by Steve Broyles. Direct Line Software, 71 Neshobe Road, Newton, MA 02468. (617) 527-9566. <http://users.rcn.com/deeds/> DeedMapper maintains all deeds for a project in a single file and displays, prints, and exports multiple plats.

Hughes, Sarah S. *Surveyors and Statesmen: Land Measuring in Colonial Virginia*. Richmond: The Virginia Surveyors Foundation, Ltd. and The Virginia Association of Surveyors, 1979. Part II, "The Science of Surveying in the Seventeenth Century," is an excellent overview of the state of the "science" throughout the colonies.

Merriam-Webster's New Collegiate Dictionary. The classic, big red dictionary you bought for school contains many of the words you'll encounter in land records.

Pronto Land Measure, P.O. Box 279, Northville, MI 48167. (248) 347-3145. <www.prontolandmeasure.com> Carries a variety of land-platting tools and forms, including a Land Measure Compass with arm.

SCALE

Unless you are trying to use a specific map, such as a county highway map or an old map, you do not need to calculate the scale. Simply use the USGS quadrangle (1:24000) scale. However, if you do need to match a specific map—or if the distances on the deed are not given in poles, rods, or perches—use the following instructions.

USGS Scale

The scale of most USGS quadrangle maps is 1:24,000. The "divide by" number for a 1:24,000 map is 4.772130756, which we round to "divide by 4.8" (the difference is less than the width of a pencil line). Use the USGS scale 1:24,000 (1 millimeter = 4.8 poles) unless you have a reason to use a different scale. (Using this scale all the time helps you develop a sense of "how big" specific pieces of property are.)

To convert poles, rods, or perches (they're all the same thing) to millimeters at the USGS scale, divide the poles by 4.8. (If you don't have a calculator and have to divide by hand, divide the number of poles by 5 for a rough sketch in millimeters.)

Calculating the "Divide by" Number for Other Scales

All but old maps should provide a scale (a 1:x number, such as 1:6000). To figure out what number you should divide the number of poles by if you are using a ruler with millimeters, divide the big number of the scale of the map by 5029.2.

If you want to know how we calculated that magic number, here's the math:

$$\frac{1 \text{ unit on the map}}{x \text{ units on the ground}} \times \frac{16.5 \text{ feet}}{1 \text{ pole/rod/perch}} \times \frac{12 \text{ inches}}{1 \text{ foot}} \times \frac{2.54 \text{ cm}}{1 \text{ inch}} \times$$

$$\frac{10 \text{ mm}}{\text{cm}} = \frac{16.5 \times 12 \times 2.54 \times 10 \text{ mm on the map}}{x \text{ poles on the ground}} = \frac{5029.2 \text{ mm on the map}}{x \text{ poles on the ground}}$$

If the Map Doesn't State the 1:x Scale

If your map doesn't have a 1:x scale in the legend, you may have to calculate that also. For example, if it says 1 inch = 1 mile,

$$\frac{1 \text{ inch on the map}}{1 \text{ mile on the ground}} \times \frac{1 \text{ mile}}{5280 \text{ feet}} \times \frac{1 \text{ foot}}{12 \text{ inches}} =$$

$$\frac{1 \text{ inch on the map}}{5280 \times 12 \text{ inches on the ground}} = \frac{1 \text{ inch on the map}}{63,360 \text{ inches on the ground}}$$

The scale is 1:63,360, so you would calculate 63,360 ÷ 5029.2 and get 12.5984252 (use 12.6 for the divide-by number for poles).

	Corner markers	Neighbors	Direction	Distance	mm
corner	Beginning at:				
line					
corner					
line					
corner					
line					
corner					
line					
corner	to the beginning				

Grantor:
Grantee:
Acreage:
Waterways:
Citation:
Scale: USGS (1:24000); divide poles by 4.8 to get mm

Thumbnail sketch:

Figure 11-6 Photocopy this form for your own use.

TWELVE

Public-Land Survey System

P ublic land is land transferred directly from the *federal* government to individuals. States comprised primarily of such land are called *public-land states*. In public-land states, the land was surveyed before it was se-

\di'fin\ *vb*

Definitions

PUBLIC-LAND STATES

- Alabama
- Arizona
- Arkansas
- Alaska
- California
- Colorado
- Florida
- Idaho
- Illinois
- Indiana
- Iowa
- Kansas
- Louisiana
- Michigan
- Minnesota

- Mississippi
- Missouri
- Montana
- Nebraska
- Nevada
- New Mexico
- North Dakota
- Ohio
- Oklahoma
- Oregon
- South Dakota
- Utah
- Washington
- Wisconsin
- Wyoming

Definitions

DEFINITIONS

Meridian   North-south (vertical) line from which Ranges are counted east and west. Sometimes mentioned in records but not required for platting; the reference is unambiguous without it.

Range   Six-mile-wide strips counted east and west from a meridian.

Baseline   East-west (horizontal) line from which Townships are counted north and south.

Township   Six-mile-wide strips counted north and south from a baseline.

township   Six-mile-square unit of land (thirty-six square miles), defined, for example, as T5N, R5W (Township 5 North, Range 5 West). Occasionally in local practice the direction is omitted. A *named township* often approximately coincides with a township, but named townships are political boundaries.

section   ⅟₃₆ of a township; equal to 640 acres (1 square mile); numbered from 1 to 36, beginning in the upper right corner and snaking to the lower right corner.

quarter-section   160 acres, the amount that could be homesteaded according to the Homestead Act of 1862—theoretically enough to support a family.

---

lected for purchase, using the *rectangular-survey system*, which we generally refer to as the *township-range system*. This system defines six-mile-square townships, comprised of 36 one-mile-square sections. After the land was *opened*, it was disposed of in a planned, orderly manner in predefined rectangular lots.

LAND DESCRIPTIONS

Rectangular-survey land is located on a map by reading the description backward—from *right to left*.

Example: The northeast quarter of the southwest quarter of section twenty-six of Township Four South Range Nine West of the third Principal Meridian.

NE¼	of the SW¼	section 26	T4S	R9W	3rd PM
⑥	⑤	④	③	②	①
40 acres	160 acres	640 acres	23,040 acres		
⅟₁₆ sq. mi.	¼ sq. mi.	1 sq. mi.	36 sq. mi.		
		(1 mi.×1 mi.)	(6 mi.×6 mi.)		

The Meridians and Baselines

The first step in surveying was to establish the meridian and baseline and determine what area they would define. There are more than two dozen meridians (with their associated baselines). The earliest meridians were numbered, one through six, but most of them have names. Some cover several states, such as the fifth and sixth meridians, which opened up much of the central states, but some are small, such as those for several Indian reservations in the West.

The Townships and Ranges

Once a meridian and baseline were established, the next step was to survey the ranges (west and east from the meridian) and the townships (north and south from the baseline). Don't confuse these townships with named townships.

T3N R3W	T3N R2W	T3N R1W	T3N R1E	T3N R2E	T3N R3E
T2N R3W	T2N R2W	T2N R1W	T2N R1E	T2N R2E	T2N R3E
T1N R3W	T1N R2W	T1N R1W	T1N R1E	T1N R2E	T1N R3E
T1S R3W	T1S R2W	T1S R1W	T1S R1E	T1S R2E	T1S R3E
T2S R3W	T2S R2W	T2S R1W	T2S R1E	T2S R2E	T2S R3E
T3S R3W	T3S R2W	T3S R1W	T3S R1E	T3S R2E	T3S R3E

Figure 12-1 Townships are numbered east and west from the meridian line. Ranges are numbered north and south from the baseline.

Visitors to Salt Lake City (particularly genealogists focused on research at the Family History Library) may never have noticed the obelisk outside the wall at the southeast corner of Temple Square. This is the meridian marker for the Great Salt Lake Base and Meridian. The meridian runs north-south along the east side of Temple Square, and the baseline runs east-west on the south side of Temple Square. Thus, on a typical lunch hour, many researchers may have been in Township 1 North Range 1 West (Temple Square and the Family History Library), Township 1 South Range 1 West (Crossroads Mall), Township 1 South Range 1 East (ZCMI Mall), and Township 1 North Range 1 East (the Joseph Smith Memorial Building).

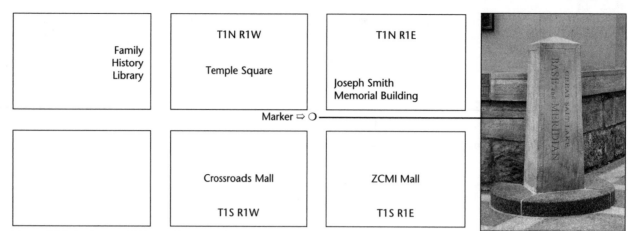

	T1N R1W	T1N R1E	
Family History Library	Temple Square	Joseph Smith Memorial Building	

Marker ⇨ ○ ━━━━━━━━━━━━

	Crossroads Mall	ZCMI Mall	
	T1S R1W	T1S R1E	

Figure 12-2 In August 1855 David H. Burr, First US Surveyor-General for Utah erected this stone pillar, marking the Great Salt Lake Baseline and Meridian. The pillar sits outside the southeast corner of the wall surrounding Temple Square in Salt Lake City.

Sections

Each township-range combination is six miles on each side. The next step was to survey it into 36 sections, each of which is one mile on a side, containing 640 acres. Section corners also were marked physically. At first it seems like the section numbering doesn't make sense because it isn't always from left to right. The surveyor numbered the sections as he walked them, as shown in the illustration (why he couldn't remember where he was and number them logically is beyond me). (See figure 12-3.)

Figure 12-3 Section numbering begins in the upper right corner of a Township-Range and snakes its way down to the lower right corner.

Section 36	Section 31	Section 32	Section 33	Section 34	Section 35	Section 36	Section 31
Section 1	↓ Section 6	← Section 5	← Section 4	← Section 3	← Section 2	← Section 1	Section 6
Section 12	→ Section 7	→ Section 8	→ Section 9	→ Section 10	→ Section 11	↓ Section 12	Section 7
Section 13	↓ Section 18	← Section 17	← Section 16	← Section 15	← Section 14	← Section 13	Section 18
Section 24	→ Section 19	→ Section 20	→ Section 21	→ Section 22	→ Section 23	↓ Section 24	Section 19
Section 25	↓ Section 30	← Section 29	← Section 28	← Section 27	← Section 26	← Section 25	Section 30
Section 36	→ Section 31	→ Section 32	→ Section 33	→ Section 34	→ Section 35	Section 36	Section 31
Section 1	Section 6	Section 5	Section 4	Section 3	Section 2	Section 1	Section 6

Because the earth is round, sections are a bit narrower at the top than at the bottom. You may notice some land descriptions for public land that show decimal values in the acres. This reflects the fact that a section did not contain quite 640 acres.

Public roads—which I grew up calling "section roads"—were often run between each section, hence one mile apart.

Quarter Sections

Most of our ancestors couldn't afford to buy a whole section of 640 acres, therefore the sections were further subdivided into quarter sections (160 acres), halves of quarter sections (80 acres), and quarters of quarter sections (40 acres).

Often deeds contain descriptions for what seem like several parcels of land. When you draw them out, it may be that they are contiguous but that the legal descriptions required each to be stated separately. Or you may find that they are checkerboarded. If your ancestor was optimistic, he may have hoped to purchase the in-between parcels as he acquired more funds and was willing to live with the inconvenience of unconnected land (and the chance that someone else would purchase the intervening parcel). (See figure 12-4.)

T4S R9W section 26

NW¼ of section 26		E½ of NE¼ of section 26
160 acres		80 acres
N½ of SW¼ of section 26 80 acres		
		SW¼ of SW¼ of sec. 26 40 acres

Figure 12-4 A section was one square mile (one mile on each side). It contained 640 acres, hence a quarter section contained 160 acres. Land sales were often in units as small as 40 acres (a quarter of a quarter section).

Finding Public Land on the Map

It is easy to locate a parcel of land in a public-land state on a map. Tax maps and county atlases are arranged by township and range. USGS quadrangle maps have the township, range, and section information already drawn on them in red (look in the margins for the change in township or range numbers). You will just have to calculate the location of your ancestor's forty-acre quarter of a quarter section.

ANOMALIES
Public-Land States With Nonstandard Systems

Much land had been granted in Ohio prior to the *Ordinance of 1785*. These sections (see Appendix A: Locality Reference), were, therefore, not surveyed under the system described in this chapter. Florida—the only Atlantic seaboard state to be a public-land state—had two areas surveyed nonstandard ways, as did Indiana.

In many areas, metes-and-bounds surveys survive that are holdovers from preemption claims arising from when early settlers (more popularly called *squatters*) or individuals receiving grants directly from an earlier government were able to retain their original property.

Figure 12-5 On the bottom portion of the county copy of the Monroe County, Illinois, plat book, you can see metes-and-bounds surveys arising from the early settlements at Prairie du Rocher, which lay mostly in Randolph County.

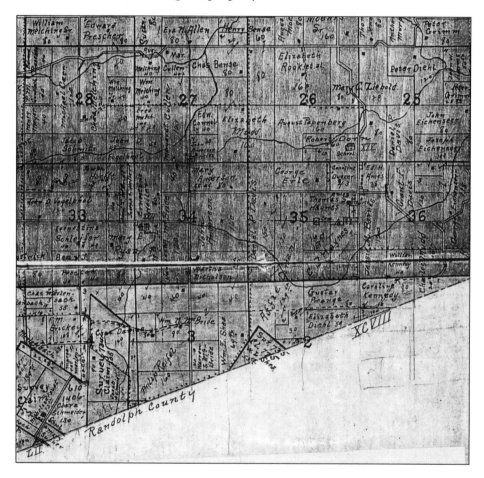

State-Land States With Rectangular Systems

In state-land states, a number of areas were presurveyed into rectangular plots, usually because they were part of a particular land act, such as a lottery. In some cases, they even used the terminology of *township* and *range*. However, these were not part of the public-land rectangular survey system as carried out by the federal government. Some examples:

Maine, New Hampshire, Vermont: Discontinuous portions of land were presurveyed rectangularly using the terms *township, range,* and *section* or *lot,* but the orientation and numbering systems were not consistent.

Georgia: The portions of Georgia that were part of the land lotteries were presurveyed on a somewhat rectangular basis, with lot numbers, but much of this system fell dormant.

Kentucky: The Jackson Purchase, Kentucky's westernmost portion, and the last to be opened for settlement following an Indian treaty, was presurveyed in a rectangular system, using the terms *township, range,* and *section.* Many of the early metes-and-bounds surveys were severely flawed and overlapping, so they were either abandoned or settled through the court system.

New York: Land companies in western parts of the state presurveyed the land, usually in a rectangular configuration with numbered lots.

Pennsylvania: The so-called "donation lands" (bounty land for Revolutionary War service) are laid out in a rectangular configuration and are numbered by lot.

Tennessee: North Carolina's western lands (Tennessee) were to have been ceded to the Confederation after the Revolution. However, it turned out that most of the Tennessee land had already been encumbered by often-overlapping Revolutionary grants made by North Carolina. It took years to iron out the conflicts. The western portion of the state was presurveyed in a rectangular system, using the terms *township, range,* and *section,* but it did not match the layout used in the federal system. It had the important advantage mentioned previously, however, of allowing simple and unambiguous transfer of property.

Texas: In the vast, empty reaches of Texas, a rectangular-survey system was found to be practical, but it was not used uniformly.

RESOURCES

Cazier, Lola. *Surveys and Surveyors of the Public Domain: 1785–1975.* Washington, D.C.: U.S. Department of the Interior, Bureau of Land Management, 1976.

Ernst, Joseph W. *With Compass and Chain: Federal Land Surveyors in the Old Northwest: 1785–1816.* New York: Arno Press, 1958, 1979.

Stewart, Lowell O. *Public Land Surveys: History, Instructions, Methods.* Minneapolis: Meyers Printing Co., 1935, 1976.

Locality Reference

The following references provide background information or are statewide references. Most land records are found at the county or local level. A literature survey of the first two items will point to many additional references.

The Church of Jesus Christ of Latter-day Saints. The Family History Library Catalog in FamilySearch. <www.familysearch.org> A fast and easy-to-use CD-ROM version is available for purchase from the Web site at the extremely reasonable price of five dollars (as of this writing). Also published on microfiche and available at the Family History Library and Family History Centers (the microfiche is no longer available for purchase); microfiche is the fastest version to scan to learn what is available on a locality.

Periodical Source Index (PERSI). An enormous project of the Allen County (Fort Wayne, Indiana) Public Library, which has a substantial periodical collection. PERSI identifies the primary topic of each article in each publication. More than 1.5 million entries (PERSI 2000), available on CD-ROM and online subscription at <www.ancestry.com>.

Read about your state of interest in the following publications:

Eichholz, Alice, ed. *Ancestry's Red Book: American State, County and Town Sources.* Rev. ed. Salt Lake City: Ancestry Incorporated, 1992. Organized by state, with each state covered by a local expert.

Luebking, Sandra Hargreaves. Chapter eight, "Research in Land and Tax Records." In *The Source*, rev. ed., edited by Loretto Dennis Szucs and Sandra Hargreaves Luebking. Salt Lake City: Ancestry Incorporated, 1996.

These online sources are the best way to locate the variety of Web sites that can help you use land records. The content of Web sites varies widely. You may find mailing addresses and office hours, articles, indexes, abstracts, and imaged documents.

Cyndi's List. <www.cyndislist.com>, created by Cyndi Howells, is the starting point for exploring what land information is available online and for accessing local Web sites of courthouses, archives, and libraries.

RootsWeb. <www.rootsweb.com>, an organized, linked system of Web sites created by volunteers, some of which include land-related information or information on research in the locality; now owned and hosted by Ancestry with free access.

The USGenWeb Project. <www.usgenweb.org>, an organized, linked system of Web sites created by volunteers, some of which include land-related information or information on research in the locality.

Land records of specific localities often are the subject of lectures at major conferences. Taping at major genealogical conferences is done by:

Repeat Performance, 2911 Crabapple Lane, Hobart, IN 46342. (219) 465-1234. <www.audiotapes.com>.

Public Land

The Bureau of Land Management has custody of most of the records relating to the transfer of property from the federal government to individuals. The Eastern States office ("eastern" is defined as east of or bordering on the Mississippi River) has been aggressive about making many of its records available to the public by providing indexes and sometimes images. Because the patents are indexed online for the eastern states, earlier published works listing names are not included here; however, they're worth seeking out, especially for the information in the introductions.

Bureau of Land Management (BLM)—Eastern States, General Land Office (GLO) Records Automation. Its Web site <www.glorecords.blm.gov> lets you search in a variety of ways and access more than two million federal land patents issued between 1820 and 1908 for the eastern states and more than two million serial patents issued after 1908 for all public-land states. You can even order a copy of the patent on plain or parchment paper. Additional indexing and imaging is in process. The BLM maintains survey plats and field notes for many states, which are not on the Web site. General Land Office Records Access Staff, Bureau of Land Management—Eastern States, 7450 Boston Blvd., Springfield, VA 22153-3121.

Bureau of Land Management (BLM)—Western States, U.S. Department of the Interior, 5353 Yellowstone Road, P.O. Box 1828, Cheyenne, WY 82003-1828.

National Archives and Records Administration (NARA) in Washington, D.C., maintains the entry files for the Eastern States.

McMullin, Phillip W. *Grassroots of America*. Salt Lake City: Gendex Corp. 1972; reprinted Greenville, S.C.: Southern Historical Press, 1993. Consolidated index to *American State Papers*.

Szucs, Loretto Dennis, and Sandra Hargreaves Luebking, eds. *The Archives*, Salt Lake City: Ancestry Incorporated, 1988. See state-by-state table for holdings of regional branches for public-land states.

U.S. Congress, *American State Papers, Public Lands*. Washington, D.C.: Gale and Seaton, 1832–61; reprinted Greenville, S.C.: Southern Historical Press, 1993. These include claims (preemptions) presented by individuals already settled on public land (squatters). For index, see McMullin, *Grassroots of America*.

Alabama   **public-land state**

See Public Land above. Alabama has two meridians: the St. Stephens Meridian and the Huntsville Meridian. However, because the southern border and the border of the Tallahassee Meridian survey did not match, some far-southern Alabama lands are surveyed from the Tallahassee Meridian. Land records at the county level are in the Office of the Probate Judge.

LAND OFFICE	OPENED
St. Stephens	1803
Nashville, Tennessee	1807
Huntsville	1807
Milledgeville, Georgia	1815
Cahaba	1815
Tuscaloosa	1820
Sparta	1820
Mardisville	1832
Montgomery	1832
Demopolis	1833
Lebanon	1842
Elba	1854
Centre	1856
Greenville	1856
Mobile	1867

Barefield, Marilyn Davis, comp. [also Hahn, Marilyn Davis]. *Old Cahaba Land Office Records and Military Warrants, 1817–1853.* Birmingham: Southern University Press, 1986. *Old Demopolis Land Office Records and Military Warrants, 1818–1860, and Records of the Vine and Olive Colony.* Easley, S.C.: Southern Historical Press, 1988. *Old Huntsville Land Office Records and Military Warrants, 1810–1854.* Easley, S.C.: Southern Historical Press, 1985. *Old Mardisville, Lebanon, and Centre Land Office Records and Military Warrants, 1834–1860.* Greenville, S.C.: Southern Historical Press, 1990. *Old Montgomery Land Office Records and Military Warrants, 1834–1869.* Birmingham: Southern University Press, 1991. *Old Sparta and Elba Land Office Records and Military Warrants, 1822–1860.* Easley, S.C.: Southern Historical Press, 1983. *Old St. Stephen's Land Office Records and American State Papers, Public Lands.* Easley, S.C.: Southern Historical Press, 1983. *Old Tuskaloosa Land Office Records and Military Warrants, 1821–1855.* Easley, S.C.: Southern Historical Press, 1984.

Alaska   public-land state

See Public Land *on page 159. Some of Alaska's public lands weren't surveyed until relatively recently. Three of its surveys were done at the beginning of the twentieth century (Copper River Meridian, Fairbanks Meridian, Seward Meridian), and two were not established until 1956 (Kateel River Meridian and Uniat Meridian). Records for transfers between individuals are in the Office of the Recorder for each judicial district.*

LAND OFFICE	OPENED
Sitka	1884
Juneau	1902
Nome	1907
Fairbanks	1907
Anchorage	1923

Alaska BLM Office, Anchorage Federal Office Building, 222 W. Seventh Avenue, #13; Anchorage, AK 99513-7599. (907) 271-5960.

Arizona   public-land state

See Public Land *on page 159. Arizona's land is surveyed from the Gila and Salt River Meridians, except for land in the Navajo Reservation, which is surveyed from the Navajo Meridian. Land records at the county level are in the Recorder's Office.*

LAND OFFICE	OPENED
Prescott	1868
Florence	1873
Gila	1873
Tucson	1881
Phoenix	1905

Arizona BLM Office, 222 North Central, Phoenix, AZ 85004-2203. (602) 417-9200.

Arkansas   public-land state

See Public Land *on page 159. When the first land office opened in July 1820, there were already many private, preemption, and territorial claims made as early as 1803. Arkansas's land is surveyed from the Fifth Principal Meridian. Lovely Purchase Donation Claims are in northwest Arkansas. Bounty land for the War of 1812 was awarded by lottery. Land records at the county level are in the Office of the County Clerk or the Clerk of the Circuit Court.*

LAND OFFICE	OPENED
Little Rock	1818
Batesville	1818
Washington	1832
Fayetteville	1832
Helena	1834
Clarksville	1838
Champagnolle	1845
Huntsville	1860
Little Rock (reopened)	1866
Washington (reopened)	1867
Clarksville (reopened)	1867
Dardanelle	1870
Harrison	1870
Camden	1871

Allen, Desmond Walls. *Arkansas Donation Lands; 14 December 1876–30 April 1880.* Conway, Ark.: Arkansas Research, Inc., 2000. *Arkansas Donation Lands; 1 May 1880–30 June 1882.* Conway, Ark.: Arkansas Research, Inc., 2000.

———. *Arkansas Swamp Land Sales 1855–1868*; *Arkansas Swamp Land Sales 1868–1879*; *Arkansas Swamp Land Sales 1879–1921*; *Arkansas Swamp Land Sales 1921–2001*. Conway, Ark.: Arkansas Research, Inc., 2001.

———. *Arkansas School Lands Sales, 1853–1997*. Conway, Ark.: Arkansas Research, Inc., 2001.

———. *Arkansas Land Patents: County Series*. Conway, Ark.: Arkansas Research, Inc., 1991. Fifty-seven volumes covering all seventy-five Arkansas counties.

Christensen, Katheren. *Arkansas Military Bounty Grants (War of 1812)*. n.p.: Arkansas Ancestors, 1971.

California   public-land state

See Public Land *on page 159. There were substantial private claims, about 30 percent of the state's land, based on Spanish and Mexican grants. California is surveyed from the Humbolt, Mount Diablo, and San Bernardino Meridians. Land records at the county level are in the Recorder's Office.*

LAND OFFICE	OPENED
Los Angeles	1853
Benicia	1853
Marysville	1853
San Francisco	1857
Humboldt	1858
Stockton	1858
Visalia	1858
Sacramento	1866
Aurora, Nevada	1868
Susanville	1871
Shasta	1871
Independence	1873
Bodie	1878
Redding	1890
Eureka	1899
Oakland	1906

California BLM Office, 2800 Cottage Way, Sacramento, CA 95825-1885. (916) 978-4400.

Colorado   public-land state

See Public Land *on page 159. Colorado's land is surveyed from the Sixth Principal Meridian and the New Mexico Meridian, plus a tiny portion from the Ute Meridian. Much of its land was homesteaded. Land records at the county level are in the Office of the County Clerk and Recorder.*

LAND OFFICE	OPENED
Golden City	1863
Denver	1864

Fair Play	1867
Central City	1867
Pueblo	1870
Del Norte	1874
Lake City	1877
Leadville	1879
Durango	1882
Gunnison	1882
Glenwood Springs	1884
Lamar	1886
Montrose	1888
Akron	1890
Sterling	1890
Hugo	1890

Colorado BLM Office, 2850 Youngfield St., Lakewood, CO 80215-7093. (303) 239-3600.

Connecticut   original colony

Original grants were by the town proprietors. Deeds are recorded at the town level by the Town Clerk.

Melnyk, Marcia D., ed. *Genealogist's Handbook for New England Research.* 4th ed. Boston: New England Historic Genealogical Society, 1999.

Delaware   original colony

Delaware was originally the "three lower counties" of Pennsylvania, and all early grants were made by the Penn Proprietary. However, the grants were usually at least referenced in county court records, loose land papers were turned over to Delaware, and the "Fugitive Records Project" repatriated or copied most of the remaining records, so research should begin in Delaware. The boundary dispute between Delaware and Maryland resulted in many early grants and deeds for Sussex County land being recorded in Maryland. Land records at the county level are in the office of the Recorder of Deeds. However, the earlier deeds are now in the possession of the Delaware Public Archives and have been microfilmed.

District of Columbia

The District of Columbia was established in 1792. Land transactions prior to that time are in Virginia or Maryland. Deeds after the district was formed are in the Office of the Recorder of Deeds.

Angevine, Erma Miller. "Research in the District of Columbia." *Research in the District of Columbia.* Arlington, Va.: National Genealogical Society, 1992. See especially "Land Records."

Gahn, Bessie Wilmarth. *Original Patentees of Land at Washington Prior to 1700.* Baltimore: Genealogical Publishing Company, 1969.

Florida   **public-land state**

See Public Land *on page 159. Florida, although on the east coast, is a public-land state. Florida's land is surveyed from the Tallahassee Meridian. There were many early Spanish grants. There was a small amount of donation land in East Florida, granted by an act of 1842 to persons settling and bearing arms during the Seminole War. Florida has some homesteaded land. Land records at the county level are in the Office of the Clerk of Court.*

LAND OFFICE	OPENED
Tallahassee	1823
St. Augustine	1823
Newnansville	1842
Tampa	1854
Tallahassee (reopened)	1866
Gainesville	1872

Davidson, Alvie L. *Florida Land: Records of the Tallahassee and Newnansville General Land Office, 1825–1892.* Bowie, Md.: Heritage Books, Inc., 1989.

Historical Records Survey. *Spanish Land Grants in Florida.* 5 vols. Tallahassee: State Library Board, 1940–41.

Georgia   **original colony**

Headrights were used in Georgia in the statehood period to promote settlement in the eastern part of the state where bounty land was also granted for Revolutionary War service. Land lotteries in 1805, 1807, 1820, 1821, 1827, 1832 (Cherokee), 1832 (Gold), and 1833 were used to promote settlement in the western and northern portions of the state. The lists of lottery winners have been published; the 1805 list names all applicants. Lottery land was presurveyed as rectangular lots for each lottery. Land records at the state level are in the Office of the Surveyor General; at the county level they are in the Office of the Clerk of Superior Court or the Ordinary Court.

Davis, Robert Scott. "Research in Georgia." *National Genealogical Society Quarterly* 80 (1992): 89–114. See especially "Land Records."

Wood, Virginia S., and Ralph V. *1805 Land Lottery of Georgia* (Cambridge, Ga.: Greenwood Press, 1964). Lucas, Silas Emmett Jr. *1807 Land Lottery of Georgia*; *1820 and 1821 Land Lotteries of Georgia*; Houston, Martha Lou, *1827 Land Lottery of Georgia*; Smith, James F., *1832 Cherokee Land Lottery*; Lucas, Silas Emmet *1832 Gold Lottery of Georgia*; Davis, Robert Scott, *1833 Land Lottery of Georgia* (Easley, S.C.: Southern Historical Press, 1968, 1973, 1975, 1968, 1976, 1991). "1807 Land Lottery Eligibles, Oglethorpe County." *The Georgia Genealogist* 32 (1977)–36 (1978).

Hawaii   **state-land state**

Prior to the 1840s, land in Hawaii was considered to belong to the king, in a feudal system not unlike that in Europe. There were extensive private claims made when the system changed in the 1840s. Land records for the transition and the modern period are in the Bureau of Conveyances.

Idaho   **public-land state**

See Public Land *on page 159. Idaho's land is surveyed from the Boise Meridian. Land records at the county level are in the Office of the County Recorder.*

LAND OFFICE	OPENED
Boise	1866
Lewiston	1866
Oxford	1879
Hailey	1883
Coeur d'Alene	1884
Blackfoot	1886

Idaho BLM Office, 1387 S. Vennell Way, Boise, ID 83709-1657. (208) 373-4000.

Illinois   **public-land state**

See Public Land *on page 159. Illinois's land is surveyed from the Second, Third, and Fourth Principal Meridians. There were earlier claims, especially along the Mississippi River. Bounty land for the War of 1812 was awarded in central Illinois. Land records at the county level are in the Office of the County Recorder or County Clerk.*

LAND OFFICE	OPENED
Kaskaskia	1804
Shawneetown	1812
Edwardsville	1816
Palestine	1820
Vandalia	1820
Springfield	1822
Danville	1831
Quincy	1831
Chicago	1834
Galena	1834
Dixon	1840

Illinois Public Domain Land Tract Sales database. <www.sos.state.il.us/depart ments/archives/data_lan.html>.

Indiana   **public-land state**

See Public Land *on page 159. Indiana's land is surveyed from the First and Second Principal Meridians. Early claims existed along the Ohio River, particularly near Vincennes. Bounty land was given to officers and men under George Rogers Clark in the Revolutionary War along the Ohio River. Land records at the county level are in the Recorder's Office.*

Cincinnati Land Office, Indiana Land. Some patents for "the Gore" in southeastern Indiana were issued by the Cincinnati Land Office (they are indexed on the BLM Web site as Ohio).

LAND OFFICE	OPENED
Vincennes	1804
Jeffersonville	1810
Terre Haute	1819
Brookville	1819
Crawfordsville	1819
Indianapolis	1820
Fort Wayne	1822
La Porte	1833
Winanac	1840

Iowa   public-land state

See Public Land *on page 159. Iowa's land is surveyed from the Fifth Principal Meridian. There were many settlers in Iowa before the land offices opened who formed "land claim clubs" in an attempt to keep their land. More land was claimed in Iowa by virtue of bounty-land scrip than in any other state. Land records at the county level are in the Office of the Recorder.*

LAND OFFICE	OPENED
Dubuque	1838
Burlington	1838
Fairfield	1842
Marion	1843
Iowa City	1846
Chariton	1852
Des Moines	1852
Council Bluffs	1855
Fort Dodge	1855
Sioux City	1855
Decorah	1855
Osage	1855

Kansas   public-land state

See Public Land *on page 159. Kansas's land is surveyed from the Sixth Principal Meridian. Land records at the county level are in the Office of the Register of Deeds or the County Clerk.*

LAND OFFICE	OPENED
Lecompton	1854
Doniphan	1857
Kickapoo	1857
Ogden	1857
Fort Scott	1857
Junction City	1859
Atchison	1861
Topeka	1861
Mapleton	1861

Humboldt	1861
Augusta	1870
Salina	1870
Concordia	1870
Neodesha	1871
Independence	1871
Cawker City	1872
Wichita	1872
Kirwin	1874
Larned	1874
Hays City	1874
Wakeeny	1879
Oberlin	1880
Garden City	1881
Dodge City	1893
Colby	1893

New Mexico BLM Office, 1474 Rodeo Road, Santa Fe, NM 87505. (505) 438-7582.

Kentucky   state-land state

Kentucky's land belonged to Virginia before it ceded the remaining ungranted land to the Confederation. Like many of the transitional states, Kentucky's land was granted through a variety of programs. Fortunately, the indexes to the eighteen early series have been published by Jillson (below). When searching for a pioneer ancestor in the printed volumes, check all eighteen lists, and be aware that several lists are only somewhat alphabetical, because they were taken directly from the indexes and not realphabetized. Land in the Jackson Purchase was surveyed using a rectangular-survey system. Land records at the county level are in the Office of the County Clerk or Recorder.

Jillson, Willard Rouse. *Old Kentucky Entries and Deeds.* Originally published in 1926; reprinted Baltimore: Genealogical Publishing Co., 1987. Transcripts of the indexes of nine separate series of early Kentucky land records. Lincoln Entries (1779–1787); Fayette Entries (1782–1794); Jefferson Entries (1779–1785); Military Warrants (1782–1793); Military Entries (1784–1797); Court of Appeals—Grantees (1783–1846); Court of Appeals—Grantors (1783–1846); Court of Appeals—Wills (1769–1850); Court of Appeals—Attorneys (1781–1853). *The Kentucky Land Grants.* 2 vols. Originally published in 1925; reprinted Baltimore: Genealogical Publishing Co., 1971. Transcripts of the indexes of nine additional series of early Kentucky land records. Volume 1: Virginia Grants (1782–1792); Old Kentucky Grants (1793–1856); Grants South of Green River (1797–1866); Tellico Grants (1803–1853); Kentucky Land Warrants (1816–1873); Grants West of Tennessee River (1822–1858); Grants South of Walker's Line (1825–1923). Volume 2: Warrants for Headright (1827–

1849); Grants in the County Court Orders (1836–1924). *Kentucky Land Records*. A convenient, consolidated CD-ROM publication by Family-TreeMaker (now Genealogy.com) of the Jillson publications.

Louisiana   public-land state

See Public Land on page 159. About 12 percent of the land was claimed successfully by individuals before the land could be granted. Louisiana's land is surveyed from the Louisiana and St. Helena Meridians. Low-lying swampland made the surveying difficult and the square grid patterns somewhat impractical in terms of ownership. Land records at the parish level (counties existed only briefly in the state) are in the Office of the Clerk of Courts.

LAND OFFICE	OPENED
New Orleans	1811
Opelousas	1811
Ouachita	1811
St. Helena	1819
Monroe	1821
Greensburg	1837
Natchitoches	1838
Baton Rouge	1844

Maine   state-land state

Until 1820, Maine was part of Massachusetts and land was granted by the town proprietors. Before the Revolution, it had only one county—York. Some very early transactions may be found in Ipswich Deeds and Old Norfolk County Deeds. After the Revolution, land was surveyed in townships and ranges (most of the northern portion of the state) and sold to pay for war debts. Through 1824 these records are in the Massachusetts State Archives. Land records at the county level are in the Registry of Deeds.

Melnyk, Marcia D., ed. *Genealogist's Handbook for New England Research.* 4th ed. Boston: New England Historic Genealogical Society, 1999.

Maryland   original colony

Land in Maryland was granted under the proprietorship of Lord Baltimore, who collected quitrents. These early tracts were usually named, sometimes providing clues to origins or family connections. Maryland granted land that was later determined to be in Delaware, so both grants and deeds for parts of Sussex County, Delaware, are found in Maryland records at the state level and in several counties. Land records at the county level are in the Office of the Clerk of Court.

Bond, Beverly W. "The Quitrent System in Maryland." *Maryland Historical Magazine* 5 (1910): 350–65.

Coldham, Peter Wilson. *Settlers of Maryland.* Vol. 1 (1679–1700), vol. 2 (1701–1730), vol. 3 (1731–1750), vol. 4 (1766–1783), vol. 5 (1751–1765). Baltimore: Genealogical Publishing Company, 1995–96.

Massachusetts   original colony

Land in Massachusetts was granted by the crown to the Plymouth Colony and the Massachusetts Bay Colony, who in turn "planted" towns. The proprietors of each town were responsible for distributing the land, usually by drawing lots, creating random initial settlement patterns. Initial grants are at the town level. See Melnyk (below) for the current location of records. Two groups of early deeds—Ipswich Deeds and Old Norfolk County Deeds—are often overlooked for transactions in Essex County and in present-day New Hampshire and Maine.

Galvin, William Francis. *Historical Data Relating to Counties, Cities, and Towns in Massachusetts.* 5th ed. Boston: New England Historic Genealogical Society, 1997.

Melnyk, Marcia D., ed. *Genealogist's Handbook for New England Research.* 4th ed. Boston: New England Historic Genealogical Society, 1999.

Registry of Deeds, Southern Essex District, has put images of its early deed books online <www.salemdeeds.com>. Although the site mentions indexes, these deeds are not indexed and must instead be accessed from the "Historic" icon by book and page number. The page numbers are those of the restored copies, which may not agree with a page number you have found through a citation or an index. Both page numbers are visible on the images, so it is possible to find the entry you wish. (Hint: Early pages were folio numbered— one number for every two pages—so try doubling the number.)

Thwing, Annie Haven. *The Crooked and Narrow Streets of Boston 1630–1822* (Boston: Marshall Jones Company, 1920) and "Inhabitants and Estates of the Town of Boston 1630–1800" (the augmented Thwing card file at the Massachusetts Historical Society), published together on CD-ROM (Boston: New England Historic Genealogical Society, 2001). Provides an extensive history of the land-settlement of Boston, as well as details about early landholders and land transactions.

Michigan   public-land state

See Public Land *on page 159. Michigan's land is surveyed from the Michigan Meridian. Land records at the county level are in the Office of the Register of Deeds.*

LAND OFFICE	OPENED
Detroit	1804
Old Monroe	1829
White Pigeon Prairie	1831
New Monroe	1834
Kalamazoo	1834
Genesee	1836
Ionia	1836
Sault Ste. Marie	1847
Duncan	1854
Marquette	1857
East Saginaw	1857

Mackinac	1858
Traverse City	1858
Reed City	1878
Grayling	1888

Minnesota   public-land state

See Public Land *on page 159. Minnesota's land is surveyed from the Fourth and Fifth Principal Meridians. Land records at the county level are in the Office of the County Recorder (formerly Register of Deeds).*

LAND OFFICE	OPENED
Stillwater	1847
Sauk Rapids	1852
Brownsville	1854
Winona	1854
Minneapolis	1854
Red Wing	1854
Chatfield	1856
Buchanan	1856
Henderson	1856
Faribault	1857
St. Cloud	1858
Forest City	1858
Cambridge	1858
St. Peter	1858
Otter Tail City	1859
Duluth	1859
Sunrise City	1860
Taylor's Falls	1861
Winnebago City	1861
Greenleaf	1866
Alexandria	1868
Jackson	1869
New Ulm	1870
Litchfield	1870
Redwood Falls	1872
Oak Lake	1872
Detroit	1872
Worthington	1874
Benson	1876
Fergus Falls	1876
Crooksten	1878
Tracy	1880
Marshall	1889
Cass Lake	1903

Warren, Paula Stuart. "Research in Minnesota." *National Genealogical Society Quarterly* 77 (1989): 22–42; reprinted as *Research in Minnesota*. Arlington, Va.: National Genealogical Society, 1992. See especially "Land Records."

Mississippi   public-land state

See Public Land *on page 159. Mississippi's land is surveyed from five meridians: the Chickasaw Meridian, Choctaw Meridian, Huntsville Meridian, St. Stephen's Meridian, and Washington Meridian. Land records at the county level are in the Office of the Clerk of the Chancery Court.*

LAND OFFICE	OPENED
Washington	1803
Augusta	1819
Jackson	1819
Mount Salus	1827
Columbus	1833
Chocochuma	1833
Pontotoc	1836
Grenada	1840
Paulding	1860

Missouri   public-land state

See Public Land *on page 159. Part of the Louisiana Purchase, Missouri's early French settlements meant it had a not-insignificant amount of land along the Mississippi River that was settled (sometimes with grants and surveys in metes-and-bounds). Missouri's land is surveyed from the Fifth Principal Meridian. Bounty land for the War of 1812 was awarded in northern Missouri. Land records at the county level are in the Office of the Recorder of Deeds or County Recorder.*

LAND OFFICE	OPENED
Franklin	1818
St. Louis	1818
Jackson	1818
Lexington	1823
Palmyra	1824
Fayette	1832
Springfield	1834
Plattsburg	1842
Clinton	1843
Milan	1849
Warsaw	1855
Boonville	1857
Ironton	1861
Springfield (reopened)	1866

Kliethermes, Sharon A. *Missouri School Land Sales.* Loose Creek, Mo.: Dogwood Publications, 1987.

Porter, Pamela Boyer, and Ann Carter Fleming. "Research in Missouri," reprinted as *Research in Missouri.* Arlington, Va.: National Genealogical Society, 1999; originally published in *National Genealogical Society Quarterly* 87 (1999): 85–116. See especially "Land Records."

Rising, Marsha Hoffman. *Opening the Ozarks: 1835–1839* (to be published). This study of the first one thousand men and women to patent land at the Springfield Land Office will help greatly in our understanding of the mobility patterns of frontier settlers.

Montana   public-land state

See Public Land *on page 159. Montana's land is surveyed from the [no number] Principal Meridian. Land records at the county level are in the Office of the County Clerk and Recorder.*

LAND OFFICE	OPENED
Helena	1867
Bozeman	1874
Miles City	1880
Lewistown	1890
Missoula	1890
Kalispell	1897
Great Falls	1902
Billings	1906
Glasgow	1907

Montana BLM Office, P.O. Box 36800, Billings, MT 59101-6800. (406) 896-5000.

Nebraska   public-land state

See Public Land *on page 159. Nebraska's land is surveyed from the Sixth Principal Meridian. The first land homesteaded under the act of 1862 is in Gage County near Beatrice in southeastern Nebraska, which today is Homestead National Monument. The Kinkaid Act of 1904 allowed homesteads of 640 acres in the arid sand hills of western Nebraska. Railroad lands cut a broad swath across the state. Land records at the county level are in the Office of the Register of Deeds.*

LAND OFFICE	OPENED
Omaha City	1854
Brownsville	1857
Nebraska City	1857
Dakota City	1857
Beatrice	1868
Lincoln	1868
Grand Island	1868
West Point	1869
Lowell	1872
North Platte	1872
Norfolk	1873

Bloomington	1874
Niobrara	1875
Neligh	1881
Valentine	1882
McCook	1882
Sidney	1886
Chadron	1886
O'Neill	1888
Alliance	1890
Broken Bow	1890

Wyoming BLM Office; 5353 Yellowstone Road, P.O. Box 1828; Cheyenne, WY 82003-1828; (307) 775-6256. Nebraska is under the Wyoming office.

Nimmo, Sylvia. "Research in Nebraska." *National Genealogical Society Quarterly* 77 (1989): 260–76. See especially "Land Records."

Potter, James E. *U.S. Government Land Laws in Nebraska 1854–1904.* Nebraska State Historical Society Reference Information Guide No. 7.

Nevada   public-land state

See Public Land *on page 159. Nevada's land is surveyed from the Mount Diablo Meridian. Most land transactions focused on minerals, rather than ground, and some transactions are recorded by mining district. Land records at the county level are in the Office of the County Recorder.*

LAND OFFICE	OPENED
Carson City	1862
Austin	1867
Aurora	1868
Belmont	1868
Elko	1872
Eureka	1873
Pioche	1874
Reno	1911

Nevada BLM Office, 1340 Financial Blvd., P.O. Box 12000, Reno, NV 89520-0006. (775) 861-6400.

New Hampshire   original colony

Early deeds are found in Ipswich Deeds and Old Norfolk County Deeds. Initial transfers of land were done by town proprietors. Shortly before the Revolution, land records began being recorded at the county level in the Office of the County Recorder.

Boulton, Nathaniel. *Documents and Records Relating to Towns in New Hampshire,* vols. 8 and 9 in *New Hampshire Provincial and State Papers.* Concord: Charles C. Pearson, printer, 1875.

Melnyk, Marcia D., ed. *Genealogist's Handbook for New England Research.* 4th ed. Boston: New England Historic Genealogical Society, 1999.

New Jersey   **original colony**

The proprietors of East Jersey and West Jersey granted land to individuals. These proprietors records are private records. Generally, colonial-era deeds were recorded by the proprietors; federal-era deeds are found in the Office of the County Clerk or County Register.

New Mexico   **public-land state**

See Public Land *on page 159. Large portions of New Mexico land had been granted by Spain and by Mexico. Federal-period land was granted as Donation Lands and through other federal programs, such as homestead and cash sales. New Mexico's land is surveyed from the New Mexico Principal Meridian. Land records at the county level are in the Office of the County Clerk or County Recorder.*

LAND OFFICE	OPENED
Santa Fe	1858
La Mesilla	1874
Las Cruces	1883
Folsom	1888
Roswell	1889
Clayton	1892

New Mexico BLM Office, 1474 Rodeo Road, Santa Fe, NM 87505. (505) 438-7400.

New York   **original colony**

New York's earliest grants were Dutch, in the area of present-day New York City, Long Island, and the Hudson River Valley. Unlike other colonies, New York used a manorial system in some areas, in which farmers simply leased land from the "lord of the manor." Unfortunately, manor records are private and, since they did not transfer ownership of land, were not necessarily of long-term value and rarely survive. Some land in central New York was given by lottery as bounty land to Revolutionary War soldiers who served for New York; few settled on the land. Land in what became the Holland Land Company was presurveyed into rectangular lots. A fire destroyed many early land records. Land records at the county level are in the Office of the County Recorder.

Kim, Sung Bok. *Landlord and Tenant in Colonial New York: Manorial Society, 1664–1775.* Chapel Hill, N.C.: University of North Carolina Press, 1978.

Livsey, Karen E. *Western New York Land Transactions.* 2 vols. Baltimore: Genealogical Publishing Co., 1991, 1996. These volumes index records of the Holland Land Company, which are available on microfilm.

O'Callaghan, E.B. *Calendar of New York Colonial Manuscripts; Indorsed Land Papers 1643–1803.* Harrison, N.Y.: Harbor Hill Books, 1987.

North Carolina   **original colony**

North Carolina originally was governed by Lords Proprietors, who made the land grants. When North Carolina became a royal colony, Earl Granville did not give up (sell) his proprietorship and continued to make grants. Both groups used headrights to promote settlement. Land grants in North Carolina are indexed in a card file at the Land Grant Office. Land records at the county level are in the Office of the Register of Deeds.

Hofmann, Margaret M. *The Granville District of North Carolina 1748–1763, Abstracts of Land Grants.* 5 vols. Weldon, N.C.: Roanoke News Co., 1986–95.

Hofmann, Margaret M. *Colony of North Carolina, 1735–1764, Abstracts of Land Patents; Colony of North Carolina, 1765–1775, Abstracts of Land Patents.* Weldon, N.C.: Roanoke News Co., 1983, 1984.

Leary, Helen F.M., ed. *North Carolina Research: Genealogy and Local History.* Raleigh: North Carolina Genealogical Society, 1996.

North Dakota   **public-land state**

See Public Land *on page 159. North Dakota's land is surveyed from the Fifth Principal Meridian. Land records at the county level are in the Office of the Register of Deeds.*

LAND OFFICE	OPENED
Pembina	1870
Fargo	1874
Bismarck	1874
Grand Forks	1880
Devils Lake	1884
Minot	1890
Dickinson	1904
Williston	1906

Montana BLM Office, P.O. Box 36800, Billings, MT 59101-6800. (406) 896-5000.

Ohio   **public-land state**

See Public Land *on page 159. Ohio was the state in which public-land surveying was defined . . . and redefined . . . and redefined. It has several variations on the township-range-section system, plus several special districts or purchases, the largest or most confusing of which are described below. Land records at the county level are in the Office of the County Recorder.*

Cincinnati Land Office, Indiana Land. Some patents for "the Gore" in southeastern Indiana were issued by the Cincinnati Land Office (they are indexed on the BLM Web site as Ohio).

Connecticut Western Reserve. This bounty-land area in northeastern Ohio was administered by Connecticut. Records are at Connecticut State Archives; there are no records at BLM.

Donation Tract. Land in southern Ohio under an act of 1792 given to men who would bear arms to serve as protection against the Indians to promote settlement for the Ohio Company.

Fire Lands. This area was granted to residents of nine towns in Connecticut that were burned by the British in the Revolutionary War.

First Seven Ranges. This was supposed to be the first area in the public domain opened for sale, but only the first four ranges were surveyed when the office opened in September 1787 and no section lines had been run. The range numbering began at the Pennsylvania border. The township numbering began at the Ohio River and ran northward; however, it started over each time at the Ohio River, thus, for example, the township to the west of T8N R1W is T12N R2W (instead of T8N R2W, as became the standard). The sections were numbered in the pattern used in the rest of the public domain.

Ohio Company Purchase. This was part of the Ohio River Survey. Like the first seven ranges, this land abutted the Ohio River and was therefore settled early. Because of the fractional pieces along the Ohio River, land title was often conveyed by lot number.

Ohio River Survey. This survey continued the system established in the First Seven Ranges, numbering ranges westward from the Pennsylvania border and the townships northward from the Ohio River. This survey is discontinuous, with part of it north of the U.S. Military District and part of it south.

Symmes Purchase (Miami Purchase or Land between the Miami Rivers). The records of this private purchase are lost, although a few local records survive.

U.S. Military District. This was granted as bounty land to officers and soldiers of the Continental Army under an act in 1796.

Virginia Military District. Land in this large district was granted by Virginia. Most of the land in this bounty-land area in central Ohio is surveyed in metes-and-bounds, as is Virginia. There are very few records for the district in BLM possession.

LAND OFFICE	OPENED
Steubenville	1800
Marietta	1800
Chillicothe	1800
Cincinnati	1800
Zanesville	1803
Canton	1807
Wooster	1809
Delaware	1819
Piqua	1819
Tiffin	1819
Bucyrus	1819
Wapakoneta	1819
Lima	1835
Marion	1836
Upper Sandusky	1843
Defiance	1848

Bell, Carol Willsey. *Ohio Lands: Steubenville Land Office, 1800–1820.* Youngstown: the author, 1983.

Berry, Ellen Thomas, and David A. Berry, comps. *Early Ohio Settlers: Purchasers of Land in Southeastern Ohio, 1800–1840* and *Early Ohio Settlers: Purchasers of Land in East and East Central Ohio, 1800–1840.* Baltimore: Genealogical Publishing Company, 1984, 1989.

Ohio Lands: A Short History. This booklet is regularly produced by the Auditor of the State of Ohio for use in Ohio schools. The newest version, for students, called *Along the Ohio Trail: A Short History of Ohio Lands* is available at <www.auditor.state.oh.us>, with an interactive CD version planned.

Smith, Clifford Neal. *Federal Land Series.* 5 vols. Chicago: American Library Association, 1972–86.

Oklahoma   **public-land state**

See Public Land *on page 159. Oklahoma's land is surveyed from the Cimarron and Indian Meridians. It opened each new area for settlement with a flamboyant land rush (who says marketing hoopla is a modern concept?), except the final area, which was allocated through a lottery. Land records at the county level are in the Office of the County Clerk.*

LAND OFFICE	OPENED
Guthrie	1889
Kingfisher	1889
Oklahoma City	1890
Beaver	1891
Alva	1893
Enid	1893
Perry	1893
Woodward	1893
Mangum	1897
El Reno	1901
Lawton	1901

New Mexico BLM Office, 1474 Rodeo Road, Santa Fe, NM 87505. (505) 438-7400.

Oregon   **public-land state**

See Public Land *on page 159. The 1850 Oregon Donation Lands Act (and the anticipation thereof) prompted significant settlement. Oregon's land is surveyed from the Willamette Meridian. Land records at the county level are in the Office of the County Recorder or County Clerk.*

LAND OFFICE	OPENED
Oregon City	1854
Winchester	1855
Roseburg	1855
La Grande	1866

Linkville	1872
The Dalles	1875
Lakeview	1877
Burns	1888
Drewsey	1888
Portland	1905
Vale	1910

Oregon BLM Office, 1515 SW 5th, Portland, OR 97201. (503) 952-6003.

Lenzen, Connie. "Research in Oregon." *National Genealogical Society Quarterly* 79 (1991): 33–55; reprinted as *Research in Oregon*. Arlington, Va.: National Genealogical Society, 1992. See especially "Land Records."

Oregon and Washington Donation Land Files. 1851–1903 NARA M815 (108 rolls). They are indexed and abstracted in Genealogical Forum of Oregon, *Genealogical Material in Oregon Donation Land Claims*, 5 vols. Portland: Genealogical Forum of Oregon, 1957–75, but there are significant differences between the microfilm and the publication.

Pennsylvania   original colony

Colonial-era grants were made by the Penn Proprietary but were largely considered public records. Some early tracts were named, which occasionally provides clues to origins or family connections. Soldiers in the Pennsylvania Line during the Revolutionary War received bounty land, known as "donation land," in western Pennsylvania, or were eligible to purchase discounted "depreciation land." Land records at the county level are in the Office of the County Recorder.

Lemon, James T. *The Best Poor Man's Country; A Geographical Study of Early Southeastern Pennsylvania*. Baltimore: John Hopkins Press, 1972.

Munger, Donna Bingham. *Pennsylvania Land Records: A History and Guide for Research*. Wilmington: Scholarly Resources, 1991.

Rhode Island   original colony

Rhode Island followed the New England model of granting land to town proprietors, who then distributed the land to individuals. This distribution will be found in the town proprietors records, possibly in a separate land-records book. Land transfers in Rhode Island are called "land evidences." Subsequent records will be found at the town level.

Melnyk, Marcia D., ed. *Genealogist's Handbook for New England Research*. 4th ed. Boston: New England Historic Genealogical Society, 1999.

Rhode Island Land Evidences, 1648–1696. Providence: Rhode Island Historical Society, 1921; reprinted Baltimore: Genealogical Publishing Company, 1970.

South Carolina   original colony

South Carolina used headrights to promote early settlement. Early landholders had to pay quitrents. In the mid-eighteenth century, when land changed hands, the new landowner filed a memorial—a detailed chain of title and description, including waterways and names of adjoining property owners. These are in-

dexed in the COM Index (see below). Before 1785 all South Carolina deeds were recorded at the state level, abstracted by Langley and Holcomb (see below).

Land records at the county level are in the Office of the Register of Mesne Conveyance (South Carolina's term for deeds) or the Clerk of Courts.

Hendrix, Ge Lee Corley. *Research in South Carolina.* Arlington, Va.: National Genealogical Society, 1992. See especially "Land Records."

Holcomb, Brent Howard. *Guide to South Carolina Genealogical Research and Records.* Columbia, S.C.: the author, 1986.

Langley, Clara A. *South Carolina Deed Abstracts, 1719–1772.* 4 vols. Easley: Southern Historical Press, 1983–84. Holcomb, Brent H. *South Carolina Deed Abstracts, 1773–1778; 1776–1783; 1783-1788.* 4 vols. Columbia: SCMAR, 1994–96.

South Carolina Department of Archives and History. *Combined Alphabetical Index* (CAI, but usually called COM index). This computer index (also available as a microfilm publication) indexes a dozen different series of land-related records.

South Dakota   public-land state

See Public Land on page 159. South Dakota's land is surveyed from the Fifth and Sixth Principal Meridians and from the Black Hills Meridian. Land records at the county level are in the Office of the Register of Deeds.

LAND OFFICE	OPENED
Vermillion	1861
Springfield	1870
Yankton	1872
Sioux Falls	1873
Deadwood	1877
Watertown	1879
Mitchell	1880
Aberdeen	1882
Huron	1882
Rapid City	1888
Pierre	1890
Chamberlain	1890

Montana BLM Office, P.O. Box 36800, Billings, MT 59101-6800. (406) 896-5000.

Tennessee   state-land state

The area that is now Tennessee was originally held by North Carolina, which issued numerous grants and warrants for its western lands. Much of this land was not actually surveyed and granted for decades, so although much of Tennessee should have been included in the public domain, by the time all claims were resolved, only a small portion fell under the jurisdiction of its one land office. Some land in Tennessee was surveyed in a township-range system but was never public land. Land records at the county level are in the Office of the Registrar of Deeds.

Bamman, Gale Williams. "Research in Tennessee." *National Genealogical Society Quarterly* 81 (1993): 99–125; reprinted as *Research in Tennessee*. Arlington, Va.: National Genealogical Society, 1993. See especially "Land Records."

———. "This Land is Our Land! Tennessee's Disputes with North Carolina." *Genealogical Journal* 24 (1996): 101–26.

Griffey, Irene M. *Earliest Tennessee Land Records and Earliest Tennessee Land History*. Baltimore: Clearfield Publishing Company, 2000.

Texas   state-land state

Early land grants were made by Spain and by Mexico. The Republic of Texas granted land from 1836 until statehood in 1845, including headrights and bounty land. Texas also used a proprietary system in the nineteenth century called "colonies." Although Texas was never a public-land state, some of its vacant lands are surveyed using a rectangular-survey system. Land records at the county level are in the Office of the County Clerk.

Bockstruck, Lloyd DeWitt. *Research in Texas*. Arlington, Va.: National Genealogical Society, 1992. See especially "Land Records."

Gould, Florence C., and Patricia N. Pando. *Claiming Their Land: Women Homesteaders in Texas*. El Paso: Texas Western Press, 1991.

Land Commission. *Abstract of All Original Grants and Locations Comprising Texas Land Titles to August 31, 1945*. Vols. 1–8; supplements A–H. Austin: General Land Office, 1941–45.

Miller, Thomas Lloyd. *Bounty and Donation Land Grants of Texas, 1835–1888*. Austin: University of Texas Press, 1967.

Miller, Thomas Lloyd. *The Public Lands of Texas, 1519–1970*. Norman: University of Oklahoma Press, 1971.

Utah   public-land state

See Public Land on page 159. Until 1869, Utah's land was granted by The Church of Jesus Christ of Latter-day Saints (Mormons). Utah's land is surveyed from the Salt Lake and Uintah Meridians. Land records at the county level are in the Office of the County Recorder.

LAND OFFICE	OPENED
Salt Lake City	1868
Beaver City	1876
Vernal	1905

Utah BLM Office, 324 S. State Street, Suite 301, Salt Lake City, UT 84145-0155. (801) 539-4001.

Vermont   state-land state

Vermont followed the New England model of granting land to town proprietors, who then distributed the land to individuals. However, New Hampshire and New York had both made earlier grants within its boundaries, and a border dispute continued for many years with New York. Some Vermont towns were surveyed using a township-range-lot system, which was a precursor to the rectangular-survey system used in the public domain. Distributions will be found in the town proprietors records, possibly in a separate land-records book. Subsequent records will be found at the town level.

Batchellor, Albert Stillman. *The New Hampshire Grants . . . Townships . . . Within the Present Boundaries of the State of Vermont, From 1749 to 1764.* Concord: Edward N. Pearson, printer, 1895; reprinted Boston: New England Historic Genealogical Society, 1998.

Melnyk, Marcia D., ed. *Genealogist's Handbook for New England Research.* 4th ed. Boston: New England Historic Genealogical Society, 1999.

Virginia   **original colony**

Virginia's lands were granted by the colony or state and by proprietors, the most significant of these being the Northern Neck (Fairfax) Proprietary. Land records at the county level are in the Office of the Clerk of the Circuit Court.

Gentry, Daphne S., comp., revised by John S. Salmon. *Virginia Land Office Inventory.* 3d ed. Richmond: Virginia State Library and Archives, 1981, 1988. The introduction gives a detailed explanation of the land-granting process in Virginia, with important comments on which records survive, which do not, and why.

Gray, Gertrude E., comp. *Virginia Northern Neck Land Grants.* 2 vols. Baltimore: Genealogical Publishing Co., 1987, 1988. The index provides information about adjoining property owners, surveyors, and chain carriers.

Grundset, Eric G. "Research in Virginia." *National Genealogical Society Quarterly* 82 (1994): 179–206; reprinted as *Research in Virginia.* Arlington, Va.: National Genealogical Society, 1998. See especially "Land Records."

Harrison, Fairfax. *Virginia Land Grants: A Study of Conveyancing in Relation to Colonial Politics.* Richmond: Old Dominion Press, 1925; reprinted Westminster, Md.: Willow Bend Books, 2000.

Hudgins, Dennis Ray. *See* Nugent.

Joyner, Peggy Shomo, comp. *Abstracts of Virginia's Northern Neck Warrants and Surveys.* 5 vols. Portsmouth, Va.: the author, 1985–95. These are manuscript documents at the Library of Virginia that have not been microfilmed.

The Library of Virginia Web site. <www.lva.lib.va.us> The library has automated the consolidated card file index to all Virginia colonial patents, Virginia grants, and Northern Neck grants with links to scanned images of the original patent books.

McGinnis, Carol. *Virginia Genealogy: Sources and Resources.* Baltimore: Genealogical Publishing Co., 1993.

Nugent, Nell Marion. *Cavaliers and Pioneers. Abstracts of Virginia Land Patents and Grants.* 3 vols. Richmond: Virginia State Library, 1732–74. (Continued by Dennis Ray Hudgins. 4 vols. Richmond: Virginia Genealogical Society, 1994–99.) These volumes cover the entire colonial period; continuation of the project into the federal period is planned. The detailed index in each volume provides access to information about headrights, adjoining property owners, and waterways.

Washington   public-land state

See Public Land *on page 159. Washington was part of Oregon for its early settlement years; land in Washington was included in the Oregon Donation Lands Act (see "Oregon" on page 177). Washington's land is surveyed from the Willamette Meridian. Land records at the county level are in the Office of the County Auditor.*

LAND OFFICE	OPENED
Olympia	1854
Vancouver	1860–61
Walla Walla	1871
Colfax	1876
Yakima	1880
Spokane Falls	1883
North Yakima	1885
Seattle	1887
Olympia (new)	1890
Waterville	1890

Oregon and Washington Donation Land Files. 1851–1903 (NARA M815, 108 rolls). They are indexed and abstracted in Seattle Genealogical Society, *Washington Territory Donation Land Claims* . . . Seattle: Seattle Genealogical Society, 1980.
Oregon BLM Office, 1515 SW 5th, Portland, OR 97201. (503) 952-6003.

West Virginia   state-land state

West Virginia was part of Virginia until 1863. Its prestatehood grants are Virginia records (see "Virginia" on page 181). Records at the county level simply remained with the county when statehood was granted. Land records at the county level are in the Office of the County Clerk or Clerk of the Circuit Court.

Wisconsin   public-land state

See Public Land *on page 159. Wisconsin's land is surveyed from the Fourth Principal Meridian. Land records at the county level are in the Office of the Registrar of Deeds.*

LAND OFFICE	OPENED
Mineral Point	1834
Green Bay	1834
Milwaukee	1836
Muscoda	1841
St. Croix River Falls	1848
Hudson	1849
Menasha	1852

La Crosse	1852
Stevens Point	1852
Superior	1855
Eau Claire	1857
Bayfield	1860
St. Croix Falls	1860
Wausau	1872
Ashland	1886

Wyoming   public-land state

See Public Land *on page 159. Wyoming's land is surveyed from the Sixth Principal Meridian and the Wind River Meridian. Railroad lands cut a broad swath across the state. Land records at the county level are in the Office of the County Clerk.*

LAND OFFICE	OPENED
Cheyenne	1870
Evanston	1876
Buffalo	1887
Douglas	1890
Lander	1890
Sundance	1890

Wyoming BLM Office, 5353 Yellowstone Road, Cheyenne, WY 82003. (307) 775-6256.

General Resources

Specialized resources are found in the appropriate chapters or in Appendix A: Locality Reference.

General Information

Bentley, Elizabeth Petty. *County Courthouse Book*. 2nd ed. Baltimore: Genealogical Publishing Co., 1995.

The Church of Jesus Christ of Latter-day Saints. The Family History Library Catalog in FamilySearch. <www.familysearch.org> A fast and easy-to-use CD-ROM version is available for purchase from the Web site at the extremely reasonable price of five dollars (as of this writing). Also published on microfiche and available at the Family History Library and Family History Centers (the microfiche is no longer available for purchase); microfiche is the fastest version to scan to learn what is available on a locality.

Cyndi's List. <www.cyndislist.com>, created by Cyndi Howells, is the starting point for exploring what is available online.

Eichholz, Alice, ed. *Ancestry's Red Book: American State, County and Town Sources*. Rev. ed. Salt Lake City: Ancestry Incorporated, 1992. Organized by state, with each state covered by a local expert.

Elliott, Wendy B., and Karen Clifford. "Printed Land Records." In *Printed Sources: A Guide to Published Genealogical Records*, edited by Kory L. Meyerink. Salt Lake City: Ancestry Incorporated, 1996.

Everton Publishers. *The Handy Book for Genealogists*. 10th ed. Logan, Utah: Everton Publishers, 2002.

Everton Publishers, Web site. <www.everton.com>. This Web site lists courthouse addresses and other valuable information.

Greenwood, Val D. *The Researcher's Guide to American Genealogy*. 3d ed. Baltimore: Genealogical Publishing Co., 2000.

Hinckley, Kathleen W. *Locating Lost Family Members and Friends*. Cincinnati: Betterway Books, 1999. Chapter nine, "Real Estate Records," 103–6, discusses some twentieth-century land-related records.

———. *Your Guide to the Federal Census*. Cincinnati: Betterway Books, 2002.

Hone, E. Wade. *Land and Property Research in the United States*. Salt Lake City: Ancestry Incorporated, 1997.

Luebking, Sandra Hargreaves. Chapter eight, "Research in Land and Tax Records." In *The Source*, rev. ed., edited by Loretto Dennis Szucs and Sandra Hargreaves Luebking. Salt Lake City: Ancestry Incorporated, 1996. The latter part of the chapter has state-by-state discussions of land sales and records. Be advised, however, that the metes-and-bounds platting instructions in both the original edition and the revised edition are incorrect.

Meyerink, Kory L., ed. *Printed Sources: A Guide to Published Genealogical Records*. Salt Lake City: Ancestry Incorporated, 1996. You can find information of value in many chapters in addition to the chapter focused on land and tax records.

Mills, Elizabeth Shown. *Evidence! Citation and Analysis for the Family Historian*. Baltimore: Genealogical Publishing Company, 1997.

National Archives and Records Administration (NARA). <www.archives.gov>. They hold bounty-land records and many of the records for purchases of federal lands.

National Union Catalog of Manuscript Collections (NUCMC). Washington, D.C.: Library of Congress, 1962–94. Recent entries are at <www.lcweb.loc .gov/coll/nucmc/nucmctxt.html>. NUCMC is a descriptive catalog of the manuscript holdings of reporting archives, which might include such items as deeds, proprietors records, and surveyors' records.

Periodical Source Index (PERSI). An enormous project of the Allen County (Fort Wayne, Indiana) Public Library, which has a substantial periodical collection. PERSI identifies the primary topic of each article in each publication. More than 1.5 million entries (PERSI 2000), available on CD-ROM and online subscription at <www.ancestry.com>.

RootsWeb. <www.rootsweb.com>, an organized, linked system of Web sites created by volunteers, some of which include land-related information or information on research in the locality; now owned and hosted by Ancestry with free access.

Rose, Christine, and Kay Germain Ingalls. *The Complete Idiot's Guide to Genealogy*. New York: Alpha Books, 1997. Chapter twelve, "A Little Traveling Music, Please," can help you prepare for effective on-site research. The first part of chapter thirteen, "Courthouses: Gateway to the Past," concerns land records.

Smith, Juliana Szucs. *The Ancestry Family Historian's Address Book*. Salt Lake City: Ancestry Incorporated, 1997.

Szucs, Loretto Dennis, and Sandra Hargreaves Luebking, eds. *The Source*. Rev. ed. Salt Lake City: Ancestry Incorporated, 1996. You can find information of value in many chapters in addition to the chapter focused on land and tax records.

The USGenWeb Project. <www.usgenweb.org>, an organized, linked system of Web sites created by volunteers, some of which include land-related information or information on research in the locality.

Warren, Paula Stuart, and James W. Warren. *Your Guide to the Family History Library*. Cincinnati: Betterway Books, 2001. Video: Paula Stuart Warren and James W. Warren. "The Video Guide to the Salt Lake City Family History Library." Hurricane, Utah: The Studio, 2002.

Historical Background

Akagi, Roy Hidemichi. *The Town Proprietors of the New England Colonies: A Study of Their Development, Organization, Activities, and Controversies, 1620–1770*. Philadelphia: University of Pennsylvania Press, 1924; reprint Gloucester, Mass.: William Smith, 1963.

Billington, Ray Allan. *Westward Expansion: A History of the American Frontier*. 5th ed. New York: The Macmillan Company, 1982. Great maps and thumbnail explanations of the causes and events of migration. Often used as a college textbook, it discusses the push, pull, and pathways as migration spread into new regions.

Bond, Beverley W., Jr. *The Quit-Rent System in the American Colonies*. New Haven: Yale University Press, 1919.

Hughes, Sarah S. *Surveyors and Statesmen: Land Measuring in Colonial Virginia*. Richmond: The Virginia Surveyors Foundation, Ltd. and The Virginia Association of Surveyors, 1979. Part II, "The Science of Surveying in the Seventeenth Century," is an excellent overview of the state of the "science" throughout the colonies.

Keim, C. Ray. "Primogeniture and Entail in Colonial Virginia." *The William and Mary Quarterly* Series III, 25 (1968): 545–86. Useful beyond Virginia.

Price, Edward T. *Dividing the Land: Early American Beginnings of Our Private Property Mosaic*. Geography Research Paper No. 238. Chicago: University of Chicago Press, 1995. Excellent maps, photographs, and bibliography.

Reps, John W. *Town Planning in Frontier America*. Princeton: Princeton University Press, 1969.

Salmon, Marylynn. *Women and the Law of Property in Early America*. Chapel Hill: University of North Carolina Press, 1986. Extremely useful for understanding how women's lives were restricted by the statute and common law that "protected" them.

Seiler, William H. "Land Processioning in Colonial Virginia." *The William and Mary Quarterly* Series III, 6 (1949): 416–36. Useful beyond Virginia.

Shammas, Carole, Marylynn Salmon, and Michel Dahlin. *Inheritance in America from Colonial Times to the Present*. New Brunswick: Rutgers University Press, 1987; reprinted Cooperstown, N.Y.: Frontier Press, 1996. Useful tables for inheritance by intestacy.

Slatten, Richard. "Interpreting Headrights in Colonial-Virginia Patents: Uses and Abuses." *National Genealogical Society Quarterly* 75 (1987): 169–79. Useful beyond Virginia.

Sperry, Kip. "Processioning in the Southern States." *Genealogical Journal* 4 (1975): 150–54. Useful beyond Virginia.

Additional Help

Handwriting

Kirkham, E. Kay. *The Handwriting of American Records for a Period of 300 Years*. Logan, Utah: Everton Publishers, 1973, 1981.

Sperry, Kip. *Reading Early American Handwriting*. Baltimore: Genealogical Publishing Co., 1998. Video: Kip Sperry. "Reading Early American Handwriting." Hurricane, Utah: The Studio, 2000.

Stryker-Rodda, Harriet. *Understanding Colonial Handwriting*. Baltimore: Genealogical Publishing Company, 1986.

Dictionaries and Definitions

Older editions of any dictionary are even better for genealogists.

Black, Henry Campbell. *Black's Law Dictionary*. St. Paul: West Publishing Co. Includes almost all of the legal terms you are likely to encounter in your research (although some creative searching may be required). Look for a copy in a used-book store.

Lederer, Richard M. *Colonial American English, a Glossary.* Essex, Conn.: Verbatim Books, 1985.

Merriam-Webster's New Collegiate Dictionary. The classic, big red dictionary you bought for school contains many of the words that you'll encounter in land records.

Oxford English Dictionary. Defines historical use of terms in great detail. Originally issued in 1933 in thirteen volumes, it has been reprinted and updated (including a CD-ROM edition). The more recent two-volume *New Shorter Oxford English Dictionary* provides a less-cumbersome alternative.

Ryskamp, George R. "Common-Law Concepts for the Genealogist: Real-Property Transactions." *National Genealogical Society Quarterly* 83 (1996): 165–81.

Glossary

Abstract: A skeletal summary of the important information in a document; the act of creating an abstract. *See also title abstract.*

Abutters: Adjoining landowners.

Acknowledge: A statement by the maker of an instrument (document) that he made and signed it. The *acknowledgment* section usually follows a deed in the deed book. *See also prove.*

Acre: A common measure of area, 43,560 square feet. There are 640 acres in a square mile.

Administration/administrator/adminstratrix: Adminstratrix is the feminine of *administrator.* When a person dies *intestate* (without a will), the estate is administered by an appointed administrator. An intestacy is often called an *administration.* The administrator usually is the person who sells the deceased's land. Sometimes a land sale may be indexed under the administrator's name rather than that of the deceased.

Affirm: Quakers do not swear oaths. When they sign as witnesses or makers of a document, they affirm. The use of the terminology is a flag that the person is a Quaker (although occasionally it means that the clerk or most of the area's residents were Quaker and the terminology was used out of habit).

Agent: A person who has been given the right to act for another person, usually to transact specific business. An agent would usually have a *power of attorney* giving and defining the right.

Agreement: Type of instrument (document) often related to land and recorded in deed books.

Alienate: Transfer ownership of something from one person to another.

Aliquot part: Fraction. When a tract cannot be described in a single township-range-section-part description, then the legal description of the tract requires all of the aliquot parts to be complete.

Appurtenance: An intangible right associated with land, such as an easement or right-of-way.

Arpent: A French measure of area, exact value varied, generally equivalent to approximately .85 acres; sometimes a measure of distance.

Assign: To transfer the rights belonging to an instrument (document)—such as a warrant or bounty-land scrip—to another person, usually by signing (endorsing) the back, as we do today with car titles, for example. The transaction is called an *assignment;* the person to whom the document is assigned is called the *assignee;* oddly, the person who does the assigning never seems to be called the assignor.

Assigns: The phrase generally found in deeds "his heirs and assigns forever," meaning anyone to whom the grantee might assign the property in the future. This means that the property is owned in *fee simple.*

Baseline: Each major survey in the public-land system is centered at a baseline (the east-west line) and a *meridian* (the north-south line). Townships were numbered north and south from the baseline.

Block: Subdivisions often are identified by block and then by *lot* within block. Once a valid subdivision plat has been filed with the proper authority, title to individual lots can be legally transferred by referencing the subdivision name and lot/block number(s).

Bond: An agreement to pay a penalty if a certain obligation is not filled. Bonds sometimes are recorded in deed books, especially if the security for the bond is land.

Boundary: The edge (bounds) of a piece of property.

Bounds: See metes-and-bounds.

Bounty land: Land (or the right to land) given to a man to get him to do something (or, less correctly, to reimburse him for something he already did). In reference to land, the bounty was always for military service. *See also warrant.*

Cadastral maps: A *cadastre* is an official register of the quantity, value, and ownership of real estate, used to apportion taxes. Cadastral maps are what we usually call tax maps, and they typically show subdivisions, boundaries, and buildings. A number often correlates to the cadastre to identify the current owner.

Calls: General term for the metes-and-bounds descriptions (lines and corners) in a deed or survey.

Caveat: A complaint filed to halt the grant process, usually because the person filing the caveat feels he already has a right to some portion of the land involved.

Certificate: Similar to a *warrant;* varies by time and place, usually preceded by a term describing what type of certificate, such as *cash certificate.*

Chain: A *Gunter chain* was the tool used to measure distances by a surveyor in early America. It was made of one hundred straight pieces of metal (about seven inches long), connected by three small loops. The length between the center loops, a *link,* was 7.92 inches. The Gunter chain was sixty-six feet long; which is defined as the distance *chain.* In New England, where lots were typically smaller, sometimes half chains were used that were only thirty-three feet in length, but this does not affect the distance *chain.* One hundred links equals four *rods* (which are the same as *poles* and *perches*), each of which is sixteen and a half feet long. The Gunter chain had convenient tags that hung from the center loop to mark significant distances.

Chain carriers: Two people required to hold each end of the surveyor's *chain* used to measure distances. The chain carriers (abbreviated "CC") are sometimes identified on a *survey.* Because the person getting the survey would have to pay for the services of the chain carriers, he usually provided them himself. We often find a chain carrier who is a teenager or young man of the family (who would serve without pay) or another person getting a survey done at the same time (in an exchange of services). Some surveyors used additional helpers, such as a *pilot* or a *marker.*

Chancery court: The court that heard causes (cases) in *equity* (disputes over issues of fairness) between individuals. Both acrimonious land disputes and friendly land divisions appear *in chancery.*

Clear title: A title that has no liens and has a documented chain of transfer from first owner to current owner.

Colony: The unit of government before the Revolutionary War.

Commissioner: Similar to a *trustee.* Land transactions for entities such as towns were often done by commissioners. Sometimes a land sale may be indexed under the commissioners' names.

Common: Land could be *held in common,* meaning that the owners owned an unspecified portion of the whole, also called *undivided interest.*

Compass: The instrument with a needle that points north *or* the instrument with two legs and a hinge that allows the transfer of distance on a drawing *or* a *land measure compass,* used in modern platting.

Compass rose: The symbol on a survey showing which direction is north, and so on. They sometimes are very elaborate. On old surveys and plats, north often is not at the top. Also a *compass card,* the mariner's compass with thirty-two points of direction.

Consideration: The amount of money or other item of value that's exchanged for land. Consideration includes love and affection.

Convey: To transfer title or ownership from one person to another; *conveyance* is the term for the instrument (document).

Corner: The geographical anchor between two lines in a metes-and-bounds survey. Usually, but not always, this is the point at which there is a change of direction in the lines. The description usually mentions physical features, such as "a clump of pines," "a pile of stones," "the mouth of the branch," or "the crossroads," but it isn't unknown for it to be identified simply as "a corner." The corner may mention adjoining (abutting) landowners, whose property may run along one or both lines or may simply touch at this corner.

Credit entry: Between 1800 and 1820, public lands could be sold on credit entry. The buyer had four years to pay the government in installments, but there were many defaults due to economic difficulties.

Curtesy: If a child was born alive to a woman with rights to property, the husband automatically received a *life interest* in her property, called a *tenancy by curtesy.* It was based on the life of the husband—not that of the wife or child—so if the wife died and the child died, the husband still retained a life interest in the property (no matter how unfair that sounds).

Curtilage: Ground around a house, but within the fence. Also seen as *courtledge* and other variations.

Deed: An instrument (document) used to transfer title or ownership from one person to another.

Deed of gift: A deed in which the monetary or practical consideration (if any) is less than the value of the land and in which "love and affection" may be mentioned. This often was used to transfer land to children before the deaths of the parents. *See also maintenance agreement.*

Deed of trust: A deed in which the grantee does not have full legal ownership. In some times and places, it was used instead of a *mortgage.*

Direct index: The direct index is the grantor index. Why they couldn't just say grantor index is beyond me; I can never remember which is which, partly because it is logically backward to me. The grantee index is called an *indirect index.*

Discriminate: Land surveyed before the granting process. *See indiscriminate-survey system.*

Division: The legal process by which a parcel or lot of land is divided between or among its several owners. Also called a *partition.* The division process went something like this: One or more of the owners would appear in a probate court (if the joint ownership was the result of inheritance) or *chancery court* and request a division. The court would appoint persons to examine or survey the property and return an opinion about whether or not it could be divided without destroying its value, and if so, how. A plat might be recorded in the court record at this point. If the court ordered the division accepted, then each owner was assigned a portion, which was now his or hers to sell outright. If the land would not support division, this often precipitated a series of transactions in which one or more of the owners bought out the other owners. Death of the widowed mother, a planned move, or financial difficulties often prompted a division request, as did a desire on the part of one or more owners who were farming all or a portion of the land to be better able to manage their farming efforts.

Do.: The abbreviation for "ditto," often found in deed indexes.

Donation land: Lands given to promote settlement in specific, limited areas. The federal government gave donation lands in Arkansas, Florida, Oregon, and New Mexico.

Dower or *dower rights:* The lifetime interest that the law allowed a widow to retain in the real property of her deceased husband in order to maintain herself and her children. This is commonly called *widow's thirds.*

Dower release: The specific statement, usually recorded directly following a deed, that the wife has been examined "privily" (alone, without the husband in the room) and has agreed to the sale of the land, including her *dower rights.*

Dowry: The property a wife brings to her husband in marriage. Not to be confused with *dower.*

Drains: Old terminology referring to land that drains into the named waterway; watershed. *See waters of.*

Easement: See right-of-way.

Ejectment: "At common law, this was the name of a mixed action . . . which lay for the recovery of the possession of land, and for damages for the unlawful detention of its possession. The action was highly fictitious, being in theory only for the recovery of a term for years, and brought by a purely fictitious person, as lessee in a supposed lease from the real party in interest. The latter's title, however, had to be established in order to warrant a recovery, and the establishment of such title, though nominally a mere incident, was in reality the object of the action. Hence this convenient form of suit came to be adopted as the usual method of trying titles to land." [*Black's Law Dictionary,* 4th ed.] These types of chancery court actions involved such fictitious characters as Aminidab Seekright, Alice Notitle, Ferdinand Dreadnought, John Doe, and Richard Roe.

Endorsement: The signature assigning the rights in the instrument (document), such as a warrant, to another person.

Entail: The restrictions placed on the transfer of real property. *See fee tail.*

Entry: The record that reserves a specific piece of land for a person who is in the process of obtaining a grant. In Virginia, for example, it meant that the person had a valid warrant to have vacant land surveyed. The entry serves two purposes: It "stakes a claim" for the warrantee, reserving the land for him pending the survey; it also gives notice that if another person believes that he has a prior right to the land, then he needs to file a *caveat.*

Equity: Justice administered according to fairness, in a *chancery court* or court of equity. Equity cases are between individuals.

Escheat: The process of transferring ownership of land from the hands of an individual back to the government or proprietor. Property usually escheated because the owner died without heirs, the owner didn't pay the taxes or quitrents, or the owner failed to comply with some provision of the grant or sale, such as building a home and planting crops.

Estate: A broad term covering whatever type of land ownership or possession a person might have. Thus, both a lease and a title in *fee simple* are a person's estate.

Et al., et als.: Latin shorthand for *et alius* (singular) or *et alii* (plural), which means "and others."

Et ux.: Latin shorthand for *et uxor,* which means "and wife."

Evidences: Rhode Island used the phrase *land evidences* for grants and deeds.

Executor: The person or persons named by the *testator* in a will to carry out the terms of the will. The executor usually is the person who sells the testator's land. Occasionally, in an index, the transaction may be indexed under the executor's name rather than that of the deceased.

Extract: A *transcription* of a document, but with boilerplate text omitted and replaced with ellipses points (. . .).

Fee simple: The type of title or ownership in which the owner can do whatever he wants with the land and can dispose of it in any way he likes; also called *fee simple absolute.* Contrast with *fee tail.* This use of *fee* is a modern derivative of the medieval *fief* and relates to the granting of a freehold. It doesn't relate to money.

Fee tail: The type of title or ownership in which the title or ownership is limited, defined, or specified by a document created by a prior owner. For example, a will stating "to my son William and then on his death to his son John" creates a fee tail for William, who cannot sell the land. If there were no additional wording, John would hold the land in *fee simple* and could sell it after he came into possession, if he so chose. If, however, the words "and the male heirs of his body forever" were added, then the land was still *entailed,* a specific type called *fee tail male.* Other deed restrictions could be made, such as liquor could never be sold on the property, or the property was transferred only as long as a specified use continued (such as a church or school), or that a cemetery must be preserved.

Feme covert: The aspect of English common law that says that a woman was covered by her husband, that they were one person, for whom he acted. The husband acted for his wife and was responsible for her actions. This is why the husband is found selling land that the wife "owned" in our modern understanding.

Feme sole: A woman who for some reason (usually the lack of a husband through death, divorce, or abandonment) is acting on her own. See *feme covert.* It is uncommon to find feme sole transactions (the words are not used in the transaction), but when you do, they can be very interesting.

Feoffment: The grant of an estate held in *fee.* Residual medieval language.

Field notes: The notes made during the survey process for public-land surveys. They often contain interesting details about physical features, both geographical and man-made.

Foreclose: To take over property when a mortgage is not paid.

Free and common socage: See socage. Residual medieval language.

Freehold: An estate held in *fee.* Residual medieval language.

Furlong: 660 feet; ⅛ of a mile.

Grant: The instrument (document) by which land is transferred from a government or proprietor to an individual; the act of transferring the land. The term means the same thing as *patent,* but the preferred usage varies by time and locality.

Grantee: The party to whom title of land is transferred (the buyer in a sale). It applies to both grants and deeds. The term, however, never appears directly in a deed; the grantee is often called the *party of the second part.*

Grantor: The party who is transferring the title in a deed (the seller in a sale), sometimes called the *party of the first part.*

Guardian: Someone who's responsible for protecting the property (not the person) of a person who cannot act for himself or herself, either because of age or incompetence. Sometimes a land sale may be indexed under the name of the guardian, rather than that of the child or other person.

Gunter chain: See chain.

Head: The place at which a body of water originates.

Headright: A common method of encouraging settlement in some of the early colonies. A person who was imported into a colony was worth a certain number of acres of land, which could be claimed by whoever paid for the transporting (or bought the headright by "reimbursing" the captain, transportee, or owner of the right). There was no paper issued upon entry; the person wanting to claim the headright went into court and simply named the rights he had. There was much abuse of the system, but it also promoted settlement.

Heirs: Persons who have a right in property (or a potential right), due to inheritance, whether through a *testacy* or an *intestacy.* The phrase often seen in deeds, "heirs and assigns forever," means that title is in *fee simple* and that the land can go to the heirs of the grantee or to whomever he might assign (sell) it to.

Hereditaments: Property that can be inherited. Terminology that is often found in the boilerplate section near the end of a deed.

Homestead: The *Homestead Act of 1862* allowed a settler to claim 160 acres by improving it and paying a fee. Over the next century, 10 percent of America's *public land* was homesteaded. Also refers to a house in which such an individual resides.

Indenture: Originally, an instrument (document) that is written twice (or more) on the same sheet of paper, and then the copies were cut apart with a curvy or jagged line (to prevent forgery). This type of instrument (usually a form of a contract) was used when both parties continued to have an interest in the terms of the agreement. Thus, a *mortgage* or *lease* might be an indenture, but a *fee simple* sale shouldn't be. Eventually, the term came to apply to the instrument, even if it wasn't done with the two copies and a jagged cut.

Indirect index: The indirect index is the grantee index. The grantor index is called a *direct index.*

Indiscriminate-survey system: The system so-called because the land was chosen indiscriminately (independently) of the survey system. We generally call this the *metes-and-bounds survey system.*

Interlined: Written between the lines. The scribe might add at the bottom of a deed "and the barn interlined" to indicate that place where he put a ^ and then squeezed "and the barn" above the line is not a later addition by someone else.

Intestate, intestacy: A person who dies without a valid will is said to have died *intestate.* The resulting process is then called an *intestacy.* The terminology "he dying intestate" is often found in deeds in which the *administrator* or children are selling his land.

Joint tenants with rights of survivorship: When there are multiple owners to property, they are called *joint tenants with rights of survivorship* if upon the death of one of the tenants, the other owners divide the portion of the deceased. If his heirs inherit instead, this is called *tenants in common. See also undivided interest.*

Jointure: A freehold estate to be settled on a widow, on death of her husband.

Jurisdiction: The government entity that had authority over the land transaction. You must determine the jurisdiction in order to know where to look for the records.

Lady Day: Annunciation Day, March 25. Occasionally, Lady Day (the first day of the year prior to 1752) was designated as the date on which payments or taxes were due.

Land causes: A case (cause) in chancery that involved land. *See ejectment.*

Land entry file: The file created when an individual filed to patent public land. A typical file might contain the application and receipts. Depending on the act under which the claim was made, the file can sometimes contain valuable genealogical information about naturalization, residence, and family structure. Land entry files are in the custody of the National Archives and Records Administration. You must have specific information before requesting the file, including the full legal description of the land (meridian, township, range, section).

Land measure compass: The instrument used in modern land platting (actually a type of protractor). It is circular, with 0° at top and bottom, and 90° at left and right.

Land office: The office responsible for transferring ownership from government to individual.

Lease: The transfer of possession but not ownership. Any agreement that gives rise to a relationship of landlord and tenant.

Lease and release: The type of transaction used, especially in areas under proprietorships, to transfer *estate* or possession. It involved two transactions, executed one day after the other, between the same two parties, one of which is for a nominal sum, such as one dollar. It was used there as a way of accommodating the English system of landownership (*see seisin*).

Lease for three lives: A type of lease used briefly in the Northern Neck of Virginia and the New York manors in which the term of the lease was until the last of the three named *grantees* died. It was most common for the three individuals to be related. For example, the lease might be in the names of a man, wife, and son (who often was very young, if he was an only son and they were optimistic he would survive).

Lien: A claim against a piece of property stating that the filer of the lien has some type of claim against the property, usually a debt related to the land or an improvement thereon, but sometimes a *bond* or other type of *security*.

Life interest, life estate: This means that a person possesses land only during their lifetime. He or she cannot sell or will the land. After the person dies, the title transfers according to the document creating the life interest, or according to law.

Line: The "sides" in a land description. A typical line description included direction, distance, and possibly adjoining (abutting) landowners. It might however, specify a feature, such as "along the road/ridge/creek." Occasionally (and annoyingly), it had little specific information.

Link: 7.92 inches, 1/100 of a pole. *See chain.*

Lis pendens: This means "suit pending." A notice of lis pendens is published to inform people that property is under the jurisdiction of the court until the suit is resolved. Sometimes separate books are maintained for lis pendens.

Lodged: When an instrument (document) has been submitted to the proper authority, but action is on hold, often awaiting payment of fees. If nothing further happens, the document may eventually be identified in an archives as *unclaimed* or *not acted upon.*

Longlot: Many early predetermined land divisions were in the form of long narrow lots, with the short end(s) abutting on a road and/or waterway. This was to equalize the general value of each lot in terms of both access and land type and to prevent a few individuals from obtaining all the best land in an area.

Lot: The individual properties within a *subdivision,* each of which has a separate title. Once a valid subdivision plat has been filed with the proper authority, title to individual lots can be legally transferred by referencing the subdivision name and lot number.

Maintenance agreement: Instrument (document) by which someone, usually a child of the grantor, agrees to care for the grantor, usually elderly parents, in exchange for certain property.

Manor house: Technically, the house of the lord of the manor, but since the lord of the manor was simply the property owner, it's just an ordinary house, possibly with a dirt floor and no glass in the windows.

Meanders: The winding turns of a waterway; found in land descriptions as "along the meanders of the creek." Used as a general term in land platting to describe a line that does not have both a distance and a direction. *Down the meanders* means with the direction of water flow (which may be northwards); *up the meanders* means against the direction of water flow.

Mechanics lien: The type of *lien* filed by a contractor or repairman to assure that he will be paid for work on the property.

Memorials: Term used in South Carolina for the registration of land title by recitation of transfers and other evidence.

Meridian: Each major survey in the public-land system is centered at a meridian (the north-south line) and a *baseline* (the east-west line). Ranges were numbered east and west from the meridian. The land for each meridian survey was contained within a single state, with the exception of the St. Stephens Meridian and the Huntsville Meridian (Mississippi and Alabama) and the Tallahassee Meridian (Florida and Alabama).

Mesne: Intermediate or intervening. In South Carolina, the Register of Mesne Conveyance recorded the land *memorials*.

Messuage: A dwelling house. The wording in deeds (or wills transferring title) may be "dwelling or tenement and lands" or "messuage plantation and tract of land with the appurtenances," making it clear that it isn't merely the house or the land, but both that are being transferred. However, in some localities, the usage of the term alone seems to indicate land with a dwelling house.

Metes-and-bounds: A description specifying the measures and boundaries of a parcel of land. *See corners, lines,* and *indiscriminate-survey system.*

Michaelmas: The Feast of St. Michael the Archangel, September 29, was often designated as the date on which payments or taxes were due.

Military right, military certificate: See bounty land.

Mineral rights: The right to extract (or not) minerals from a property. The *surface rights* (the right to farm the land and dwell on it, for example) could be sold and possessed independently of the mineral rights.

Minor: Someone under the legal age.

Moiety: One half. This is the terminology used, for example, when two men purchase property together or when a man leaves his farm to his two sons jointly and then one of them sells his moiety.

Mortgage: When a person borrows money using land as security, that is a mortgage. The mortgage allows the person all rights in the land, as long as he meets the conditions of the mortgage, such as periodic repayments. Sometimes the person can sell the land, as long as the mortgage is disclosed, but this should be verified in the law of the time and place. Very often the word *mortgage* never appears in the document. If there are repayment conditions, this flags the document as a mortgage, but sometimes mortgages look just like deeds. They are sometimes recorded in a *mortgage book* separate from deeds. A *mortgage release* may be recorded as a separate instrument or written in the margin when the mortgage is paid in full.

Mortgagee: Person who takes or receives a mortgage on property he is selling; person to whom property is mortgaged. This is confusing; you will find the mortga*gee* in the gran*tor* index.

Mortgagor: Person who gives a mortgage; person who mortgages property. You will find the mortga*gor* in the gran*tee* index.

Mouth: The place where a body of water empties into a body of water.

Orphan: Infant (minor, child under legal age) whose father is deceased. The child's mother may be alive.

Orphans' Court: In some states, this is the name of the court that heard probate matters. You may find petitions for sale or *division,* including *plats* within the records of this court.

Parcel: Another term for a piece of land.

Partition: See division.

Party of the first part: The *grantor* in a deed.

Party of the second part: The *grantee* in a deed.

Party of the third part: A trustee, which usually suggests a mortgage or conditional sale.

Patent/patentee: The instrument (document) by which land is transferred from a government or proprietor to an individual, the *patentee;* the act of transferring the land. The term means the same thing as *grant,* but the preferred usage varies by time and locality.

Peppercorn: The feudal system required an annual payment. Some grants, in an attempt to break free of this in practical application, designated the payment to be a peppercorn.

Perch: 16.5 feet. Equivalent to a *pole* or *rod. See chain.*

Personalty, personal property: Anything that can be moved; anything that isn't *realty* or *real property.* For a brief period in Virginia, slaves were considered real rather than personal property, and attached to a specific piece of land, which was soon found to be impractical.

Petition: A document presented to an authority. In connection to land, we often see a petition for land to be divided or partitioned amongst joint owners. *See division, tenants in common,* and *undivided interest.*

Plantation: In a deed, this simply means property with land under cultivation or growing crops (and possibly included property used solely for grazing). It carries no connotation of size, wealth, or slaves. It didn't even have to have a house on it, so forget images of *Tara.*

Plat: The drawing and accompanying text, usually prepared by a surveyor, showing the boundaries of a piece of property, commonly showing lines with direction and distance, corners with geographical features, and adjoining property owners. Also refers to the drawing we create today from the *metes-and-bounds descriptions* found with a deed.

Pole: 16.5 feet. Equivalent to a *perch* or *rod. See chain.*

Power of attorney: The instrument (document) giving a person the right to act for another person, usually to transact specific business. Powers of attorney often are found recorded in deed books, because the most common reasons for powers of attorney were to sell land or to settle estates, which often included selling land. A power of attorney meant that it was not necessary for the person who was, for example, selling land or a warrant to be physically present. This type of document can provide important evidence of origins and family relationships.

Preemption: A claim to a prior right in land, usually based on settlement and improvement of land. Many pioneers were *squatters,* either moving onto vacant land before the governing body had authorized the area for settlement and grants, or simply occupying the land without bothering to obtain a grant (often because they couldn't pay for the land or the granting process). When the federal government took over the area that became public lands, one step in the process before they could open an area for sale was to clear the preemptions. State-land states faced the same problems as they opened their western lands, often following treaties with the Indians.

Prenuptial agreement: Agreement before marriage as to property rights. Occasionally found in deed books when a bride had a substantial amount of inherited property that she (or her family) did not want under the control of the husband.

Primogeniture: The principle of English common law under which the eldest son inherited real property. Technically, it means that he had the right to the property—i.e., it couldn't be willed by the father to other persons, and Virginia, for example, had a law stating that an eldest son could challenge a will in which his father had done so. However, since a father could sell property that wasn't *entailed,* the term is more generally used to refer to property that passes silently to the first son. No document was required to record the transfer.

Principal meridian: See meridian.

Private claim: The claim a person said he had to land because he possessed it before the area in which it lay was claimed by a government (a.k.a. *squatting*). *See preemption.*

Processioning: In areas using the metes-and-bounds survey system, which relied on natural boundaries and was often imprecise due to early survey methods, designated persons might periodically walk the boundaries of property with the owners (and often other longtime residents), refreshing markers and agreeing on the boundaries.

Proprietor: A person to whom the crown made a direct grant of a large piece of property and who then chose to lease, rent, or sell the land to individuals.

Prove: A statement by a witness that he or she saw the maker of the instrument (document) sign it. Wills, for example, must be proved by a witness in order to be probated, because obviously the signer can't appear. Deeds that are proved by a witness (in localities where they are normally acknowledged by the signer) may indicate death, illness, or migration. *See also acknowledge.* The distinction between the terminology is not maintained everywhere, however.

Public domain: The term for lands held by the federal government. Nearly one-third of the land originally obtained by the federal government is still in the public domain, most of it in the American west.

Public-land state: A state in which most of the land was granted to individuals by the federal government, rather than a colony or state. The thirty public-land states are Alabama, Alaska, Arizona, Arkansas, California, Colorado, Florida, Idaho, Illinois, Indiana, Iowa, Kansas, Louisiana, Michigan, Minnesota, Mississippi, Missouri, Montana, Nebraska, Nevada, New Mexico, North Dakota, Ohio, Oklahoma, Oregon, South Dakota, Utah, Washington, Wisconsin, and Wyoming. Non-public-land states are called *state-land states.*

Quadrangle map: A USGS (United States Geological Survey) topographical map in the scale 1:24000.

Quarter section: A common unit of land in public-land grants and deeds, equal to 160 acres, as in, for example, "the northeast quarter of section 13." A quarter of a square mile.

Quitclaim: An instrument (document) in which the grantor (or, most often, grantors) releases his or her right or interest (often called *undivided interest*) in the property. In a multiparty quitclaim, the parties usually share similar interests in the property because they have inherited it jointly, either through intestacy or a will in which the testator gave his land to "all my children." However, it isn't uncommon to find quitclaims where we can't find any real property interest; they seem to be filed "just in case." The consideration may be a nominal sum, such as one dollar, or it may be significant. Quitclaims often are found soon after the death of the widow, but it isn't unusual to find that one of the more ne'er-do-well children sells his interest many years earlier or that a child migrating westward files a quitclaim before moving, giving his or her rights to one of the other siblings.

Quitrent: A fixed annual payment or rent, somewhat like a tax, that the landholder paid to the government or proprietor. A vestige of the feudal system in Europe, it is called *quit*rent because it freed the landholder (usually one holding the land in *socage*) from other services and obligations.

Range: Generally, the six-mile-wide strips running north-south and numbered east and west from the meridian of a major survey in the public-land system.

Realty, real property: Anything that cannot be moved; as opposed to *personalty* or *personal property,* which is moveable. Realty includes land and what is affixed to the land, such as buildings, minerals, trees, fences, and so on. In an unsuccessful experiment, Virginia briefly legislated that slaves were realty so that they could be *entailed* and thereby not sold (and, theoretically, kept with the entailed land).

Record: To copy an instrument (document) into a public book.

Rectangular-survey system: The system used in public-land states (and elsewhere in some instances) in which property is surveyed before granting into townships, ranges, and sections.

Release: A general term. *See dower release, lease and release, mortgage,* and *quitclaim.*

Right-of-way: Deeds can be used to transfer elements connected to land other than the physical dirt. *Right-of-way* refers to passage over the property, usually by a path, road, railroad, or utility line. The latter is sometimes called an *easement.*

Rod: 16.5 feet. Equivalent to a *perch* or *pole*. See *chain*.

Russell index: A popular index system (well, popular with clerks, less so with genealogists) patented by Robert C. Russell, sometimes referred to (not necessarily fondly) as the *l-m-n-r-t system*.

Scilicet: The term for that funny squiggle (something like S^ct) often found above or before a deed in a deed book. It means "to wit" or "namely" or "that is to say"; used with the location, it can be interpreted as "from that place."

Scrip: A piece of paper (certificate) that entitles the possessor to a certain number of acres in a certain place. Scrip was negotiable, thus the possessor could assign it (endorse it) to someone else. Scrip for *bounty land* often changed hands several times between the soldier and the settler.

Section: One square mile, 640 acres. There were 36 sections in a given township-range in the final form of the *rectangular-survey system*.

Security: The item of value (often land) used to secure the promise that someone will perform a particular task; the person providing the security.

Seisin, seizin: A common-law term meaning possession or tenure of property. The transfer of tenure was called *livery of seizin* (delivery) and was done literally and physically, when the holder of the tenure stood on the land in the presence of neighbors and gave the new holder a piece of dirt and a twig. In very early deeds, you may find a statement such as "by delivery of Twigg and Turf" (or "turff and twig").

Sheriff's sale: The forced sale of an individual's property, usually because of failure to pay taxes or because of a court order. After appropriate public notice, the sheriff would auction the land, usually on the courthouse steps. Often the deed is indexed under the sheriff's name—or just "sheriff," sometimes found at the end of the *S*'s in the index—rather than that of the former owner.

Silent transfer: Land that changes hands without a record, almost always by inheritance. Land inherited by primogeniture would by definition be a silent transfer. Land inherited by the laws of intestacy should, in theory, have created a record through an administration, but the family often neglected to file for administration, usually for financial reasons. In some cases, the son already farming the land at the father's decease would simply continue to farm it. Sometimes a late-filed quitclaim will record the transfer; sometimes we learn of it through a recitation of title in a deed many decades later.

Socage: A tenure of lands gained by working the land and payment of a fee such as a quitrent. This is as opposed to tenure gained by providing military service to lord or proprietor. *See also quitrent.*

Squatting: See preemption.

State-land state: A state in which most of the land was granted to individuals by the colony or state. There are twenty state-land states: the original thirteen colonies (Connecticut, Delaware, Georgia, Maryland, Massachusetts, New Hampshire, New Jersey, New York, North Carolina, Pennsylvania, Rhode Island, South Carolina, Virginia), plus Maine, Vermont, West Virginia, Kentucky, Tennessee, Texas, and Hawaii. Non-state-land states are called *public-land states.*

Subdivision: The creation of smaller properties from a larger one, each of which has a separate title. This is the common method of land description in settled areas, from small hamlets to large cities. Once a valid subdivision plat has been filed with the proper authority, title to individual lots can be legally transferred by referencing the subdivision name and lot/block number(s).

Survey: The *plat* (drawing and accompanying text) prepared by a surveyor, showing the boundaries of a piece of property; the act of creating the survey (plat). The act of surveying a piece of property. For a grant, this was based on a warrant that described the general location and adjoining property owners and on the boundaries of existing property owners. As a precaution (a wise one, given the inaccuracy of many original surveys), surveys often were made for subsequent transfers of property between individual owners.

Surveyors books: A book in which a surveyor or government recorded surveys, especially for grants. Some of these are private rather than public records.

Swamp: In some areas, a term often used to refer to a creek.

Taxes: Owners were usually taxed on land. Tax records can help point to landownership and transfer, especially if the records are destroyed or not readily identifiable in an index.

Tax maps: See cadastral maps.

Tenants in common: When there are multiple owners to property, they're *tenants in common* if upon the death of one of the tenants, his heirs inherit. If the other owners divide the portion of the deceased, this is called *joint tenants with rights of survivorship. See also undivided interest.*

Tenement: A dwelling house; also used to refer to real property irrespective of the presence of a house. It is not our modern usage as a multifamily residence, often a slum dwelling.

Tenure: As an English colony, our understanding of land derived from the English concept that the crown owned the land and that anyone else held it in tenure, which meant as a result of service to the king or to whomever was next up the food chain from the tenure holder. Some colonies rejected this feudal concept, while others tried to accommodate portions of it within their own reality. It wasn't very practical, especially since it wasn't universal and many colonies offered straightforward landownership. However, we may encounter vestiges of it, especially in the wording of land transactions in the early colonial period. *See,* for example, *quitrent, seisin,* and *socage.*

Testator: The person writing a will.

Title: The ownership of a property; the document stating that ownership.

Title abstract: A list of the changes of ownership to a piece of property. The nongenealogists you see working with deed books in courthouses are usually abstractors working for title companies, but they focus on more recent time periods.

Topographical map: A map showing geographical features, often with contour lines to indicate elevations and colors to indicate type of terrain. *See quadrangle map.*

Township: In most public-land areas, townships are six-mile-wide strips running east-west and numbered north and south from the baseline of a major survey in the public-land system. Townships were basic units for granting new settlement lands in New England (but were not necessarily standard sizes). They were intended to be community entities, with church, school, and government associated with the township. *Named townships* are used in many states and usually correspond generally—but not entirely—with a six-mile-square (thirty-six-square-mile) surveyed township.

Tract book: A book used to record a summary of land transactions with public-land states. It's organized according to the land survey (township, range, section). The federal government used tract books to keep track of what land had been granted and what land was yet ungranted. Even in modern times, most localities use tract books as easy reference to identify ownership of a specific piece of land.

Transcript, transcribe: A verbatim, word-for-word copy of a document; creating a transcript.

Treasury warrant, treasury right, and *treasury certificate:* Instruments (documents) in a process in which the potential grantee had to exchange cash at the Treasury office for the right to obtain a land warrant.

Trustee: Someone who holds something in trust for one or more other persons. Trustees often did land transactions for corporate entities such as churches and towns. In some instances, a trustee may act for one or more individuals, although we are more likely to see a *guardian* than we are a trustee. Sometimes a land sale may be indexed under the trustees' names.

Turf and twig: See seisin.

Undivided interest: When land is owned jointly by more than one person, they usually own an unspecified portion of the whole. An owner can sell his or her share but cannot sell any specific part of the land. This can be inconvenient, so often an owner wishing to sell his interest petitioned for a *division.*

Unrecorded deed: There was not necessarily a legal requirement in early times that deeds be recorded in order to be legal (although the recording may have created a stronger claim in event of a controversy). You may see a reference in the chain of title in a deed to "an unrecorded deed." You may also notice that if a deed was not recorded near the time of the transaction, it will be found recorded with a later deed selling the property, if it still is in the hands of the seller. These are called *late-recorded deeds. See also lodged.*

Vacant land: Also often called *unappropriated land.* This is land that has not been granted to someone. It does not relate to whether or not it is occupied.

Vara: A Spanish measure of distance, exact value varied. As used in Texas, it was equivalent to 33⅓ inches.

Voucher: Similar to a *warrant.* Precise usage varies by time and locality.

Warrant: An instrument (document), such as a *treasury warrant, military warrant, bounty land warrant,* or *preemption warrant,* stating that the possessor had a right to a certain number of acres in a certain area. This warrant allowed him to select land and have it surveyed (if it was not in a public-land area, in which case it was already surveyed). Precise usage varies by time and locality. As a verb, it is found in *warranty deeds,* as in "warrant and defend," meaning that the seller has a *clear title* and can defend the title against challenges.

Waters of: Refers to land that drains into the named waterway. "On the waters of Cripple Creek" does not mean that the property directly touches the creek.

For example, Pittsburgh, Pennsylvania, is technically on the waters of the Mississippi River.

Widow's thirds: A common terminology for a woman's *dower rights.*

Witness: The person who observes another person signing a legal document. The purpose of a witness is that he or she can appear to *prove* the signer's signature in case the signer cannot appear to *acknowledge* that he signed the document. In some areas, however, the witnesses typically prove all deeds.

Index

Look for These Other Great Genealogy Titles From Betterway Books!

Your Guide to Cemetery Research—Cemeteries can help fill the holes in your precious family history! With this book, you'll learn how to determine when and where a person died, locate the exact cemetery in which a family or individual is interred, analyze headstones and markers, interpret funerary art and tombstone iconography, and more!
ISBN 1-55870-589-9, paperback, 272 pages, #70527-K

Preserving Your Family Photographs—Learn how to care for your family photograph collection by applying the concepts used by conservators and photocurators every day. Maureen Taylor shows you how to organize your photographs for both family history research and display, create a scrapbook using archive quality guidelines, select a restoration expert to restore damaged photos, use photo identification techniques and more.
ISBN 1-55870-579-1, paperback, 272 pages, #70514-K

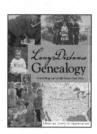

Long-Distance Genealogy—Gathering information from sources that can't be visited is a challenge for all genealogists. This book will teach you the basics of long-distance research. You'll learn what types of records and publications can be accessed from a distance, problems associated with the process, how to network, how to use computer resources and special "last resort" options.
ISBN 1-55870-535-X, paperback, 272 pages, #70495-K

Your Guide to the Federal Census—This one-of-a-kind book examines the "nuts and bolts" of census records. You'll find out where to view the census and how to use it to find ancestors quickly and easily. Easy-to-follow instructions and case studies detail nearly every scenario for tracing family histories through census records. You'll also find invaluable appendixes, and a glossary of census terms.
ISBN 1-55870-588-0, paperback, 288 pages, #70525-K

These books and other fine Betterway titles are available from your local bookstore, online supplier or by calling
1-800-448-0915.